Temps

TEMPS

The Many Faces of the Changing Workplace

Jackie Krasas Rogers

ILR Press *an imprint of*

Cornell University Press ITHACA AND LONDON

First published 2000 by Cornell University Press
First printing, Cornell Paperbacks, 2000

Printed in the United States of America

Library of Congress Cataloging-in-Publication Data
Rogers, Jackie Krasas, 1965–
    Temps : the many faces of the changing workplace /
Jackie Krasas Rogers.
        p.   cm.
    ISBN 0-8014-3638-9 (cloth) — ISBN 0-8014-8662-9 (paper)
    1. Temporary employment—United States. 2. Part-time
employment—United States. 3. Lawyers—United States.
HD5110.2.U5 R64   2000
331.25′72—dc21

                                        9-088451

Cornell University Press strives to use environmentally responsible
suppliers and materials to the fullest extent possible in the publishing of its books. Such materials include vegetable-based, low-VOC
inks and acid-free papers that are recycled, totally chlorine-free, or
partly composed of nonwood fibers. Books that bear the logo of the
FSC (Forest Stewardship Council) use paper taken from forests that
have been inspected and certified as meeting the highest standards
for environmental and social responsibility. For further information, visit our website at www.cornellpress.cornell.edu.

Cloth printing   10 9 8 7 6 5 4 3 2 1

Paperback printing 10 9 8 7 6 5 4 3 2 1

FSC FSC Trademark © 1996 Forest Stewardship Council A.C.
        SW-COC-098

For everyone who has temped

Contents

Preface

In the late 1980s, I worked in the insurance industry. I noticed that the company I worked for routinely used large numbers of temporary employees. Being in Los Angeles, many of them were entertainment industry hopefuls. Many were not. I was struck by the degree to which these workers were separated from the rest of us, the "permanent" workers. Although they worked at the same company alongside permanent workers sometimes performing the same duties, I couldn't help but wonder about the organizational reality of these "temps."

After my first year in graduate school, I had planned to work for a friend, a human resources manager in need of someone to help with her company's insurance re-enrollment period. When my friend lost her job, and consequently I lost mine, I began to panic about finding summer employment. Recalling my interest in temporary work, I convinced myself that being a temporary would serve two purposes: I would have an income for the summer months, and I could make some contacts in the local temp market. So I temped. During my first month, I was selected as the runner-up employee of the month. For this honor I was given the dubious title of "peach pit winner," a wordplay on the name of the temporary agency. I didn't have the heart to tell them the pit was what one normally threw away after finishing the peach. Nevertheless, I returned to the same agency the following year to do fieldwork and to conduct some preliminary interviews. The structure of the book reflects the difference in the richness of the data. Analysis of the temporary law labor process is introduced after a full discussion of clerical work. Where possible, I follow a parallel structure for the analysis of temporary law, noting gaps in that data. A final comparison between the two occupations is provided, drawing some preliminary, but nonetheless compelling conclusions.

Chapter 1 provides an overview of temporary employment, making the case that it is gendered work that should be explored through a gender lens. I also provide an overview of the two groups of interview subjects: temporary clerical workers and temporary attorneys.

In Chapter 2, I address the skill question in clerical work. What, in fact, is temporary work doing to the skills needed to perform clerical work? This is a different question from one that assumes technological developments to be the primary means through which workers experience changes in skill requirements for jobs. In the case of temporary clerical work, I explore the notion that a change in the social organization of work can facilitate changes in skill.

Chapter 3 provides an analysis of the organization of control in temporary clerical work. Here I explore the work process in temporary clerical employment and its implications for the allocation of power in the employment relationship. I find that organizational control, interpersonal control, and discursive control act to shift power away from temporary workers in favor of the temporary help service agency and their clients. At the same time, this triad aids in providing a measure of control over so-called permanent workers.

Using a feminist conceptualization of resistance, Chapter 4 takes a look at the ways in which temporaries resist various practices in the temporary employment relationship. Resistance in temporary employment tends to be individualistic and oriented toward coping rather than change that is due largely to constraints on resistance in temporary employment. Often temporaries' acts of resistance reproduce the negative stereotypes that so many of them wish to eschew.

Chapter 5 explores the notion of subjectivity in the temporary employment relationship. How do temporary workers subjectively experience various aspects of their work process? For example, do they experience control *as* control? One interesting irony is the way in which the "myth of the full-time job" acts to secure the cooperation of many temporaries even as their own experiences provide evidence that temporary employment is not a viable means through which to obtain permanent employment. They uphold the myth even as their experience contradicts it.

In Chapter 6, I analyze independently the labor process in temporary lawyering, echoing many of the issues elicited in the previous chapters with regard to clerical work.

Finally, Chapter 7 compares temporary clerical work with temporary lawyering so as to draw out common and differential effects of temporary status. Temporary employment for lawyers is found to be gendered, yet gendered differently from clerical work. A lawyer's "professional" status mitigates some gender effects while exacerbating others.

THIS book is a long way from that first temporary assignment. I am grateful to the many people who contributed to its completion. First and foremost, I thank all the temporary workers who so generously gave of themselves and their time so I could learn from them. I hope I have done your stories justice. I also would like to thank the agency managers for their assistance in accessing such a highly fluid workforce, and for their candor in their interviews. Others who helped me early on include Nora Hamilton, Pierette Hondagneau-Sotelo, Eun Mee Kim, Jody Miller, Jon Miller, Sally Raskoff, and Barrie Thorne. Both the University of Southern California and the Haynes Foundation provided financial support for the early phases of this project.

I also owe a debt of gratitude to my colleagues and the Department of Labor Studies and Industrial Relations at Penn State University, for providing me with the resources and time to make this book a reality. I would especially like to thank Paul Clark, Alan Derickson, and Mark Wardell for their advice throughout the editorial process. Many additional thanks to the teaching and research assistants who have helped lighten my load along the way: Matt Barrett, Stacy Davidson, Lisette Garcia, Tara Habasevich, Roshani Herath, Chris Keller, and Christine Muchi.

Fran Benson, my editor, has been invaluable in guiding me through the editorial process in a nearly pain-free manner. The manuscript reviewers she selected provided extensive, constructive, and user-friendly feedback. I thank Nancy Winemiller for her patience through the nitty-gritty of the editorial process. I also thank Vicki Smith and Mary Romero for their superlative efforts and what must have been a considerable time commitment.

Finally, I would like to thank my family, who have supported me in immeasurable ways through the completion of this project. Mom and Dad provided unending enthusiasm especially when I needed it. To Gregg, thanks for putting up with me, for proofreading my manuscript (again), and for keeping silliness alive in our house. Cecilia, my little one, you are too much for words. Thank you for making every minute of the day interesting.

Temps

1 Gender, Occupations, and Temporary Employment

Gwen Williams (a fictional composite) is a twenty-eight-year-old African American who lives by herself in the San Fernando Valley. On this Monday morning she gets out of bed early so as to leave plenty of time to shower, eat a quick breakfast, and spend a solid twenty minutes rethinking the outfit she spent forty minutes selecting last night. She checks herself several times in the mirror that hangs next to the college diploma in the bedroom. She wants to look just right today. What was to be a power breakfast evolves by necessity into a few bites of toast and a cup of coffee as she hurries to the bus stop. The butterflies in Gwen's stomach and the anxiety over her appearance can be attributed to the fact that Gwen is starting a new job today—new building, new part of town, new boss, new co-workers, new schedule, new route to work, new restrooms and lunch spots, new rules of conduct (written and unwritten). In Gwen's line of work, first impressions are often crucial, especially if she wants to keep working.

Gwen is relieved when she finally can settle into a seat on the bus that will take her to within three blocks' walking distance of her job. She checks her watch and relaxes a bit. The research she has done on the bus route seems to have paid off. She opens her briefcase, containing her brown bag lunch (Gwen's not sure if the new company has a cafeteria) and other personal items and pulls out the morning paper. After scanning the help wanted section and a few news stories, Gwen turns to the comics and looks for her favorite strip, *Dilbert*. Today Dilbert's boss has employed a temporary worker (a recent college grad) for the dubious honor of flapping his arms to prevent the motion-detecting lights from turning off automatically.

Gwen can't help but laugh. Dilbert and his co-workers always seem to have some insight into her world. They always seem to be able to make her laugh. And that's important, because tomorrow morning, if she's lucky, Gwen will get up and repeat the exact same routine she went through today. Those first-day-on-the-job anxieties and uncertainties will be waiting for her when she wakes up, because Gwen Williams is a temp.

Temporary help service (THS) agencies have existed in the United States since World War II, yet only recently have they and their workers provided material for popular comic strips, television shows, and movies. Both Scott Adams's *Dilbert* and Gary Trudeau's *Doonesbury* regularly have displayed the daily trials and tribulations of temporary workers. On NBC's drama series *ER*, a seemingly oblivious and (of course) incompetent temporary worker interrupts emergency surgery to get her timecard signed. Adolescent cartoon misfits Beavis and Butt-head pass unnoticed as temporary workers as they insult callers while answering the phones, misspell every word in typing assignments, and nearly destroy the office building. Four inept, self-centered temporaries who can't even type are the focus of a burglary investigation in the film *Clockwatchers*, while a sexy, psychotic, power-hungry temporary worker brutally murders her co-worker to secure a permanent job in *The Temp*.

As the producers of our popular culture have taken notice of temporary employment, so have social scientists. Since 1990, scholarship on nonstandard forms of work, particularly temporary employment, has surged. Nevertheless, this area of inquiry is still in its infancy. Scholars have supplied historical, statistical, and descriptive material on temporary and other contingent work (for example, see Henson 1996; Parker 1994; and Polivka 1996).

My objective in this book is to move away from simplistic conceptualizations and generalizations and toward a more nuanced understanding of temporary work as something more than a subsection of workers who can be summed up by the outdated idea of "the Kelly Girl."[1] Temporary employment has many faces, thus significant portions of what we think we know about temporary employment need to be reworked. Based on my research on temporary clerical workers and temporary lawyers, I endeavor to move gender and race to the center of the discussion of temporary work, emphasizing the need to recognize the range of experience in temporary work. Moreover, I investigate how certain labor processes affect, and are affected by, the unique dynamics involved in the temporary employment relationship. While some may view temporary work as a fringe element in the labor force, a closer look reveals one of the fastest growing industries in the business world today, an industry that may very well reshape gendered and racialized hierarchies within a variety of occupations.

Temporary Employment and Its Discontents

In 1993, a *Time* magazine article announced the "temping of America." *Forbes, Fortune,* and *Inc.* told us to invest in THS companies. *Personnel Journal, Sales & Marketing Management,* and *Black Enterprise* schooled professionals on how to manage their "temporary" careers. *The Nation, Newsweek,* and *The Utne Reader* lamented the long-term effects of reliance on "contingent" staffing. While almost no one agreed whether temporary employment was "good" or "bad," one thing was certain: The discussion was off and running and was not going to slow down soon.

One explanation for the recent focus on temporary workers may lie in the fact that they are but one piece of the larger "contingent" workforce[2] that also includes part-time workers, independent contractors, and leased employees. Workers of all sorts have experienced downsizing, right-sizing, and re-engineering, which may have led them to nontraditional work arrangements. The survivors often find themselves in an organization increasing its use of one or more types of contingent worker. We are all becoming more personally familiar with the phenomenon.

Although contingent work comes in different forms, many contingent workers share similar concerns and problems. As the name indicates, contingent employment is marked by its instability. Contingent forms of employment are different enough, however, that sweeping characterizations often turn out to be incorrect. There is no reason to assume that part-time workers, subcontractors, and temporaries can be fused into one category for meaningful analysis. Therefore, my focus is on only one portion of the contingent workforce—temporary workers.

We know that over two million temporaries go out to work each day, and the trend toward expanding our usage of temporary workers shows no sign of reversing or even slowing (Parker 1994). Additionally, an increasing proportion of these workers can be classified as "involuntary" temporaries,[3] supporting the idea that these trends are employer- rather than employee-driven (see Golden and Appelbaum 1992). Although individuals may engage in temporary employment on a voluntary basis, the bulk of temporaries would prefer less "contingent" employment (Polivka 1996) and a better chance at a full-time job.

Temporary workers as a group earn less money than traditional workers and are less likely to have a pension plan or health insurance from any source (Hipple and Stewart 1996). Some of the problems temporary workers experience, however, are less likely to lend themselves to easy quantification. These seemingly intangible issues have been shown to be quite prominent in the everyday lives of temporary workers. Temporaries often find themselves stigmatized or isolated, uncertain of the duration of their assignment, and with little recourse when problems such as sexual harassment occur in the workplace (Henson 1996; Parker 1994; Rogers 1995; Rogers and Henson 1997). Even the supposed flexibility of temporary employment has been revealed as largely mythical, as workers must often work their schedules around the employer's needs (Martella 1991; Negrey 1993). What we do not know is how these issues might differ or be shared by temporary workers in different occupational groups.

A New Direction

Although clerical work still can be considered the mainstay of the industry, temporary employment has branched out to nearly all occupational categories. Although most of the discussion surrounding the problems of temporary employment has focused on clerical or light industrial workers, many THS companies now specialize in one or more technical or professional areas. For instance, On Assignment is a THS firm specializing in placing biological scientists, and Butler International specializes in temporary computer programmers and engineers. We cannot assume, however, that the temporary work experience is the same for professional/technical workers as it is for clerical or industrial workers. To date, there is little information available on nonclerical temporaries (a notable exception is Smith 1998). Although the primary focus of this project is to rework what we do know about clerical temporaries, I also incorporate data on temporary attorneys so as to illuminate areas of overlap and dissimilarity while I set an agenda for much-needed future comparative work.

While much remains to be explored, research on temporary employment is growing, as evidenced by two notable books. R. E. Parker's *Flesh Peddlers and Warm Bodies: The Temporary Help Industry and Its Workers* (1994) provides us with a thorough and detailed overview of temporary employment and its history. We get a clear sense of where temporary employment has been and how its uses have changed. Touching on issues of power and uncertainty, Parker lays out an astutely critical interpretation of the boom in temporary employment, wherein the temporary industry is revealed as something other than an innocent bystander.

While Parker's data expose many problems associated with temporary work, reasons as to why temporaries experience these problems remain unclear. Data on both clerical and industrial work are offered with roughly the same conclusion for both groups: Temporary work is problematic in a variety of ways for workers. Owing to the limited presentation of the interview data, detailed comparison across these two occupations is difficult at best. Clerical work and industrial work have divergent histories, union densities, and demographic compositions—differences that are often downplayed in favor of an encompassing evaluation of temporary work as exploitative. While both types of work may be exploitative, to date we are left with little evidence to tell us *why* they are both exploitative even though the work itself is very different. Are they exploitative in the same way? Do workers in male-dominated industrial work experience temporary employment and its associated problems in the same way as workers in female-dominated clerical work? Answers to questions such as these are complex, because workers within each of these occupational groupings are heterogeneous.

K. D. Henson's *Just a Temp* (1996) provides us with an ethnographically richer account of temporary clerical work through the voices of temporary clerical workers. Temporary workers have difficulty with the excessive demands of the agency as well as with co-workers who hold little respect for them. Not surprisingly, temporaries find the work exploitative and damaging to their self-image. Although problems with temporary employment are stated, it is still difficult to ascertain *why* temporary work is so problematic for so many workers. Is it the "temporary" or the "work" that makes it so? And just what *is it* that temporary employment does?

One aspect missing from recent literature is the obvious and crucial gendered dimension of temporary employment. There has been some implicit gender analysis, but no sustained focus on gender in relation to temporary work. Henson (1996) provides some useful examples ripe for a more gendered analysis. He details the industry's use of images such as the "gregarious grandma" and the "chipper co-ed" that can be more closely tied to gendered experiences of temporary employment.[4] No current analysis moves gender into a central place in the discussion, and discussion of racial inequality is glaring in its absence.

A gendered analysis is not something that simply can be pasted onto existing research. Incorporating gender significantly changes the picture of temporary employment. Many of the issues uncovered in recent literature are not new to female-dominated work. When temporary workers are described as having to learn deference (Henson 1996), the process actually being described is one that many women workers already know how to do. Women workers don't have to *learn* deference; they are schooled in it from the time they are born. Men—particularly white, middle class men—are the ones who must *learn* deference. The process of humiliation described may apply only to workers who otherwise might expect to receive displays of deference. Perhaps some of the strongest reactions to the indignities of temporary employment are due more to the tension of being a white man in a female-dominated, low-level clerical job than to the temporary employment relationship per se. Perhaps not. We do not know for sure.

To address such questions fairly and completely, we need a sustained gender analysis that makes comparisons within and across occupational groups, recognizing the many differences among temporary workers. This study should help to fill in some of the gaps in the types of analyses seen to date. V. Smith (1998) has begun a fresh approach to understanding the broader heterogeneity and similarity of experience among temporary workers. Her study of temporary workers and their managers in a high-tech firm demonstrates a significantly more complex and positive portrayal of temporary employment within the context of the high-tech industry. She found that supervisors and mid-level managers sought to draw temporary workers into a team-based, rather egalitarian system despite official directives that temporary workers were to be excluded from certain types of activities. Always mindful of the larger disadvantages of temporary employment for workers, Smith demonstrates that under somewhat unique conditions (in this case, long-term temporaries in a participative workplace), temporary workers enjoy their jobs, feel integrated, and would continue to work at their temporary job even if a permanent job were offered elsewhere. This analysis urges us to go beyond prevailing assumptions and reconsider how aspects of temporary employment interact with organizationally specific dynamics to produce the outcomes we might attribute solely to the temporary employment relationship.

Understanding the Work Process

To address the lack of an occupationally comparative approach and a presumably gender- and race-neutral approach in analyzing temporary employment, we can take an in-depth look at the work process. A work process includes all the physical, technical, and social aspects of doing a job. The research must be designed to capture information bearing on the interactions among the various components of specific work processes. To understand a work process, one must look at how the work is done, what "machinery"[5] is used, how tasks are divided, who holds what responsibilities, who wields what power, who relates to whom, and so forth. By attending to social as well as technical and physical dimensions of work, we can draw a clearer understanding of the experience of that work for the worker, including the attendant power dynamics. Such studies almost always necessarily are case studies and use participant observation or in-depth interviews.

The aforementioned approach, known as labor process theory, derives from the work of Harry Braverman who, in 1974, explored the ways in which the organization of modern work arrangements tended to deny workers the ability to use or even learn work skills. With the publication of *Labor and Monopoly Capital*, Braverman re-invigorated the critique of modern work processes, which had been eclipsed by the dominant streams of both scientific management and the human relations movement. Braverman hypothesized that capitalism would create a general tendency toward the deskilling of jobs, the "degradation of work," and the expansion of the working class.

Over the past twenty-five years, social scientists have come to appreciate the continuing relevance as well as the limitations of Braverman's work. Braverman has served to remind us that work relations are neither inevitable nor controlled by any "natural laws." Rather, work relations are social relations forged by people, and they must be investigated and understood as such. For instance, the THS industry often characterizes its growth as a nearly spontaneous reaction to changes in the labor market. As a result, temporary employment is made to seem a naturally occurring product of market forces. At least one researcher, however, has revealed how the THS industry was actively engaged in promoting its own growth and preventing regulation (see Gonos 1997).

Other investigators have incorporated some elements of labor process theory in their analyses of temporary employment; but there has not been a concentrated look at the "temporary" labor process.[6] The theory is simply background for the studies, and the story goes something like this: "Temporary work is part of modern capitalism, which Braverman and others like him have critiqued as exploitative. Therefore, temporary work is exploitative in the following ways." This simple juxtaposition of theory with observations leaves us wondering whether temporary work is just part of the same old story of capitalism, or if there is something uniquely problematic for workers in temporary versus traditional employment. Such theoretical simplicity is unconvincing based on the research I have seen thus far, including some of my own (see Rogers 1995).

One way to tackle the issue is to carefully draw out exactly how the temporary employment relationship differs from traditional employment relationships, being careful to closely link the data to the theory. Therefore, assumptions that temporary work is different from traditional work must be put aside; indeed, this is the research question. Similarities to traditional work are bound to arise and must be accounted for.

Another way to assess the unique effects of temporary employment is to do comparative work. In the broadest sense, comparative work includes comparisons both within and across groups. However, the understanding of temporary employment would be advanced by comparing temporary work in different contexts, including different occupations. If similarities in temporary employment can be drawn between two or more vastly different occupations, then we have some evidence that it is the *temporary* aspect of these jobs that has a unique effect.

Inequality and the Labor Process

Much of the current research on temporary employment shares a considerable neglect of social structures of inequality. Poor treatment of temporary workers is identified in an individualized, case-by-case manner and seems to occur independent of larger social structures such as capitalism, patriarchy, and racial inequality. Research conducted in the interactionist tradition of Erving Goffman (1959) can be especially problematic. Although providing a meaningful gendered analysis is quite possible in this tradition, if "all the world's a stage," we risk getting lost in the symbolic, neglecting the relation of the symbolic to the material realm or larger social structures, including the labor market.

Labor process theory does an effective job of linking microsocial behaviors to macrosocial structures. Yet the problem remains that there is nothing inherently gender- or race-sensitive about research done in the tradition of labor process theory. Much of the field has proceeded as though workers were the same undifferentiated mass that labor process theorists accuse capitalists of trying to create. Workers' location on the losing side of capitalism was justification enough to render great generalizations about work experience in modern capitalism. Everyone on the "losing side" is thought to lose in the same way, and therein lies the short-coming of such research. Not surprisingly, some of the staunchest criticism of labor process theory has been feminist criticism, which cites either the complete absence of gender from analysis or the unquestioned acceptance of gender inequality as "natural" in discussions relating to both technical and social aspects of the work process (Acker 1990; Cockburn 1983, 1985; West 1990; Westwood 1985).

Nevertheless, because labor process theory provides the means for connecting what happens on the shop or office floor to the influence of social institutions that surround and permeate the shop, the approach has been used successfully to address the absence of a gendered and racialized approach. One area of intense debate is the notion of skill. A fairly common theme among labor process theorists concerns the effects of an increased division of labor on job degradation. Such changes are said to increase the number of deskilled workers to the benefit of a smaller, more skilled segment of workers whose skill is maintained or increased (Braverman 1974; Thompson 1983). Quite often, an intangible technological change is cited as a scapegoat. But these changes are not gender-neutral: "Women may push the buttons, but they may not meddle with the works" (Cockburn 1985, 12). In other words, skill can be distributed unevenly between women and men. Real differences exist in the content of women's and men's work. In fact, women tend to perform most of the world's truly monotonous and labor-intensive work, and the increasing divisions of labor have tended to aid men in maintaining their skill advantage over women (Sassen-Koob 1984; West 1990).

Without disputing the real differences in men's and women's work, other feminist researchers remind us that "skill" is a slippery concept. What constitutes skill is, at least in part, socially constructed (Acker 1990; Milkman 1987; Phillips and Taylor 1980; Steinberg 1992). The very notion of "skill" is gendered—often by definition, men's work involves skill; women's does not. Analyses of job evaluation schemes have shown how supposedly "objective" gender-neutral skill valorizations have systematically disadvantaged women (Acker 1990; Steinberg 1992). The skills most often used in female-dominated jobs are consistently rated lower than those of typically male jobs. So depending on one's perspective, women's work actually may be deskilled, or it simply may be defined as unskilled and thus devalued. Men are better able than women to retain skilled jobs and to define their jobs as "skilled" regardless of the job's actual content. Both scenarios lead to a polarization of skill by gender.

Gender is embedded in the strategies that organizations use to achieve flexibility. "Enabling" strategies of flexibility (those that upgrade skill and the employment relationship) are most often pursued in male-dominated workplaces, while "restrictive" strategies (those that downgrade labor processes and the employment relationship) pervade female-dominated workplaces (Smith 1993). The fact that we are dealing with "multiple and indeterminate" labor processes rather than a singular, pre-ordained, unidirectional process is becoming increasingly apparent (Smith 1994).

With the overrepresentation of white women and African Americans in temporary employment, there is reason to believe that temporary employment represents a restrictive strategy. Yet there is no reason to believe that temporary employment has not or cannot be used as a form of enabling flexibility, at least for some workers. We should *expect* the nature and experiences of temporary work to vary by class, gender, and race, or in other ways. If we assume that the "temporary" component of temporary employment is the primary identifying factor for these workers, we will not discover or engage the heterogeneity that exists within temporary work. We lose the opportunity to develop a more complex understanding of this increasingly important phenomenon.

Thus far, the literature is filled with untapped opportunities. Although Henson (1996) tells us that two-thirds of his interviewees are women, some of the themes that emerge from quotations from the men he interviewed obviate the need for additional analysis. I was fascinated to find that Henson's quotes from "side bet" temporary workers (those who use temping to support an alternative career) are almost exclusively from men. Is this a peculiarity of the data, a chance selection of quotes, or a reflection of a deeply gendered process?

The Studies

This book is the culmination of two separate but related studies of temporary employment. The first looks at temporary clerical work, the most familiar variety of temporary employment. I conducted thirty-five interviews of temporary clerical workers and temporary help service staff between 1993 and 1996. Most of the interviews took place in Los Angeles; a few were conducted in Pennsylvania.[7] In addition, I did fieldwork as a temporary clerical employee in Los Angeles for several months of 1993 and 1994 and draw on my experiences. Archival data, including industry newsletters, advertisements, forms and policies, rounds out the research.

The second project involves temporary attorneys.[8] Securing interviews with temporary lawyers was significantly more difficult than securing the interviews with clerical workers. I also experienced many more rejections and cancellations when trying to interview the lawyers. There are several reasons for this.[9] First, there simply are fewer temporary attorneys. In addition, most of the lawyers I approached cited unexpectedly heavy workloads or family conflicts, and some simply did not feel they had the time to engage in such activity. The attorneys I did finally interview, however, were gracious with their time despite pressing obligations.

Interview guides for the two studies were quite similar, although the data gleaned were not always directly comparable. The interviews were flexibly structured around various aspects of the labor process, and the course of the interviews with the attorneys often took on a different dynamic than those with the clerical workers. In one lawyer interview, for instance, between the time I introduced myself and could sit down, the interviewee had begun telling me what he thought I needed to know. He spoke for nearly ninety minutes with scarcely a pause. I had a difficult time guiding the interview; however, he did manage to cover each area of concern quite thoroughly. Fortunately, not all the interviews with attorneys went this route. As a group, though, they were much more concise than the clerical workers in their response to my questions, and much more given to attempting to steer the interview toward their particular interests.

For these reasons, I have used caution in my analysis and cannot make a sustained systematic comparison between the clerical workers and the attorneys. The scale of the research on lawyers is not intended to be the same as that on clerical workers; rather, the data on lawyers are there to point the way toward further empirical work. In many areas, the data are rich enough for comparisons that demonstrate some ways in which specification of occupation may be of importance in the analysis of temporary employment. In other areas, the data from the lawyers is much thinner and meaningful comparisons cannot be drawn.

Seeking to investigate how specific labor processes affect, and are affected by, the unique dynamics of the temporary employment relationship, I chose to look at the organization of work in two very different occupations. In a sense, law and clerical work can be seen as representing two distant points on a number of spectra. Clerical work is a female-dominated occupation with a comparatively long history of temporary employment, while law is a male-dominated profession in which the words *temporary* and *lawyer* almost seem at odds. In addition to the gender composition of these two occupations, class differences, differing educational and "skill" requirements, the presence or absence of licensing and professional organizations, and unique occupational histories provide a context in which we would expect very few similarities. My study allows us to address the question of whether temporary employment changes the labor process in each of these occupations, and whether it changes them in similar ways. Highlighting areas of overlap between these disparate occupations should prove useful in deciphering just what it is about temporary employment that has drawn the critical eye of social researchers.

The professional/technical sector of temporary employment is growing rapidly, yet it remains a small portion of the overall business. The professional temporary, however, has been garnering the headlines of late, because the phrase "temporary professional" is somewhat of an oxymoron. Clever headlines such as "Lawyers à la Carte," "Brains for Rent," and "Experimenting with Test-tube Temps" have graced the pages of *Forbes* and *U.S. News & World Report.* Writing for *Inc.* magazine, Ellyn E. Spragins remarks, "You can hire everyone from cost accountants to road-and-tunnel engineers for as long as you need them" (1991, 133). In *Forbes,* we find Jerry Flint stating that Edward Kopko of Butler International (a "high-end" temporary employment business) "leases out engineers, computer programmers and managers to big companies for assignments that usually last six to nine months" (1994, 54). Also in *Forbes,* R. Lee Sullivan assures readers that "we're not talking about paralegal temps. We're talking law-degree-and-briefcase-carrying attorneys supplied by temp help agencies, *much as secretaries and mailroom clerks are*" (1995, 44; my italics).

Data

Studying a highly mobile population such as temporary workers poses some unique methodological issues involving access. I used several sources to reach potential interview subjects. Because my research was not covert, I was able to interview temporary workers I met during my own temping experience. My agency recommended a few possible candidates, whom I interviewed. Because I was concerned about the possible selection of the "best" temporaries on the part of the agency, and because I wanted the interviews to be truly voluntary, I told the agency I preferred to make information sheets available to all the temporaries so that they could contact me confidentially. I did make use of some "snowball" sampling; however, many temporaries were not in regular contact with other temporary workers to whom they could refer me. Interviews with agency representatives served to provide additional access to more temporary workers. Finally, I placed an ad in the regional monthly magazine *Working World,* which is free and aimed at office workers. The result is that no one source provided the bulk of my interviews.

Each of the interviews lasted between an hour and an hour and a half, although, on average, the interviews with the lawyers were shorter. Temporary clerical workers told me that they performed a range of functions for the client companies from reception and filing to word processing and executive secretarial duties. Some individuals found most of their assignments to be of one consistent type, while others were given a variety of assignments. Pay rates ranged from five to twelve dollars per hour and often varied by assignment. The THS agency typically billed the client company a 40 to 60 percent "markup" in addition to the hourly rate paid to the temporary clerical worker.

Of the thirty-five temporary clerical workers I spoke with, fifteen were men and twenty were women. Ranging in age from twenty to sixty-three, twenty of the interviewees were white, seven were African American, two were Asian American/Pacific Islander, and three were Latino/Latina. Three other interviewees did not identify only one racial or ethnic category. Of the thirty-five, seven interviews were with agency representatives. The clerical interviews were loosely structured to cover different areas of temporary work experiences but allowed for flexibility and digression to aid in my understanding of the temping experience and to establish some rapport.

Access for all of the attorney interviews was obtained through the manager of a Los Angeles temporary attorney agency. The agency is typical of temporary attorney agencies in that it provides the full range of temporary placements, from one-day appearances to two-year stints. Although the agency is small, its size does not make it atypical of agencies that handle temporary placement of lawyers. While a few agencies are considerably larger with multiple locations, most provide the same basic range of services. I interviewed fourteen attorneys and two agency representatives from a broad range of ages and legal assignments. I also had access to the one hundred fifty-four case files of active temporary attorneys at the placement agency. Five of the attorneys I interviewed were white men, and nine were white women. I made numerous attempts to interview nonwhite attorneys, but I had to rely on the agency manager to provide introductions to attorneys, and the case files did not (and could not) contain each lawyer's race or ethnicity; thus I was unsuccessful in finding even one nonwhite temporary lawyer. This may reflect the overall racial composition of the law profession, or it may be a symptom of racialized processes within temporary employment,[10] or it may be a case of a white agency manager connecting a white researcher with "appropriate" (white) research subjects.

The interview subjects ranged in age from twenty-six to fifty-four, some holding prestigious law degrees and some holding not-so-prestigious law degrees. There is no compelling reason to suspect that the attorneys interviewed are not representative of their temporary colleagues, but without nationwide data, there is little evidence to show that they are. They are, however, representative of the attorneys working through that agency. Additionally, from my analysis of the agency's case files, I can judge that the gender and age composition of the attorneys registered with this agency is similar to what appears in newspaper interviews with high-profile agency owners.

The bulk of both sets of interviews were collected in Los Angeles at a time when the local economy lagged behind most of the nation in its recovery from the recession. Reports of massive layoffs were not uncommon, particularly within the defense industry. While only one or two individuals interviewed had any connection to the defense industry, agency representatives reported a significant influx of applicants from closing defense plants. Both the clerical temporary agencies and the legal temporary agency reported having an overabundance of applicants and could not possibly place all the individuals who applied. My findings may have differed in important ways if the interviews were conducted under different labor market conditions.

The People

What follows are brief biographical sketches of some of the individuals interviewed.[11] I provide these sketches because I wanted to "put a face" on otherwise anonymous temporary workers as well as to show how diverse this group of workers truly is. So many people have worked with temporaries, yet by temporary workers' accounts, few take the time to get to know them. I did not want to reproduce that experience in this research by using disembodied quotations.

The Clerical Workers

Linda Mejia is a thirty-one-year-old Latina who was laid off from her job over seven years ago and has been working intermittently as a temporary ever since. She likes the fact that she can visit her family in Northern California for several weeks at a time in between temporary assignments. She is disappointed, however, at the number of times she has been assured that an assignment would become a full-time position, when in fact it does not. She also feels that temporary workers should be entitled to the same benefits and bonus earnings as "regular" workers.

Harold Keonig is a twenty-nine-year-old white man who works as a temporary while trying to launch his screenwriting career. He had a "real job" when he came out of college but gave it up to pursue his dream. He feels that he is treated poorly because he is a temporary, yet vows to stick with it a bit longer in case his talents are discovered while on a temporary assignment. He feels that temping is harder for men because society still expects more from them in terms of achievement.

Ramona Geary is a forty-eight-year-old white woman who has temped on and off for more than ten years of her thirty years of secretarial experience. She has been working only temporary positions for the past two years since she was laid off from her clerical position in a large downtown law firm. She says she doesn't miss the stress of her old job, but that temping brings its own stresses—daily or weekly changes in work environment and difficulty in managing personal finances. She has found that one of the best ways to get an assignment after a lull with an agency is to file for unemployment.

Larry Landers is a thirty-eight-year-old African American who returned to temporary work when the business he worked for was destroyed by the 1994 Los Angeles earthquake. He believes that working temporary is a survival skill he will use until he can get his own medical correspondence business up and running. He doesn't like to be treated as "just a temp," so he is very outgoing and hardworking on his assignments. Although he would accept a good offer of full-time employment, Larry feels that long-term jobs are becoming obsolete.

Mark Cranford is a twenty-year-old white man with six months' experience as a temporary worker. He prefers temping over his previous job of delivering pizza. Mark likes his current assignment at a large computer company because they are pretty "cool" about letting him play computer games when he runs out of work to do. He is disappointed, however, that his assignment will end when the company moves its operations out of the Los Angeles area in a few months. For the time being, he feels that temporary work is OK because the work is easy and he doesn't have to look for a full-time job.

The Lawyers

Robert Andersen is a white man in his early forties. A graduate of University of Southern California Law School, he worked for a large law firm in San Francisco and several smaller firms in Los Angeles. He works out of the house he shares with his fiancé, who provides him clerical and research assistance while she finishes law school. He enjoys the flexibility and only rarely has had to worry about meeting his monthly financial obligations. He feels that he gets the choice assignments that really challenge his ability as an attorney and that will help him build his own practice. He also feels that his friends are simultaneously envious and suspicious of his employment arrangement.

Diane Kraft is a married white woman in her late thirties with two children. She graduated from the University of San Francisco Law School and worked for a "top-ten" law firm in downtown Los Angeles. She wanted to spend more time with her children, so she started accepting assignments for one-day appearances. She works between ten and fifteen hours a week. Although Diane doesn't find the work terribly interesting, it allows her the time she needs. Still, a close friend has made comments that make her feel bad for working outside the home at all. She feels she is paid well compared with other women she knows, but she sometimes feels she is wasting her education.

So as workers like Gwen Williams prepare for another day at *an* office, we next look at the question of skill in clerical work, and the effect that temporary work is having on those skills. We shall see that a change in the structure of the employment relationship may facilitate a change in skill.

2   Deskilled and Devalued

Doug Larson is a thirty-nine-year-old white man who occasionally gets work as an extra on a popular soap opera. After losing a secure managerial job with a trucking company, he took six months off to find direction in his life. Three years earlier, he came to Los Angeles to pursue an acting career. Divorced, with no children, he feels he can accommodate the instability of both his lines of work, temping and acting. He described one of the aspects of temping that is most troubling to him:

> Usually they think of temps as being morons for some reason. And they give you very little work to start out. I'd be done in a matter of minutes and they look at you like, "Why did you do that so quickly?" I didn't find any of the work difficult. It was quite numbing on the brain. It wasn't creative. It wasn't challenging. It was just mundane work.

I asked him what made him think people thought of temporary workers as morons:

> The type of work they give you and how they present it to you. They present it to you like you're a third grader. You have to do this and make sure you don't fold the corner of the envelope to the left. And if you lick that stamp, be careful you don't cut your tongue!

Although Doug's sense of humor shows through in this exchange, he was greatly troubled by what he described as the monotony of the work and his sense that others looked down on him. Many temporaries in this book as well as those in other studies[1] complain about the lack of interesting or challenging work. Without invalidating these findings, I found that unskilled work is only part of the story. Not all workers felt that the work was unskilled at all times. In fact, some felt they had the opportunity to really "show their stuff" while on an assignment. These workers felt, however, that they were not being paid an appropriate wage for the highly skilled work they were performing. Temporary clerical work contains within it two kinds of work: unskilled/low-paid and highly skilled/low-paid. In this sense, temporary work can be seen as a lose-lose situation—an abundance of monotonous work that requires little or no skill or the use of high-priced skills in a setting that pays only a low-price wage.

In this chapter, I sketch out two different dynamics in the organization of temporary jobs. One is deskilling. By that I mean the shifting of monotonous and low-skill tasks on to temporary clerical workers. The second dynamic, devaluing, refers to the circumstance of temporary clerical workers who perform highly skilled work with little recognition. Both deskilled and devalued work are low-paid; however, devalued work more closely resembles high-end clerical work or work that could easily be argued to fall outside clerical work altogether, such as human resource management, advertising, or supervision. Outside the context of temporary employment, these tasks are typically higher paid than what these workers made. In the context of temporary employment, the performance of special tasks draws no more pay for the temporary, nor is it cause for changing the worker's title or job classification.

Understanding the simultaneous existence of these two dynamics can help us to reconcile opposing reports regarding the effects of temporary employment, the temporary industry's efforts at defining the situation, and the salience of gender, class, and race in disentangling the range of experience. Let us explore in depth the first claim, that temporary work is unskilled.

Changes in the Technical Work Process: Deskilling

The jury is still out with regard to whether clerical work has become deskilled since the change from a male-dominated to a female-dominated workforce. Clerical work has always been an amalgam. As a male-dominated field at the turn of the century, clerical work offered good pay, autonomy, and a chance for advancement for many men (Crompton and Jones 1984). Many men were able to use clerical work as an entry point to a managerial career; however, many clerical jobs even at this time could be considered low-skill and even monotonous for the men who performed them. As women entered the occupation in large numbers, they were typically found in the lower strata without paths into management. Today, most types of clerical work are female-dominated, and since the 1970s people of color have increased their representation in clerical work (Hartmann et al. 1986).

Much ado has been made about the degradation or "proletarianization" of the clerical workforce. The growth of clerical work after World War II and the introduction of new technologies spurred criticism that clerical work was being "degraded" to become more like assembly line factory work.[2] At the same time, others have argued that the advent of technology such as computers has increased the skill level in certain kinds of clerical work.[3] Both points of view seem to have some validity. Much of clerical work *is* routinized; however, significant pockets of skill do exist. The use of word processors has removed some skill from letter composition, yet a new set of skills is required to use the software package (Machung 1984). The diversity of jobs within the occupation is such that generalizations about deskilling or upgrading become nearly meaningless. Two more fitting questions to ask may be "Who is doing which jobs?" and "To what extent are those jobs skilled?"

We know that many clerical jobs are truly monotonous, and that these types of jobs, along with "back office" clerical jobs, are disproportionately reserved for women of color.[4] Then there are those clerical jobs that are highly skilled, requiring not only technical ability and organizationally specific knowledge, but also deftness at handling interpersonal communications.[5] Regardless of the work, however, the skills of clerical workers often are not acknowledged. Because skills are at least partly socially constructed, any "skill" can be passed off as a talent, a knack, a personality trait, or as an ability inherent in a particular social group, such as women, thus diminishing the value of that skill. Cultural beliefs enter into even our most "scientific" evaluations of job skill, such as the Hay System.[6] When a job is primarily performed by women, several cultural assumptions enter into its valuation. First, women's jobs historically have been seen as providing supplemental income to a family with a male breadwinner, allowing for the payment of lower wages that can in part be justified by constructing the job as low-skill.

Second, the skills of women are considered to be merely reflections of natural, "feminine" abilities. Typing sixty words per minute is not seen so much as a valuable skill that has been honed as it is simply something that women tend to do well. Therefore one can look at a female-dominated job and easily surmise that the competencies are but a reflection of women's natural abilities. Why else would so many women be crowded into the same job? Women are said to be "good with people," thus the secretary's savvy with clients can be accounted for as a gender trait rather than a skill to be valued and thus rewarded.[7]

Men and male-dominated jobs historically have been associated with skill, while women and female-dominated jobs have not. Men have contributed to the naturalization of women's skills because they have had the power to define their jobs as skilled, sometimes at the expense of women's jobs.[8] The ideologically based process through which work (usually women's work) comes to be labeled as unskilled or semi-skilled is called *devaluing*. What could arguably be seen as a skill is labeled in a way that makes the competency seem less of an achievement and more of a natural talent. The failure to acknowledge skill devalues competencies by casting them as trivialities—something an entire gender tends to do well—and they don't see the need to pay for that. They pay for skill.

Investigating the concept of skill in clerical temporary work is an onerous task because the diversity of jobs within clerical temporary work nearly mirrors the diversity in the larger occupation. Temporary clerical work encompasses such diverse assignments as data entry and filing to receptionist and executive secretary; therefore the skill involved in temporary work cannot be characterized in singular terms. Neither are temporary jobs immune from the ideological processes that are often involved in skill definition. There is no reason to assume that temporary clerical jobs use the same skills even when labeled as their traditional counterparts. Nor can we assume that the ideological defining of "skill" in temporary clerical work is identical to that of traditional clerical work. What may be assumed as skill in a full-time receptionist job is often different from the definition of skill in a temporary receptionist job. It therefore makes sense to compare the skill content of "permanent" jobs with their temporary counterparts. In other words, to what extent is the skill content of a job related to the fact that it is a temporary rather than a "permanent" job? Does temporary employment upgrade or deskill clerical work?

All of the temporary clerical workers I interviewed reported at least some assignments in which they felt they were given the worst work in the office. They referred to this type of work with a variety of terms, including (but not limited to) "shit work," "dreg work," or "scut work." Regardless of the specific moniker, one is able to infer the quality of this type of work and the way the temporaries who often performed it felt about being assigned such work. Many of the workers I spoke with identified a consistent pattern of dreg work while only occasionally being called in for the use of their "special skills."

> A lot of times you'll be called to do, you'll have to know this program and it's supposed to be a lot of word processing but it ends up being like opening the mail and answering phones all day. (Harold Koenig, twenty-nine-year-old white man)

> And at this assignment now I'm processing declination and reply letters for insurance. And it's basically all I do. And when it's done, I don't have anything to do. And when I was at the other assignment I was keeping a log of various telephone accounts because I was working in the telecommunications department. And keeping logs of the telephone bills and sending out the telephone bills to the customers. Very simple phones, nothing difficult. No real brains involved. Or at least the bare minimum. (Albert Baxter, thirty-one-year-old white man)

> I worked in a bank and stuffed envelopes for five days straight. It was terrible; it was *sooo* monotonous. [My supervisor] delegated me these huge boxes of stuff, so like I would only have to go to him two days later. I'd just go to him when I ran out of stuff to stuff. (Sarah Tilton, twenty-five-year-old white woman)

The probability of being assigned to such tedious tasks and the abundance of dreg work did not seem to vary based on one's human capital. Despite the range of educational and work backgrounds of my interviewees, they seemed to share frequent feelings of overqualification for the work that they were performing. Most jobs, it seemed to them, did not require even a high school diploma much less a college degree. Yet temporary agencies routinely test for a host of skills, including math, spelling, and computer software skills. A quick check of publicly available temporary agency materials found on the Internet demonstrates the emphasis that agencies place on their skills evaluation systems. One agency boasts their applicant testing procedures were developed by a highly prestigious consulting firm. Another claims the best skills-testing software in the business. But is this all just hype to lure potential temporaries to work for agencies, only to assign them later to the surplus of low-skill jobs available? Many temporary workers were unable to see any point to the screening process when they are routinely placed into jobs below their capability levels.

> They give you spelling tests, math tests, yeah, they do that, too. The ten-key test [data entry of numbers]. And most of the time when you go to

a job, you never basically do those things. I mean, it's like the ten-key. Unless you're really doing an accounting job and you have to add up, I can see that. But the jobs I mostly got weren't like that. I was always overqualified for the jobs. (Linda Mejia, thirty-one-year-old Latina)

So while temporary workers are tested to determine their individual skill level (that is, the maximum skill of the person), like Linda, many of my informants were seldom given assignments that required the use of their maximum skills. In this sense, temporary work can be understood to be a form of underemployment for many (Parker 1994). Indeed, temporary workers can experience temporary work exclusively in this fashion. Take Ellen Lanford for example. Her agency told her that she was one of their most "placeable" temporaries because of her extensive educational background. While she was given many assignments from the agency, Ellen expected the work to be different.

Yes, there were some days when I thought, this is ludicrous. I am so miserable. I can't believe that I'm however many years old, thirty-six, thirty-seven, and I'm making nine thousand copies of this script or something. I have two masters' degrees. (Ellen Lanford, thirty-eight-year-old white woman)

Again, to the degree that the temporary industry focuses on the human capital that temporaries bring to the job rather than the job itself, the industry can misrepresent temporary workers' experiences by equating the skill of the worker with the job. The worker and the job are treated as virtually the same, when in fact the worker may possess (and often is required to posses) a bundle of skills ranging from computer to social knowledge. Having extensive qualifications is no guarantee of receiving work that will match the temporary worker's needs.

From the client company's perspective, Ellen may appear to be the perfect match for the job. Based on her extensive educational background, the company may assume that she's capable of doing the work, she needs minimal supervision, and she shows up on time. That the particular assignment might not utilize her skills to the fullest is of little concern. Overqualification poses less of a problem for the client than for the temporary worker, unless it results in undesirable behavior on the part of the temporary worker. From the temporary's point of view, there is a disjuncture of their skills and the job tasks they are required to perform. They see the matching process as oriented toward meeting the client's needs. Because overqualification is not typically framed as problematic by the agency, finding a challenging assignment is seen by temporary workers as a lucky happenstance rather than an outcome of a managed matching process.

If temporary clerical workers believe the work they are asked to perform is lacking in skill, then to what end is this occurring? Is it simply a byproduct of a general tendency toward deskilling? Or is there a trend toward some workers maintaining or increasing the skill content of their jobs at the expense of temporary workers? Either implicitly or explicitly, temporaries acknowledge that their performance of dreg work insulates permanent employees from having to perform those low-skill tasks that they find unsavory.

> Yeah, the temp is the one who gets the shit work. And the temp is the one who is last considered for anything. (Michael Glenn, twenty-five-year-old Asian American)

> When you're a temp, you get all the shitty work. . . . You usually got stuck in the back to do the work that either someone put off or was on maternity leave or sick. Work that no one else wanted to do. (Doug Larson, thirty-nine-year-old white man)

This idea that the work assigned to temporaries is work that has been sitting untouched because no one else in the office would do it is a commonly held belief among temporary workers. My fieldwork supports what many of my informants described. I found myself doing this kind of work in several assignments. On one assignment, I was asked to replace pages in reference manuals. The manuals held information on various pension and legal codes. There were several sets of manuals on many topics. Each month, the companies that printed the reference manuals would send replacement pages (anywhere from thirty to one hundred pages per set) that required someone to go to the correct binder, pull out the old page, and insert the new page. Complicating matters was the fact that the pages were tissue-thin and separating them was quite tedious. When I was hired, the replacement pages had backed up for over fourteen months because none of the permanent workers would do this work. It had been assigned in turn to two or three permanent workers who told me (with a knowing smile) that they could just never get to it. That is why I was "the lucky one" (field notes, June 1994).

These research findings also suggest that the deskilling process in temporary clerical work is not conducted by management alone. Deskilling of temporary clerical work takes place not simply as part of a management strategy but as part of the social relations of the workplace, which may include management prerogatives as well. Therefore we see that "permanent" workers also participate in the assignment of less desirable, simple tasks to temporary workers.

> In fact, [my supervisor] was really gung ho about giving me all this grunt work to do, and I spent the entire time typing in there while she was pigging out on Doritos and whatnot. So it seemed as though she had taken the opportunity to give me all her crap work. (Irene Pedersen, twenty-four-year-old white woman)

Temporaries with similar experiences report that their entrance into an office is seen as a signal for the permanent clerical workers to transfer the work they do not want to do and have been putting off onto the temporary workers. Ironically, literature from the temporary industry demonstrates a similar understanding of this role being one of the functions of temporary work.

> Companies often call on temporary help companies for supplemental staffing during peak production periods, special projects, transitions, the introduction of new products or technology, and *to relieve "core" employees of excess overtime and tedious work.* (pamphlet from a temporary help firm; my italics)

This is a notable contradiction to the scenario portrayed by temporary agencies in which temporary workers are hired as short-term experts. Thus it seems that the "expert" notion of the temporary worker is not always applicable beyond the role of pumping up the agency's reputation in its literature, at least in the case of clerical work.

While temporary work does not necessarily change the overall technical labor process of clerical work, it can result in two categories of jobs, and differential experiences of work for permanent and temporary workers. Temporary employment can therefore serve as a type of occupational segregation that "pushes up" the skill level in the core of workers (who delegate low-skill dreg work) while "pushing down" the skill level in the periphery of temporary workers. Permanent workers are relieved from monotonous work, and (happily for the employer) these higher-paid core workers do not spend their time doing routine tasks.

Using temporary workers in this way provides a further realization of the Babbage principle.[9] Under the Babbage principle, work is divided so that highly skilled, high-priced workers spend their time exclusively on high-priced tasks, while unskilled, low-priced workers spend their time on low-priced tasks. Thus, implementing the Babbage principle is said to reduce overall labor costs. If the work was not divided, one would have to find and employ higher-skilled workers and pay the higher rate to ensure the capability of the worker for performing the high-end tasks. For example, if I am proficient at desktop publishing, having me make photocopies is not an economical use of my time. According to the Babbage principle, my time doing desktop publishing should be maximized, and someone else should be hired and paid less to do the photocopying. If the work is not divided and I must also do the photocopying, unfortunately for my employers, it will cost them the higher rate to have me perform this low-price task.

Temporary employment can then be seen as a means for bringing in low-priced workers to do low-priced work. The permanent core is where high-skilled, high-priced work is done. Therefore, it seems that the deskilling and the upgrading of clerical jobs are occurring simultaneously with the introduction of temporary workers. The overall content of clerical work may be unchanged, but the distribution of tasks now takes place with regard to the temporary/permanent division. While this is good news for core individuals who are buffered by the temporary ring, every silver lining does have its cloud. That core of skilled workers seems to be shrinking, for even in times of economic recovery the use of temporary help is rising (Parker 1994).

Changes in the Technical Work Process: Devaluing

The image of temporary work as widening the division between higher-skilled jobs and lower-skilled jobs is only partially correct. Not all temporary work is unskilled. In some cases, clerical temporaries perform complex, skilled work that is either equivalent or superior to the work of "permanent" employees. In these instances, the only distinguishing factors between permanent and temporary work often seems to be that temporary work is lower-paid and brief or uncertain in duration. Moreover, the skilled work of temporaries is not recognized as such—it is devalued or ideologically stripped of skill. This ideological deskilling can result in temporary workers receiving lower compensation[10] than permanent workers for similarly skilled work. The following description, although seemingly extreme, is reflective of the type of skilled labor that temporary workers may be called on to perform. Michael was hired for the long-term assignment as a word processor:

> Nine dollars an hour. I am publication coordinator. I do all the billing for the magazine. I do all the billing for the advertisers, which means I'm sort of accounts receivable. I answer phones. I'm front office for phones. I do the filing of course for certain things. I place the ads. I cut and paste and place all the ads. I proof the entire magazine before it goes to the printer. (Michael Glenn, twenty-six-year-old Asian American)

For those temporaries who come to the labor market highly skilled, their skills do not necessarily provide them with "market power" that translates into job security, high pay, and promotional opportunities when they enter temporary employment. While his duties required in-depth knowledge and tremendous responsibility in addition to his clerical skills, Michael was unable to increase his hourly pay rate or to become permanent in the position. If the need arises, companies can get highly skilled individuals like Michael at "bargain basement" rates by paying for a clerical temporary worker and using the full range of that worker's abilities.

Ludy describes a situation in which she wrote speeches for her temporary boss. While he showed gratitude for help, he did not offer to increase her pay:

> He was just used to having a girl who would answer his phone and take messages and type his letters. That's cool. But you don't get any more money for that, you don't get any more money for being smart. (Ludy Martinez, thirty-six-year-old Filipina)

In my own temping experience, I was a human resources clerical worker. One day I was asked to bring coffee for the company's insurance representative, and to keep him occupied while the director of human resources finished up some other work. I was supposed to keep him occupied until she was ready. Not long after we started talking, he asked me why I was temping. I gave my standard answer. Then he asked what I did before graduate school and I told him I worked in insurance. The next thing you know, we were discussing self-insured plans and Preferred Provider Organizations, and it seemed like he was quizzing me. He told me about some changes he thought the company should implement when the director walked in.

Later that week, I was asked to help with the insurance plan changes because apparently, the insurance rep thought I was quite knowledgeable.

He told the director that she better use my "talents" while I was there. She was really enthusiastic about my "newly discovered" background. I thought it was nice to work with her like this. Of course, I still had to do the filing and mailing, but I could easily fit those things in (field notes, July 1994).

In addition to finding highly skilled individuals that they can hire out at low hourly rates, temporary agency representatives prefer temporaries with a willingness to do a wide variety of work, either above or below the skill level for which they were hired.

> An applicant who if we tell her you're gonna be doing some word processing and the client asked if she can do some backup on the switchboard and says, "I wouldn't do that. I'm above that. I may have a degree or I'm working on a degree, and I have good skills, why should I do that?" Well you know, in the meantime, you're out of work. *We're paying you the same rate if you're gonna be answering phones or doing a proposal*, so that would be someone we would consider a prima donna. (Manny Avila, temporary agency representative, twenty-eight-year-old Latino)

Many times in my experience and the experiences of my interviewees, the temporary was hired to perform simple clerical work only to wind up doing highly skilled clerical work or even something altogether different. Instances of temporary workers being hired to write proposals and ending up answering phones are much less common, but they do exist. For those who were hired as clerical workers, many resented being brought into the workplace under the guise (and pay) of a clerical worker while being asked to perform complex tasks that often required extensive training or experience.

> And I went to some agencies right away, and they're like, "Well, OK, so do you speak Sanskrit, do you ride a bicycle?" It's like. "Well, no, I uh, I know this program fairly well and type and . . ." Oh well, so does everyone so that's not good enough. You need to know Lotus and Windows and desktop publishing, and you need to have had a master's in finance. . . . Sometimes they get you in there and they want you to like be their junior CEO and still pay you nine bucks an hour. (Harold Koenig, twenty-nine-year-old white man)

Certain businesses find it useful to hire overqualified temps if they can find them. Because they will get those extra skills out of them even though they're just paying an hourly wage. I mean, it's like when certain businesses found out that I could at least spell and write and compose and that's how I ended up writing speeches and stuff like that. They're getting wise to the fact that not all the temps have the same skills, and that they will try to bilk you. I mean, it's like when people found out I could translate French and Spanish, and they were like "Whoa!" (Ludy Martinez, thirty-six-year-old Filipina)

Although agencies seem willing to put to use the many skills of temporary workers, many temporaries report feeling that their education and work experience are not recognized by the agency as having been instrumental in the development of the skills they use while on assignment.

I have worked as a secretary in a law firm for twenty, over twenty years now. But that didn't matter to [the agency], didn't seem to make a difference. They wanted specific programs, and I hadn't used them. Sure, I could learn them, I worked twenty years! Doesn't that count for something? (Ramona Geary, forty-eight-year-old white woman)

It was kind of depressing for me, but I needed money. I remember being given like spelling tests and very simplified math tests to make sure I had a brain even though I had a résumé that said I graduated [from college]. . . . I think they should say, "I recognize that this may be a bit condescending, but it's just a way to screen. We know you're smart and you have a degree." Some sort of acknowledgment about that. (Carol Ketchum, twenty-nine-year-old white woman)

Thus, many temporary workers bring substantial skills and "human capital" with them to jobs that are defined and remunerated as unskilled. While employers may find themselves in the fortunate position of paying for a receptionist who ends up doing accounting, computer-aided design, or translating documents from French and Spanish, the job remains defined as clerical. Temporary agencies and their clients benefit from temporary workers' education and work experience, but the temporary workers themselves do not. Therefore, in addition to deskilling, we find either no change in the technical labor process or an upgrading that goes unrewarded by money or recognition. Agencies often fail to recognize (verbally or monetarily) the types of skills developed through education or work experience, while at the same time they are happy to market those same skills to their clients.

Deskilling and devaluing might at first appear to be contradictory tendencies because one involves highly monotonous work while the other involves highly skilled work. They are better understood as complements, however: One constitutes material deskilling, and the other constitutes ideological deskilling. Together, deskilling and devaluing help construct temporary work as the most monotonous work in an office. If we attend only to the deskilling tendency, we miss an important facet of the experience of temporary workers. In effect, we buy into the devaluing of temporary workers' skills.

Although the discussion to this point has proceeded as though material and ideological deskilling are easily demarcated categories, real-life experience reflects a more complicated relationship. Some temporary workers mainly experienced deskilled work, while others mainly experienced devalued work. Many temporary workers, however, experienced a combination of the two, and even an oscillation between deskilled and devalued work.

For example, Ludy, the woman who was translating French and Spanish as well as writing speeches, also had to spend hours transcribing audiotapes of depositions. And Cheryl Hansen (a twenty-five-year-old white woman) reported filing in a bank as well as running computer-aided design software while working as a temporary clerical worker. In my own temping experience, I worked as a receptionist and at cleaning out old files as well as rewriting personnel policies. In the receptionist and filing jobs, I was hired as a clerk. In the situation where I rewrote personnel policies, I was also hired as a clerk. For all three assignments I received an identical pay rate.

Ideologies Concerning Skill

Let's take a look at the Temporary Help Services (THS) industry's rhetoric about the skills required of its workers. The understanding of skill and the messages regarding this understanding are complex and vary according to the industry's projected audience. The industry uses notions of skill to their advantage in both marketing and eliciting consent from temporary workers. On occasions when the industry's intended audience is potential clients, temporary workers are characterized as being highly skilled. In these situations, the temporary industry claims to be filling a niche left by a dearth of skilled labor in the United States. In this excerpt from a temporary agency's promotional kit aimed at generating clients, temporary workers are cast as possessing high-level yet scarce skills:

> There is a chronic shortage of skilled clerical and technical help in this country. The Occupational Outlook Handbook, published annually by the Department of Labor, has outlined this fact since at least 1974. The

forecasted growth in demand for skilled clerical and technical help is significantly faster than the growth for the workforce as a whole. At the same time, supply side factors, such as the *women's movement*, and aging workforce, the decline of the classic secretarial school, and increased labor force mobility and opportunity have created a supply imbalance/shortfall. This fact is reflected in the newspaper classified ad sections every week. . . . Rapidly changing technology in both the clerical and technical fields have created new skill requirements to which the workforce in this country responds slowly. (temporary agency promotional kit, 1994; my italics)

Business and the temporary industry are cast as responding to a shortage and a rigidity in the U.S. workforce, for which the educational system and even the women's movement are to blame. This ideological sleight-of-hand acts to shift the impetus for temporary work from the temporary industry itself and employers to workers, when in fact Golden and Appelbaum (1992) have found it to be just the opposite. The large increases in temporary work are employer- rather than employee-driven, but by focusing on the "human capital" of workers, the temporary industry dodges questions regarding their role (and employers' roles) in creating a large contingent workforce. The THS industry is the skill-matcher, the void-filler, and the workforce educator. Temporary employment agencies are seen as the savior, as entrepreneurs supplying the solution to a desperate demand rather than as a co-creator of that demand.

The industry also often likes to make use of a military analogy by portraying temporary workers as office commandos who swoop in to solve an office crisis, after which they ride off into the sunset and their next mission. One item in a public relations kit from National Association of Temporary and Staffing Services provides an example of the heroism attributed to temporary workers and, of course, the industry that supplies these courageous men and women:

> A good secretary is an executive's right arm. So what does the boss do if that right arm is home with the flu? A competent temporary employee eases executive tensions by handling a secretary's chores. And temps, as they are called, can do much more.

Temporary workers save the day by being able to pick up a job, any job, on a moment's notice or by providing scarce skills for an urgent but limited time period. For office work, knowledge of certain software packages is one of the primary office-saving devices. One company suggests that they can provide "someone who can fill in when the resident desktop publishing expert is out, or someone who can pull together a presentation using all of the latest software."

This portrayal of temporary workers does not always mesh with reports from temporaries, who often feel overqualified for assignments while they perform unskilled work despite their "human capital" or capabilities. An experience I shared with many temporaries was being called in on what had been described to me as an "urgent" assignment, only to find little actual work to perform. One particular assignment left me wondering whether the client company would have been better off renting an answering machine for the day. I think I answered the phone a grand total of five times during the course of nine hours (field notes, 1994).

Science and Math at Your Service

The temporary industry is central in the creation and maintenance of ideologies about skill. Their manipulation and deployment of these ideologies is likely aimed at shaping the perceptions of both the temporary workers and clients to their benefit. Emphasis is placed on the supposedly rational methods being used to match temporary workers with appropriate assignments, as seen in promotional materials asserting that temporary agencies are matching skilled workers with skilled jobs:

> The education and skill levels of temporary employees of today qualify them for more jobs than ever before. Through the use of state-of-the-art technology and sophisticated procedures, a temporary help company can thoroughly test and accurately match skilled temporary employees with customers' needs and requirements. (National Association of Temporary and Staffing Services 1992).

Another way that the industry attempts to shape the definition of skill is through the use of the language of quantification. Temporaries are told that they are paid according to the skills they will use on a particular assignment. If the assignment is general office, it pays a certain amount. Word processing pays a higher amount. Executive secretary pays even more.

> Once you have been evaluated, interviewed, and approved for hire, you are immediately eligible for assignments. Your rate of pay for each assignment is determined by the specific skill level required for the job, so you know you will always be paid fairly. (pamphlet from temporary help company)

Quantification places skills assessment firmly in the realm of science (see Acker 1990 for a similar discussion involving job evaluation) and legitimizes pay changes from assignment to assignment. In contrast to how the industry markets the skills of its workers, here skill is defined as belonging to the job rather than to the workers. When skill belongs to the job, agencies can justify paying a lower rate to an individual with an abundance of human capital. This seems a better bargain than what can be gleaned even under the Babbage principle. Here the agency does not pay a high rate for highly skilled workers to do less skilled work. Instead, agencies are able to pay the lower rate to the worker with greater skill based on an assessment of the assignment. The tasks define the pay, human capital be damned. If it happens that while on a lower-paid assignment a temporary worker provides more services (from their bundle of skills) than required, so much the better.[11] If temporary agencies continue to classify assignments as "general office," regardless of the skill level of the work reported being done by the temporary, who's to challenge that classification?

The portrayal of temporary agencies as benevolent matchmakers misrepresents many of the experiences conveyed by the temporary workers interviewed for this research. On two occasions, my informants reported working with the agency to find a suitable skill match; however, the context in which this occurred was repayment of a favor. Overwhelmingly, my informants shared the experience of feeling mismatched for their assignments. If skills matching is occurring, the process is invisible to the temporary workers and does not appear to place them in assignments they feel fit their skill level.

My interviewees identified the skills assessment process[12] as particularly problematic in making a "good" match. Most temporary workers reported that the "state-of-the-art technology and sophisticated procedures" referred to in agency literature consisted of basic spelling, math, and typing tests along with a brief interview. Temporaries complained that the testing seemed an inadequate way to judge their capabilities. Claims of thoroughly scientific, state-of-the art testing facilities seemed overblown to the temporaries who actually went through this process. This was true even in many of the larger agencies. A few temporary workers reported that although the literature from these agencies promoted an extensive candidate evaluation system, their evaluation as a suitable worker consisted of nothing more than a brief interview after which they were sent out on assignments.

My own evaluation process involved completion of an application form, including standard math and spelling tests. After I completed the forms and it was determined that I had passed the tests, I was asked to take a computer test on the software I claimed to know. I was actually nervous about taking the WordPerfect test. After the typing test, [the agency manager] sat me down and started a computer program that gave me directions such as, "Locate the key used to indent a paragraph, set your tabs at _ inch, change your margins to 1_ inches, and so forth." I believed that a template would have told me the same thing. Toward the end there was a question about an advanced mail merge that I did not know. I tried twice but missed it both times. Apparently, that was not enough to keep me out of work, because I had a fifteen-minute interview and was told to call in for assignments (field notes, 1994).

Like others whom I interviewed, I felt that the tests were rudimentary. The extent to which workers feel temporary agencies are incapable of evaluating and properly using their skills is reflected in a comedy skit that one temporary worker wrote based on her experiences.

> That's where I got the idea for the Absolute Power Temp Agency. You know, how does somebody at Kelly Girl know what Idi Amin's credentials meant? Just that he could type. [He says] you know I can kill people and I can administrate a country. You know it didn't matter, but can you type? (Ludy Martinez, thirty-six-year-old Filipina)

At least some temporary workers are not buying into the idea of skill matching at all,[13] and although there is much talk concerning the employment of "scientific" skills assessment and computer testing software, workers do not always experience their pay as correlated with the skill of the job. In fact, sometimes temporaries feel that their pay rate is arbitrary (Gottfried 1991) or a product of what the temporary agency knows is the minimal acceptable rate for an individual temporary.

> And what they do is kind of play with the temps and give them what they think they'll take. I know they do that because you write down what's the lowest you'll take. (Cindy Carson, thirty-eight-year-old white woman)

> If I accepted it, that means I'd have to accept jobs from now on at that pay scale. And I didn't want to go down that far. (Jean Masters, thirty-four-year-old African American)

Thus the notions of matching skills and the quantification of skill are attempts at creating ideologies about skill that may either elicit consent from temporary workers or convince clients that the matching service provided is greater than what can be handled internally. The industry markets a bundle of skills to clients while minimizing pay to the temporaries who are assigned the most mundane tasks.

As is evident from many of the preceding quotations, temporary workers do not always readily accept the agencies' viewpoint because of the disparity between the ideology and workers' immediate experiences. We should, however, consider the potential impact of these ideologies on those in the position to make changes that affect temporary workers. Without direct, firsthand experience in temporary employment, decision-makers may more readily embrace these ideologies. Therefore, the operation of this ideology outside temporary employment may prove just as important as its operation inside temporary employment because of its potential to reinforce material constraints on temporary workers' actions through inaction on behalf of legislators and other decision-makers. Proper formulation of policy requires going beneath the rhetoric to the lived experiences of temporary clerical workers. These lived experiences can conflict with industry claims.

Ideologies Concerning Upward Mobility

Yet another powerful ideology operating on temporary workers regards temporary employment as a means to upward mobility. Temporary agencies prominently advertise skill development as a benefit of temporary employment that will surely bring upward mobility for the hardworking temporary.

> The temporary help industry acts to increase the skills and real wages of the workforce through its training and upgrading programs, and through the productive experience it provides. (press release, National Association of Temporary Services, 1994)

> As workers compete in an ever changing and complex workplace, temporary help offers numerous benefits that give temporary employees an inside tract to more advanced skills and better jobs. (press kit, National Association of Temporary Services, 1994)

In cases where temporary workers continually perform deskilled work, they obviously are inhibited from acquiring or using skills on the job. And while temporary industry representatives sing the praises of the in-house computer training they offer to temporary workers, my interviewees' reports seldom matched what was advertised. Not all temporary agencies have computer training available. The hardware, software, and space required represent a substantial investment for a smaller agency. In those agencies that do have computer training available, the "training" most often consists of the worker following an on-screen, computer-led tutorial.[14] Temporary workers who have used these tutorials have found them to be inadequate because they offer little opportunity for the student to practice in a meaningful way.

> They advertise that they have the tutorial. And it's not really a tutorial that anyone teaches you. It's something that you, you hit the button on the computer and it says [speaking slowly with emphasis], "Welcome to tutorial. We will now learn about a computer. This is your keyboard. This is the screen." And it takes you step by step by step. And the software is geared specifically for that, and you type up the little thing they give you to type up or whatever. You don't have the option to write your own letter or whatever. (Bernice Katz, thirty-four-year-old white woman)

At the temporary agency where I worked (a large regional agency), computer training consisted mainly of tutorials in WordPerfect, Microsoft Word, WordStar, DisplayWrite, MultiMate, Wang, and Samna Word. Also offered were Lotus 1-2-3 (version 2.2) and dBASE III Plus. Many of the tutorials were for outdated versions of the software, and tutorials for Lotus and dBASE are not adequate to produce proficiency in those who use them. Exceptions do exist to this training scenario, and they are well-publicized. The experiences of temporary workers, however, reflect the rarity of the high-quality training opportunities.

In addition to the lack of quality training programs, not all temporary workers are eligible for the computer training that does exist. Agencies sometimes require a certain number of hours to be worked before a temporary may access these tutorials—an ironic fact considering how agency literature emphasizes qualified individuals and promises to help temporaries develop marketable skills. At the agency where I worked, temporaries are required to have a staggering 500 hours of work (almost three months full time) before they are eligible for computer training. Because most temporaries must work through more than one agency in order to secure enough hours of work, eligibility for such programs becomes more remote the more agencies a temporary worker uses.

Many temporary workers who do qualify and would like to acquire additional computer training are inhibited from doing so because of the very nature of temporary work. Temporary workers are constrained by the uncertainty of their situation and do not have the free time or flexibility that many believe they do (Martella 1991; Negrey 1993). Temporary workers who are working full time find it difficult if not impossible to take advantage of computer training because temporary agencies typically have the same hours as the businesses they service and offer training only during those hours.

> I say I like to go once a week. That would be ideal. Truth is, maybe I'm lucky if I can do it twice a month for an hour or so. But I like to go to keep up my skills and to be seen as a presence—that I'm doing something to improve my skills. (Jean Masters, thirty-four-year-old African American)

Jean found it difficult to practice her computer skills because her agency closed at 5:30 P.M. and was not open on the weekends. Most of the time, Jean's assignments ended between 5 and 5:30 P.M. With commuting time, she could not even get to the agency before they closed much less find time to practice new skills or develop new competencies.

When temporary workers are not working full time,[15] many are involved in looking for work or running their time cards to the different agencies they use. These activities can take a substantial amount of time. In addition, temporaries must be available immediately to the agencies should an assignment arise. For many, this means waiting by the phone or calling all "your" agencies to find work, rather than isolating yourself at just one agency and making use of the computer training program. As most temporary workers will tell you, if an agency calls with an assignment, you had better be accessible or you will lose the assignment. Some temporary workers I interviewed have gone so far as to carry beepers. Overall, I found very little use of agency-provided training owing to the constraints placed on temporary workers by their status as "temporary." Thus the picture of temporaries gaining upward mobility from skills development is not always accurate for these workers.

Another way in which agencies use the ideology of upward mobility is through portraying temporary work as a good way for workers to get into a desirable organization or occupation. Temporary work is represented as a vehicle for workers to demonstrate their skills so that their talents can be discovered. The industry portrays itself as providing good jobs that could lead to something better (that is, permanent) in tough economic times.

Working as a temporary can be a meaningful and useful bridge to full-time employment by providing . . . an opportunity for workers to showcase their talents to a wide variety of potential employers. (press kit from the National Association of Temporary Services, 1994)

The temporary help/staffing services industry can act as a "jobs bridge" to full-time employment. Temporary work offers workers, who may have been displaced during current workforce restructuring, a critical safety net of income, benefits, and skills training which often provides access back to full-time employment. (pamphlet from a temporary help company, 1993)

Indeed, the most common reason that temporaries consent to perform deskilled or devalued work is that they believe they may gain a "permanent" job through temporary employment.

After working three months there I'd probably have the references from the people I work with to get a permanent job there. And I guess that's kind of a starting gate. That's pretty much what I looked for. It's just too bad because the company is moving to Sacramento or something like that. (Mark Cranford, twenty-year-old white man)

I'm temping . . . because eventually somewhere I will get an offer. And I won't have to go through the interview process in the same way everyone else does. They go, "We love you, this is a formality." And you know you've got the job basically. (Michael Glenn, twenty-six-year-old Asian American)

It's temporary, and there's a possibility. The key is here, something maybe I haven't touched on, too. There's that possibility that someone might see me and say, "Hey, he would be able to do this job." Maybe not the one I'm doing, but another job. And [there's] the possibility of acting, too. (Doug Larson, thirty-nine-year-old white man)

Thus the ideology that skills gained through temporary employment are a means to upward mobility and permanency pushes temporary workers to work hard (at deskilled or devalued work) and stay with temporary employment. They come to believe that developing and using such skills on temporary assignments will lead them out of temporary employment to their dream job, whether inside or outside the corporate world. Temporary workers become workers-in-waiting, waiting for their reward, which is a "good," full-time job. Some workers take this view to the extreme, as did one man who told me that by working in the kitchen at an entertainment company, he might be discovered for his talents as a sound engineer:

> If you do well, I mean, if you're doing something in the kitchen and they really like you, and you say, "Well I work on audio," they may pull you over and say, "Here, we've got this," or something like that. . . . It's easier to find out about jobs at a particular place if you're already in the place than it is to submit unsolicited résumés. (Arnold Finch, twenty-three-year-old white man)

Unfortunately, Arnold never was hired as a sound engineer by the entertainment company. Still other workers feel that their writing skills or management skills will be recognized and they will be offered a permanent job that differs significantly from their temporary assignment.[16] In fact, among those temporary workers I interviewed who were offered permanent jobs, the jobs offered were almost exclusively the same as their temporary assignments. Thus temporary workers often turned down permanent offers because they did not represent upward mobility through temping. Rather than take a permanent position that resembled a temporary position and its attendant deskilled or devalued work, temporary workers waited in hopes that the next offer would be more in line with their expectations. They felt that they could perform deskilled or devalued work if it was a means to an end (upward mobility) but not as a permanent job.

> During the time I temped I must have been offered at least eight or nine permanent jobs at places, and like I didn't know how to tell them I would never consider working for them, not full time, not at the same job. They'd have to give more than that. (Ludy Martinez, thirty-six-year-old Filipina)

> And I was offered a lot of full-time positions from the temp jobs. But I . . . was fortunate that I didn't have to take a job right away just to make ends meet. I could wait for the job I really wanted, one that I could use my degrees and talents for. (Ellen Lanford, thirty-eight-year-old white woman)

Thus the characterization of work as "temporary" represents an effective strategy for eliciting workers to do work they would otherwise not perform because they felt it was "beneath them." This scenario is reminiscent of women college graduates feeling they could get into the management of an organization through the secretarial pool. Temporary work alters internal labor markets in such a way, however, as to significantly separate temporary workers from permanent workers and access to internal labor markets. To the extent that the secretarial pool was ever a successful route into managerial positions, it is even less so in temporary clerical employment, particularly when temporary employees are used as a buffer around permanent employees to secure their jobs and cushion them against monotonous work. As such, temporary workers find a considerable distance between temporary employment and access to the internal labor market of a company unless they specifically were hired into a position for a trial run.[17]

When temporary workers perform work that lacks skill content, they are unable to demonstrate their capability for performing a more skilled, permanent job. Temporary industry figures reflect that 35 percent of temporary workers eventually are offered permanent jobs. Of course, this leaves 65 percent, the overwhelming majority, who are *not* offered jobs. Obviously, the industry's claims about temporary work being the road to a permanent position should be tempered. When assessing the success of temporary employment for job placement, keep in mind that the industry does not provide data regarding the type of jobs offered, or whether these offers are ultimately accepted by the temporary worker. In my research, those workers who were offered permanent jobs recounted that they did not take the jobs because of low pay or low skill requirements. In other words, temporary workers who did filing for eight hours a day were not typically offered a position in the management training program. More often than not, they were offered permanent jobs that entailed filing for eight hours a day. Jobs offered to temporaries more often resembled temporary work in skill *and* pay level. To make a definitive statement about work transitions, additional research is needed to examine these transitions from temporary to permanent work. Such research must be carefully designed to discern which temporaries are offered permanent employment and how often this occurs, which temporaries accept permanent employment offers, and which reject such offers and why.

An interesting phenomenon that indicated the effectiveness of the industry's marketing claims about temporary work as the means to a desirable permanent job was that many of my informants remained hopeful for their shot at upward mobility despite having been offered deskilled or devalued jobs they did not accept.

I didn't want to go into an agency, you know, with a lot more, with being really overqualified and going to do clerical work. I felt that would be too devastating to me. Now I just don't care. I'll take ten bucks and keep my mouth shut and go home. And you never know who you're gonna meet [while temping]. (Cindy Carson, thirty-eight-year-old white woman)

This is not to say that temporaries *never* find their perfect job through temping. Indeed, this must happen often enough to perpetuate and legitimize the myth of the full-time job, which aids in securing a docile temporary workforce. Cases of "temp finds wonder job" are paraded out by temporary agencies to the media and their own workers.

In 1993, George Williams accepted a temp assignment with Ethereal Gas Company, where his cheerful smile, reliability, and willingness to work made a good impression. Within a few months, he was offered a full time position with the gas company and has since received a promotion and an opportunity for additional training. (temporary agency newsletter)

One agency even ran a contest soliciting "temp stories" from temporary workers in Los Angeles. The ad gave examples of the kinds of temp stories they were looking for. Prominently featured are the examples of temporary workers finding great jobs through temporary employment.

The client falls in love with you and you get offered a regular, full-time position with a company you've come to know and like. . . . IT REALLY HAPPENS. Just listen to [April's] story. She started off as a temporary receptionist at a literary agency in Century City, and now she heads up the entire TV literary department! (full-page, back-cover, color advertisement placed by a temporary agency)

Thus, ideologies concerning skill and upward mobility help to secure temporary workers' consent and labor in an environment of economic and structural constraints owing to changes in the organization of work. Much has been said about the declining loyalty of workers to companies that are regularly shedding employees.[18] Despite the limits on consent produced through direct, contradictory experiences, temporary workers often embraced these ideologies, at least initially in the interviews, perhaps partially as a way to justify their position to me. Continued discussion, however, revealed a measure of control that was far from complete. Indeed, the extent to which workers embraced a particular ideology seemed to be intertwined with the extent to which they perceived themselves as having other options. In this way, structural constraints and ideologies act as mutually reinforcing means for producing consent in temporary workers.

In the case where temporary workers are performing deskilled work, the lack of skill acts as a mechanism of control over the temporary employee. The worker is unable to gain any organizationally specific skills that would increase individual bargaining power with the client. Furthermore, in this context, temporary workers are unable to increase their bundle of skills. Frederick Taylor, the "father" of scientific management, understood that removing knowledge from workers was a means to better control them. While Taylor undertook this through scientific management, the same process can occur when skilled work is allocated by permanent and temporary status.

THE picture of skill in temporary work is a complex one. Employers, in conjunction with permanent employees, can divide clerical tasks in order to insulate "core" workers from routine jobs, which results in the material deskilling of jobs for temporary workers. The overall technical work process remains unchanged, while material skill is reallocated based on one's status as a periphery or core employee. Alternatively, companies can hire temporaries into clerical jobs that are clerical in name only (upgrading the content of the job while leaving the pay unchanged), which results in the devaluing of temporary jobs. We have seen that temporary work is both deskilled and devalued, with some temporary workers experiencing both material and ideological deskilling tendencies.

A significant alteration has evolved in the operation of internal labor markets. Although represented by the temporary industry as "a foot in the door," temporary jobs do not provide the route to upward mobility as promised. Relatively unskilled temporaries can be structurally inhibited from developing the very skills that may help them to acquire less marginal work, while highly skilled temporaries can be constrained from demonstrating their capabilities on the job because they are required to do relatively deskilled work. Yet even those who are able to demonstrate their skills on the job feel that potential employers have little motivation to hire them permanently because of added benefit costs and the hiring fees charged by temporary agencies, and because they are already doing the job at a relatively low rate of pay. In these cases, temporary jobs can truly be described as a lose-lose situation—dead-end jobs regardless of the human capital that temporary workers bring with them.

Consider the high-wage, high-skill workforce touted by the Clinton administration (see also Reich 1992). The temporary industry holds that it can be central to the upgrading of U.S. workers' skills.

The U.S. Department of Labor estimates that 75% of the people who lose their jobs today will have to be retrained before going back into the workforce because their skills will have become obsolete. Currently businesses are hard-pressed to fill jobs requiring specific expertise (computer operators, word processing operators, etc.). Temporary help companies have the unique ability to provide workers with distinctive or hard to find skills. By using such workers, businesses maintain their operations even as workforce skill shortages intensify. (sample letter to the editor, National Association of Temporary Services promotional material for National Temporary Help Week, 1994)

As made evident by the stories of the workers I spoke with, some of the more grandiose claims made by the industry need to be viewed with a skeptic's eye. The temporary industry's relationship to workers' skill development is more complex than portrayed here. Even when agencies make training available, the unstable nature of much temporary employment has the unintended consequence of prohibiting skill acquisition. One possible consequence of increased temporary usage explored and supported to a degree herein might be a further bifurcation of the workforce into higher-wage, higher-skill "winners" and lower-wage, lower-skill "losers."

In addition, considering the overrepresentation of women and people of color in contingent forms of employment, we should take warning that continuing increases in temporary employment may exacerbate existing gender and racial inequalities in employment, regardless of the skills one obtains through increased educational efforts. The "winners" and "losers" are as likely to be divided by race, class, and gender as they are in many other aspects of social life. Indeed, as we see in the next chapter, rewards in the world of the temporary worker often are dispersed with regard to these social categories.

3   Out of Control

Sandy is the manager and a service representative of a branch of a large national temporary employment agency. She has more than seven years' experience in temporary placement. We discussed many aspects of the temporary employment industry, and our conversation highlighted one of the central issues in temporary clerical employment—control. When I asked Sandy what is the hardest part of running a temporary agency, she said,

> Not being able to control human nature. Not being able to control your applicants, your clients, their reactions. There's so many components we have no control over. It makes it very difficult. We're dealing with human nature, and you would think that these are responsible adults. But not all the time. They don't show up; they're two hours late; they leave for lunch and don't come back. And these are things we absolutely have no control over. (Sandy Mathers, twenty-eight-year-old African American, agency branch manager)

When asked what she does about this, Sandy replied, "Apologize [to the client] and start over."

Given Sandy's comments as well as the deskilled, or devalued nature of temporary clerical work as seen in the last chapter, how can we account for the fact that temporaries work hard at their assignments on a daily basis? Indeed, the truly intriguing question here is not why some temporaries "flake out" and wander off the job in the middle of the day, but why so many of them stay at their assigned desks and work so hard until closing time. How do temporary agencies and client companies secure the cooperation of workers who are promised little other than a paycheck? Part of the answer lies in a complex and sometimes contradictory set of social controls structured to elicit hard work and agreeability. The temporary industry, temporary agencies, clients, co-workers, and even the temporaries themselves participate in creating and maintaining a powerful yet incomplete web of controls.

Trying to understand what makes workers work is not a new undertaking. Karl Marx posed what has come to be known as "the control problem" of capitalist labor processes. Control over workers is a problem because capital[1] depends on workers' efforts to generate a profit. When managers purchase "labor power" (that is, they pay a worker for his or her time) rather than a contracted amount of output, the manager has the responsibility of ensuring that enough output is generated to bear the cost of the labor power and to create the desired profit. In other words, management must control labor.

Many researchers have identified methods of control over labor.[2] One of the most considered mechanisms for control is the division of labor, which separates conception from execution, the thinkers from the doers. The minute division of labor encourages workers to focus solely on their individual task rather than the larger scheme of things.

Researchers have identified numerous other means of control, only a fraction of which are accounted for by the division of labor. There may even be a historical development of control through its simple, technical, and bureaucratic forms. Unable to use highly personalized, simple control, some capitalists turned to more structural forms such as technical and bureaucratic control as market and other conditions changed.[3]

We also recognize that an ideological component to control exists. Braverman (1974) characterized scientific management as at least partly an ideological device deployed by management for the sole purpose of wresting knowledge and control from workers. The language of scientific management legitimizes management's search for knowledge—management rightfully comes to possess the expert knowledge previously only possessed by the workers. Workers, denuded of their know-how, have little recourse but to comply with the wishes of management.

Yet control is not always something management "does" to workers. Rather than always being coerced, workers sometimes actually "consent" to cooperate with management through institutionalized games of "making out."[4] Workers are given more freedom within a narrower field of choices. Consent is generated as workers make their choices because "one cannot both play the game and at the same time question the rules"

(Burawoy 1979, 81). In a similar fashion, the concept of "responsible autonomy" indicates that control over professional workers, endangered by the inflexibility of scientific management, can be reclaimed by relaxing some of the more structural forms of control through practices that allow workers greater discretion.[5] Again featured in both of the previous two understandings is the role of ideology in securing control over workers.

While control mechanisms are varied in their construct, they also vary in terms of intended audience and outcome. For instance, control mechanisms may be gendered. Employers have used company-sponsored beauty pageants and the "company as family" metaphor to encourage stereotypically feminine behavior and thus "feminine" compliance from workers.[6] The modes of control used in any work setting may vary with the gender of the workforce as control is intertwined with gendered meanings of skill.[7] The disproportionate placement of women in peripheral or secondary labor markets subjects them to the modes of control associated with these segments.[8]

While the many forms of control are often discussed separately, they do not appear to be empirically separate. Different varieties of control can and are combined, sometimes in the simultaneous usage of seemingly contradictory methods. This phenomenon is referred to as the "fundamental tension of management" (Thompson 1983, 151). In the sections that follow, I explore the many dimensions (sometimes contradictory) of control that are at work in temporary clerical employment.

The Organization of Control in Temporary Work

Controlling temporary work poses a challenge to management because temporary workers are dispersed throughout many different locations and are loosely attached to their jobs, either voluntarily or involuntarily. Therefore the temporary industry has attempted to use indirect controls such as "employee recognition programs and employee uncertainty in the allocation of jobs" (Gottfried 1991, 706). Simultaneously, temporary agencies use bureaucratic means of control such as rationalizing jobs and the interview/skills-testing/intake process, although in the last chapter we saw the extent to which rationalization was in the eye of the beholder. The intensification of work for temporaries is virtually assured in the context of two levels of supervision: the on-site supervisor and the agency representative (Gottfried 1991, 1994). The only crack in this multivalent control structure is the potential conflict of interests between client companies and temporary agencies. Such a conflict arises because the temporary agency has an interest in placing each temporary on an assignment for as many hours as possible. Their profit comes in the form of a " markup" as part of the hourly rate paid by the client company. In contrast, the company is interested in extracting the maximum labor power from each temporary in order to shorten the number of hours for which they are billed by the temporary agency.[9]

Finally, temporary work can itself be a mechanism of control over all workers, permanent and temporary, by further dividing the workplace in a new way that can weaken the potential for labor organizing.[10] The introduction of temporary workers has the very real potential of creating uncertainty about job stability among the permanent workers and thus reducing solidarity among workers in general.

The picture of control painted here is compelling but incomplete. Not reflected is the complexity with which temporary workers experience control in their work lives. The goal here is to allow for greater complexity in conceptualizing control as well as to allow room for contradictions, conflicts, and resistance, and conceptualizing control as more fluid than static.

Control over Temporary Workers

Because control over temporary workers encompasses many disparate phenomena, we need a framework for understanding these different dimensions. Several interrelated and sometimes contradictory types emerged from my research. While temporary agencies and client companies exercised many methods of control over temporary workers, no one method was sufficient in and of itself. Therefore, we are better off describing temporary agencies and their clients as having a vast repertoire of control methods at their disposal. While these many categories are separated for analytical clarity, placing an observation neatly into just one category is often empirically difficult. Likewise, elements of each category are not necessarily distinct or separate from the others.

Structural means consist of methods derived from the organization of temporary work, and they may include bureaucratic control. Structural control, however, also includes several factors such as capriciousness and insecurity that run counter to bureaucratic ideals that require precision and impartiality. Interpersonal varieties focus on the face-to-face relationships between temporary workers and their agencies, including the use of threats, the telling of "bad temp" and "bad client" stories, the formation of "friendships," and the uses of emotional labor. Discursive control is used to shape the behaviors of temporaries and to legitimize the practices and actions of clients and temporary agencies to the benefit of temporary agencies, business, whites, and men. Rationality, the desire to work, and the myth of the full-time job combine to present a discourse that both reflects and supports highly asymmetrical power relations among temporary workers, their agencies, and clients. While the use of difference as control could easily be included within the category of discursive control, here it merits separate discussion.

Another area of control explored here is the phenomenon wherein temporary employment affects the nature of control between the client company and its "regular" workers, and between the client company and the temporary agency insofar as implications exist for the experiences of temporary workers. Finally, I look at the various attempts (some successful) at obfuscating these forms of control.

Structural Control: Division of Labor

As seen in Chapter 2, temporary employment can increase the division of labor. An increased division of labor carries implications for management's control over workers. The division of labor can limit workers' knowledge as well as workers' social contacts. Many times, the tasks assigned a temporary clerical worker are unique when compared with the work of surrounding workers (Rogers 1999), particularly when they are given monotonous or otherwise undesirable work that has been piling up on co-workers' desks. In addition, temporary work that is short or uncertain in duration provides few opportunities for workers to form relationships. Finally, temporaries frequently experience physical isolation at the workplace, often being situated away from permanent workers and even other temporaries. Separations like these (by task, time, and space) provide little opportunity for temporaries to make meaningful comparisons with other workers, either temporary or regular, in order to judge the value of their output or the quality of their experiences. Throughout my fieldwork, I found these divisions to be a frustrating feature of temporary employment. Initially, I had planned to interview the many other temporaries I thought I would meet while on the job; however, even when I was able to identify other temporary workers around me, I seldom had enough contact with them to introduce myself, explain my project, and set up a meeting. Frequently, I was gone before I could get a name or a phone number.

As a temporary worker, I often found that unless I was replacing an absent employee, I usually was relegated to a remote corner of the office. Other temporaries report working at the end of a hallway, in part of a storage room, in a basement office, and in an empty wing on the same floor as their supervisor.

Temporary workers experience social isolation as well as physical isolation (Rogers 1995) as they inevitably find themselves outside the daily office chitchat and eating lunch by themselves.[11] Both types of isolation prevent temporaries from acquiring knowledge about their working conditions. As a result, their labor can be intensified. In fact, one of the many benefits that management books tout about temporary employment is that it reduces wasted time at work, thus extracting more labor power from the worker. Less time spent socializing means more time spent working. Here is an excerpt from a book distributed by the American Management Association on how to use temporary services:

> Improved productivity and cost containment are priority human resources issues. It is precisely in these areas that the temporary help industry maintains its effectiveness. Industry experts suggest that simply eliminating idle time or nonproductive hours increases productivity. U.S. Department of Labor statistics suggest that temporary workers are productive 90 percent of the day compared to the productivity level of the regular work force that may be productive only 65 percent of the day. Temporary workers are on the job to do one thing—to complete the job. They are not distracted by the socialization [sic] or the politics of the office. They are never absent and they don't take long lunch hours. (Interestingly, the longer temporary workers are on the job, the more likely they are to be distracted by the synergy of the office.) (Lewis and Malloy, 1991, 19)

Finally, isolation increases the logistical difficulties of organizing an already fluid workforce that moves from work site to work site as assignments change, and from temporary agency to temporary agency in order to secure enough work. Having a workforce fractured in this way reduces the likelihood of workers acquiring any measure of control through collective bargaining.[12]

Yet not all temporary workers are subject to separation from their coworkers. Some companies employ a large group of temporary workers for a specific project that can last several weeks, months, or even years (for my interview subjects, this usually occurred with banks, insurance companies, and government positions). Instead of separating workers, these "temp forces" actually help bring workers together. Contrary to the divisions we saw before, these workers may share tasks and work space. In these cases, temporary workers found it easier to identify one another, and in one company temporary workers were issued special identification cards with a big green "T." Under these conditions, workers are more easily able to engage in socializing on the job.

Regular contact permits temporaries to compare their work conditions with others. As the use of temporary workers continues to rise (both a greater use of temporary workers in general and a greater use of temp forces), we might imagine a critical point at which the concentration of temporary workers acts to decrease management control rather than enhance it. Companies with especially large temporary workforces can decrease the cost of those workers through elimination of benefits and unemployment claims (one such venue for research might be the "permanent temps" employed by large universities and other organizations). Pervasive use of temporary workers may, however, eventually act to bring workers together by increasing their contacts, their knowledge, and their feelings of solidarity. Under these conditions, temporary workers would find it easier to take collective action, thus causing additional control problems for management.

Such a scenario, however, remains at this point purely speculation. Temporaries are far from forming a critical mass. Currently, only 1 to 2 percent of the U.S. workforce is employed through the temporary industry on any given day (National Association of Temporary Services 1992). Temporary work as it currently exists typically enhances management control through atomizing workers; however, certain arrangements do exist that potentially can accomplish just the opposite.

Insecurity

A second type of structural control in temporary work concerns the employment insecurity of temporary workers (Gottfried 1991) and the capriciousness with which work and rewards can be allocated by the temporary agencies. Many temporary workers I interviewed expressed feelings of insecurity regarding the unpredictable flow of temporary assignments.

Nobody has a commitment to you. They could let you go tomorrow and not tell you. So you have absolutely no security and no guarantees and no insurance and no benefits. (Albert Baxter, thirty-one-year-old white man)

Some assignments were "good" in that they lasted for several weeks or months and offered some ability for the temporary worker to plan his or her finances. However, securing a long-term assignment is not always possible. Many assignments are for a week or less. Yet even when temporary workers are placed on coveted long-term assignments, there is no guarantee that the assignment will not be cut short, as reported by many temporaries.

Most of the ones they called me for are indefinite, indefinite, indefinite. Which I know by now means two or three days because if they told you two or three days it wouldn't really be worth it. (Mike Cranford, twenty-year-old white man)

[The manager] had estimated that this job would take three days. And the woman that hired us was surprised that a three-day job got finished in a day. And she goes, "That's fantastic. Here's your reward, I'll cut the assignment short." Not "I'll give you a bonus." So our assignment got cut down. (Cheryl Hansen, twenty-three-year-old white woman)

Temporary workers are made aware by the agency that they may be "pulled off" an assignment if their work is not satisfactory or even for no reason at all. As a result, this lingering insecurity often compels temporary workers to work hard in order to be perceived as doing a good job. Some temporary workers believe it becomes necessary for them to do a better job than "permanent" workers, who have some room for slacking off because of the permanent nature of their positions.

In a way, you have to be better than the regular people. You have to behave better. You have to be more on time. You have to not take personal calls. You have to be more straight and narrow because they can, because you're a temp, dump you tomorrow. (Ludy Martinez, thirty-six-year-old Filipina)

This view is buttressed by what I was told by temporary agency personnel.

They're looking for somebody to be there when they have the need and someone who's proficient to do what's required, even more so than the regular person or a regular position would have. (Charles Morton, fifty-three-year-old white man, agency owner/manager)

Consequently, the structured insecurity of temporary work helps to secure the labor of temporary workers who would otherwise have little attachment to the client firms. Insecurity aids in the maintenance of a docile workforce, as workers who know they can be replaced at a moment's notice are less likely to assert themselves or cause trouble on the job. In fact, most temporary agencies offer their clients a money-back guarantee of satisfaction (of which the temporary worker is aware). If unsatisfied with the temporary worker, the client simply contacts the agency, and the worker is replaced immediately.

> We stand behind the quality of our temporary employees. If our client is not satisfied within the first four hours, absolutely no charge will be made to the client and [we] will immediately make arrangements for a replacement. (pamphlet from a temporary agency)

> Temporary help companies stand behind the quality of their service. If notified promptly, most temporary help services will not charge their customers for unsatisfactory hours of work and will replace the temporary employee if necessary. (press kit from the National Association of Temporary Services)

Typically the guarantee specifies that the client does not pay for the hours worked by the unsatisfactory worker.

> We feel so confident that you will be satisfied with our services . . . [that] our services are fully guaranteed. If ever, for any reason, you are not completely satisfied, call us during the first day of the assignment. There will be no charge to you for the work performed. And we will send out an immediate replacement. (pamphlet from a temporary agency)

The money-back guarantee provides a measure of control over the temporary agency for the client company, which results in the agencies' further application of control over temporary workers. Importantly, temporary workers feel constrained by the fact that the agencies' interests lie more immediately with the client than with their workers. Several temporaries expressed concern that they had been granted or denied assignments because temporary agencies fail to consider the interests of the workers along with the interests of their clients.

> What they said is if you work this job for us, when these people call, we will make sure you go back there. And they didn't. They lied. Because they were looking out for their interests, not mine. I mean, if they

thought of both people's interests, I would have gotten hired there. (Arnold Finch, twenty-three-year-old white man)

Competition between temporary agencies also compels them to exercise tight control over their workers. Clients sometimes call several agencies, which then must compete to fill the assignment as quickly as possible. Therefore it is not unusual for an agency to request that a worker be at a client company within one hour of being notified. Once placed, if the temporary worker does not meet the client company's standards in any way, the client company can choose among several other temporary agencies to replace that worker.[13] Enough disappointments can result in the temporary agency losing a client for good; thus it is to the agency's benefit (and to some degree necessary for survival) to have compliant workers. In effect, this nicely aligns the interests of the agency and the client. The agency gets happy clients who will continue to use its services, while the client gets compliant workers. The only interests not considered in the equation are those of the temporary worker.

One of the effects of this structure of interests in temporary employment is that temporary workers report feeling taken advantage of or abused without the available recourse of responding or asserting themselves because of their precarious position both in the client company and with the temporary agency. Each of the following temporary workers describes his or her inaction as a result of feelings of insecurity. The people quoted here needed to work, and the recognition that temporary agencies have no obligation to provide them with employment kept them silent.

If they call you for a week and they only end up keeping you for one day, there's nothing you can do about it. You can't change it. You can't throw a temper tantrum. I mean, nothing you're going to do is going to change it. If they say you're not working there, you ask them politely for another assignment and hope that you get one. (Arnold Finch, twenty-three-year-old white man)

[My supervisor] was verbally abusive. She would scream at me in the middle of the day. It got so bad [that] the supervisor even said something to her. I frankly didn't know what to do. If I complained to the agency, they'd just think I was a complainer. I knew this was a great account for them. (Cindy Carson, thirty-eight-year-old white woman)

In some cases the agency would probably stick up for them because they're the client. I mean, hey, if they're a big client, they're like, "Hey, this temp is expendable. If he doesn't like being yelled at and screamed at and being called shithead, there's about fifty people in line who will." And that's true. (Harold Koenig, twenty-nine-year-old white man)

Temporary workers also feel that work can be and is distributed capriciously by the temporary agency representatives. Work can be assigned as a reward for good behavior, or it can be withheld as a punishment or a way to "cool out" angry temporaries. Those temporaries seen as cooperative and compliant receive assignments, and more often the coveted assignments, while "problem" temporaries receive undesirable assignments or no work at all. A temporary's financial future may very well be at the mercy of the temporary agency. Michael was identified to me by one of my agency contacts as one of their "best temps":

I miffed one agency [by not staying in a bad situation]. I miffed them to the point that we didn't talk for a long time. They were very unhappy with me. For the agency not to go to bat for me was very, very disappointing and off-putting. And I rarely hear from them anymore on anything. And I call them and they say, "She's busy right now; she'll give you a call back." And I don't get a call back. (Michael Glenn, twenty-six-year-old Asian American)

Regarding his anger over a pay dispute, Don reflected on his decision not to pursue the issue with the agency:

I probably should have vocalized that more, but I didn't feel like I was really in a position to even say that. Because underneath it all is if they get pissed at you they can just not give you work and say, "Oh, there's no jobs." (Don Birch, twenty-four-year-old white man)

Doug reports a paucity of work after he declined an assignment in favor of an acting gig:

They don't like when you turn assignments down. After you do that . . . I mean, you can have a very valid reason, but after you do that, for a while it's like why bother calling you. So I had to turn things down a couple times, and the next time I called, they're like, "Oh, no, we don't have anything for you. Try tomorrow." So it becomes a cat and mouse game. (Doug Larson, thirty-nine-year-old white man)

The extent to which agencies consciously use these strategies is not easy to determine from this study. There is evidence, however, that temporary agencies allow only a narrow range of variation around the norm of acceptable behavior for temporary employees. The agency representatives I spoke with reported little tolerance of errors by temporary workers.

> No, they don't [work for us again]. You don't get too many opportunities to do that. I give only one strike. (Sandy Mathers, twenty-eight-year-old African-American woman, agency branch manager)

> In most cases, an employee will be given a second chance, although performance will be closely monitored for a period of time. If a service receives a second negative evaluation, it is not likely to go on placing that person in the future. (Fanning and Maniscalco 1993, 129)

> Sometimes they have that attitude, "I'm just a temp," you know. I don't have the patience for that. I'll fire a temp in no time. But if you're nice to somebody, they'll take advantage, you know. And you have to be able to let them know who's in charge here. (Manny Avila, twenty-eight-year-old Latino, agency placement manager)

Competition among Temporaries

The feelings that agencies can operate unchecked in this manner are heightened by the sense of competition among temporaries. The agency representatives I spoke with all reported that they had more "applicants" than they could possibly place in any given day.[14] Likewise, temporary workers were keenly aware that agencies had many more temporaries than they could place.

> But the temp market has changed, and there's a lot more temps, a lot more competition out there. (Ramona Geary, forty-eight-year-old white woman)

> You have to be able to commit [to an assignment]. You can't call them back. And if they let you call them back, there's the chance that the three other people that they called who are also perfect for the job will call back before you do. It's happened to me. (Arnold Finch, twenty-three-year-old white man)

> When you start out, you have to take just about anything. There's so many people doing this nowadays that are out of work; the agencies have their pick of the litter, and they can choose whoever they want. (Doug Larson, thirty-nine-year-old white man)

While some competition simply is due to economic conditions that push workers out of traditional work relationships, competition is also fostered by the temporary agencies through incentive programs (Gottfried 1991) as well as the ways they place workers. Temporary employees who hope to acquire access to health insurance or vacation benefits must work a minimum number of hours to qualify (sometimes the equivalent of working full time for two-thirds of the year). With the agents in control of the workflow, temporary workers who want employment benefits (most do) work hard and even compete with one another for the favor of the agency.

> They kept saying if you work really, really hard, we'll give you a bonus. And I worked really hard and every time I got up to a point where I should have gotten a bonus, they figured out a way not to give it to me. I'd work Monday through Thursday super hard, and on Friday they'd lay us off. And then they'd say, "Well, it wasn't a full week. You didn't work a full week, so we can't give you the bonuses." (Arnold Finch, twenty-three-year-old white man)

When temporary agencies look to place workers in an assignment, they place calls to temporaries on their "active" list. The first available temporary they reach is the one who gets the assignment. Being available for assignments means either waiting by the phone or having a beeper. Several of the temporaries I interviewed did carry beepers as a conscious strategy to secure assignments more readily than other temporaries. Temporary workers without such accoutrements felt disadvantaged:

> Yeah, [I got as many assignments] as I could. I mean, I had two things against me as far as temping goes. One, they love people with pagers, and I don't have one. If you have a pager they can get you jobs like anytime. Two, most places require you to have a vehicle. I was doing the bus, and you know it's really hard to get work even through a temp agency doing the bus. (Scott Parson, thirty-four-year-old African American)

The need to please the agency, however, can go beyond availability. Extreme but rare examples involved working extra hours without charging the client and performing extra duties for free, which secures additional labor power for the client company.

Related Institutions

Several of the temporary workers I spoke with reported what I considered a surprising interaction between the unemployment offices and temporary agencies. Some temporary workers were directed to temporary agencies by their unemployment office.

It was an unemployment office that suggested temping to me. It wasn't in California. It was in Maine. They were giving me ideas how to pick up some work. (Doug Larson, thirty-nine-year-old white man)

Even when temping was not an explicit suggestion on the part of the unemployment office, some temporaries felt pressured to take any assignment offered by the temporary agency for fear of losing any unemployment benefits to which they may have been entitled.

Basically, if someone called you for an assignment, you had to have a really good reason not to accept that assignment. Otherwise unemployment will cut you off. So basically you had to accept the job. (Jean Masters, thirty-four-year-old African American)

The structure of the temporary employment relationship is buttressed by existing employment law, which allows for the unilateral employment relationship in temporary work, as well as the lack of employment law relating specifically to temporary employment. With employment at will, "permanent" workers have little recourse to dispute what they may consider to be unfair termination. Temporary workers have even less recourse, for temporary employment is the epitome of the "at will" employment relationship. Demonstrating that termination from an assignment was anything more than a client changing his or her mind would be difficult if not impossible. Even when the client does truly shorten an assignment, there is no recourse for a temporary to collect monies he or she planned on earning from the full duration of the assignment. The best the temporary can hope for is that the agency will be able to find another assignment.

Similarly, the termination always can be justified in terms of poor work on the part of the temporary worker. The temporary worker seldom has a long-term relationship inside the client company, wherein someone could testify to the high quality of the temporary's work. Add this to the stereotypes of lazy temps and of the poor- quality work performed by temporary workers, and it's easy to see how temporary workers feel extremely constrained by their structurally precarious position in the labor market.

Interpersonal Control

In addition to forms of control that are built into the structure of temporary work, temporaries are subject to control exerted at micro levels of interaction between individual temporary workers and individual agents and between the temporary worker and individuals at the work site. While discussed separately, interpersonal controls and structural controls are interrelated. Interpersonal controls are shaped by structural factors such as capriciousness and insecurity, and the extent to which structural controls are felt depends on the qualities of the interpersonal relationships.

The first two types of interpersonal control, the use of subtle threats and storytelling, fall closer to the notion of simple control as a very direct exercise of personal power.[15] Although "interpersonal control" as conceptualized here includes simple control, it diverges from a purely despotic description to incorporate the sometimes-subtle manipulations that occur between temporary agency supervisors and workers. These relationships are much like those between domestic workers and their employers. "Friendship" often is intermingled with manipulation and even exploitation.

Subtle Threats

Capriciousness and insecurity form the background against which temporary agency representatives work to elicit worker compliance. Temporary workers report, for example, that agency representatives make subtle threats of assignment loss to workers who complain about almost any aspect of an assignment. The following account was related to me by a temporary employee who had complained about the way her pay rates were being computed:

> Only at my friend's agency was I given more money for doing something more. All the other ones, they offered to replace me if I didn't "like" the assignment. (Ludy Martinez, thirty-six-year-old Filipina)

Like many of the threats reported by my interviewees, this one is subtle because the agent frames the issue as being one of unhappiness on the part of the temporary worker rather than the shortcomings of the agency or client. The problem lies not with the agency's process for computing pay rates; rather, the temporary worker is portrayed as having an attitude problem. Also, the meaning of the agency's statement is left open for interpretation, and makes it easy for the agency manager to deny any threatening intentions.[16] Nevertheless, it is clear that for temporary clerical workers, complaining subjects them to a potential loss of the current assignment as well as future assignments and income. Temporaries come to understand that they must bring their behavior in line with what the agency desires, or they will be replaced by a "happier" (that is, more compliant) temporary.

Storytelling

The second type of interpersonal control includes what I call "bad temp stories"— anecdotes told to the worker either by the agency or the client about temporaries who performed poorly. These anecdotes always seem to involve a temporary worker who failed to live up to the standards of the agency or client by exhibiting behaviors that the agency or client wanted to eliminate (usually related to tardiness, mode of attire, attitude, or work intensity).

> As I was leaving [the agency manager] thanked me for coming to interview for the one-week temp job. Of course, I said, "No problem," and smiled. I wondered, "Why am I interviewing for a temp job?" She said [the client] likes her to check everyone out because they had a really bad experience once with a temp. (field notes, June 1994)

These tactics accomplish the conveyance of job expectations and help to ensure the compliance of the temporary worker through the presentation of an unflattering "temp" stereotype. Bad temp stories also carry the latent threat of job loss. "Bad" temps inevitably are dismissed, a fate no current temporary wants to be subjected to. When presented with the stereotype, temporary workers feel the need to distance themselves from the stigma and strive to become "supertemps." Supertemps outperform permanent workers and go beyond the tasks that are required of the job, again increasing job intensity.

In addition to "bad temp" stories, there are "bad client" stories. Bad client stories are accounts of clients who are said to be particularly difficult or demanding in some respect. These anecdotes serve to forewarn temporary workers of work conditions that may be unfavorable, and at the same time they set up a situation in which the worker agrees to "overcome" that difficulty in order to prove himself or herself to the agency or the client. Once again, the temporary employee is challenged to differentiate himself or herself from other temporary (and possibly permanent) workers by demonstrating the ability to cope with difficult and possibly abusive clients. Those temporary workers who work diligently and behave properly theoretically will minimize the chances of being abused by the problem client. Temporary workers may even gain a sense of proficiency and accomplishment in this area, as did Jean, who prided herself on her ability to handle tough cases. In fact, she told me that was one reason she received so many assignments:

> [The agency manager] knew that I always got these assignments where the people were difficult to deal with. But when I got there I was, like, I don't understand what was so difficult. So I said, "Oh, the guy's just a New Yorker. What's the problem?" You know he just has a New York attitude. There's nothin' wrong with him. (Jean Masters, thirty-four-year-old African American)

The agency I worked for told me a bad client story when they asked me to go to the client's office for an interview for a one-week assignment. Interviewing for short-term assignments is highly unusual, and I was not paid for the time I spent interviewing. The agent said it was a week-long assignment at a property management company and that I would have to interview for the position, because despite her seven years' experience in the industry, the client didn't trust her. She said the client wanted someone who was "just so" (field notes, June 1994).

I was forewarned of a difficult client, who was actually more fastidious than outright difficult, and I went beyond my duties to please the agency and the client before I ever started the assignment by interviewing on my "free time." In my field notes at that time, I described "feeling good" about the outcome, which may have mitigated my displeasure at giving my time away for free. Once on the actual assignment, I monitored my behavior more than usual.

Friendships

Still another type of interpersonal control arises because of the potential for a highly personalized relationship between temporary workers and the agency representatives. Some temporary workers actually seek out a highly personalized relationship with the agency representatives in order to secure more and better assignments. Like the domestic workers described by Romero (1992) and Rollins (1985), temporary clerical workers hope to improve their working conditions by getting friendly with agency representatives.

> And I talk to the temp [agency representatives] as if they were my friends because often they are. It's like the one I was estranged from. Well, the other day I got a call. What was one of my first questions to the

head of the temp division? "How's your tennis going?" It's like we're not personal friends but we're still on this level. (Michael Glenn, twenty-six-year-old Asian American)

Temporaries often characterize these relationships as friendships, and sometimes even liken them to familial relationships. Temporary agency promotional materials seem to encourage this outlook:

We take a personal, "family" approach to the employment relationship, fostering employees' growth and development in their work and in their community. (pamphlet from a temporary agency, 1992)

It would be disingenuous to deny that some temporary clerical workers had true feelings of friendship for their agency representatives; however, as in domestic work, these relationships are replete with ambivalence. Rollins's (1985) term *friendly exploitation* describes the mix of warm feelings *and* manipulation that domestic workers experienced at the hands of their employers. From the perspective of the agency representatives, they can use the personalized nature of this relationship to gain compliance from the temporary worker.[17] Temporary workers report "doing favors" for their agency because of their "friendship" with one or more of the representatives. Michael told me about an incident where he took an undesirable assignment with a promise from the agency that they would get him into a temp-to-perm assignment later. When this assignment never materialized and his favor was not reciprocated, Michael was understandably angry.

In fact, temporary worker self-help books encourage temps to do personal favors for their agency representatives

And you won't regret becoming friends with your assignment manager. . . . If you go on vacation, send your [assignment manager] a postcard or a Christmas card or birthday card. You want him or her to like you. . . . What are typical favors your service may ask of you? To take on a "rotten assignment"—the client is difficult. To take a lower rate than usual for an assignment. . . . To accept a boring assignment. To be at a client's place of business in less than an hour. To work at a location that is hard to reach or off the beaten path. (Lewis and Schuman 1988, 53)

. . . and place the blame on temporaries when promises are not honored by the agency.

Be warned: The [assignment manager] may promise you anything and then forget—if you allow that. Don't allow yourself to be manipulated. Speak up. It's okay to remind your service of the favor you did. Just be pleasant, and don't make it sound as though you are holding it hostage. (Lewis and Schuman 1988, 52)

Temporary workers in the subservient position of having to do favors for "friends" to secure work assignments are hardly in a position to complain or call an agency representative on the carpet when a favor goes unrewarded.

"Friendship" is seen very differently from the perspective of agency representatives I spoke with who made clear the status differences between temporary clerical workers and themselves. In contrast to the employers of domestic workers, agency representatives did not characterize their work relationships as friendships by any stretch of the imagination.

You get to know your applicants. But I try not to get too personal with them because they have to respect me and my responsibility here. My allegiance is to the agency, and as the manager of the office, you know, I would love to go out and have drinks with you, but I don't really think that's a good idea because you need to respect me as your manager, as your supervisor. (Sandy Mathers, twenty-eight-year-old African American woman, agency branch manager)

The personalized nature of their interactions with temporary workers is most accurately characterized as an application of human relations principles rather than a true friendship. While some temporary workers may interpret the relationship as a friendship, agency representatives clearly identified their actions as nothing more than techniques for maintaining morale and good office relationships.

Emotional Labor

There are many reasons why temporary employees are expected to perform emotional labor (see Henson 1996; Rogers 1995), but here I want to focus on emotional labor performed to maintain the relationship with the temporary agency. Given their precarious labor market position, temporary workers are constrained in their interactions with the agencies when disputes arise over hours, pay, treatment, conditions, and so forth. Rather than express their anger and outrage over such disputes, temporaries work very hard to suppress negative emotions, and some even replace them with empathy for the temporary agency.

Notes from my temporary experience demonstrate a similar response. One day I went to pick up my check. They couldn't find it. I asked what I needed to do to get a check today because I was leaving town and needed the money. The woman at the next desk said there was nothing that they could do and I'd have to get the check on Tuesday, and that was the soonest. I explained my problem again. She got very snitty and said there was nothing she could do and that it was not her fault. I was furious at how I was being treated. And I almost said something, but I bit my tongue. I didn't say anything because I needed more assignments and I needed to do my research. It just pissed me off that this woman didn't show one ounce of understanding. She just sat there with this cold look on her face. Like I was an annoyance. And I smiled and pleaded for my check. I even apologized for being an inconvenience. Ugh! (field notes, July 1994).

This emotional labor has a twofold effect. Surface acting mutes conflicts and secures the desired outcome for the agency (compliance), while deep acting serves to bring the temporary worker's definition of the situation into line with that of the agency. In deep acting, temporary workers suppress their anger and concern for their own best interests and eventually take on the point of view of the client or the agency.

> And I was *really* angry about [my request for a raise being denied]. But I never expressed anger. . . . I think they ought to stick by their employees. [The agencies] don't know people, so it's hard to [raise their rates]. . . . But if they do, then clients will just say, "We'll get another temp agency." (Marianne Wayne, twenty-six-year-old African American)

Thus this temporary worker who was extremely angry with her agency eventually found herself empathizing with their position and dropped her request for a pay raise. Her own interests were subjugated in favor of, or made to seem identical to, the agency's interests.

Many of the interpersonal methods of control discussed here seem to run counter to bureaucratic controls as found in Gottfried (1991), which rely on a codification of rules and expectations. While on the surface temporary employment may appear to be designed to operate more "objectively" than most employment relationships, on closer inspection we find highly personalized and sometimes manipulative relationships between temporary workers and the agency personnel.

Discursive Control

Both interpersonal and organizational structural control aid in securing the labor and cooperation of temporary workers. Discursive control, however, helps to structure both organizational control and interpersonal control by seemingly aligning the interests of temporary workers with the agencies and clients on an ideological level. Therefore, discursive control serves as an overarching ideological framework that buttresses both organizational control and interpersonal control over temporary workers. Furthermore, discursive control aims to legitimize and naturalize temporary employment and its practices.

Discursive control attempts to align perceptions of temporary workers favorably with the goals of temporary agencies and clients by employing certain ideological constructions of temporary work, including scientism and rationality, the right/desire to work, and the myth of the full-time job. While the agencies' discursive control is far from complete, its considerable effectiveness can be seen in temporary workers' internalized representations of the ideological framework supporting temporary employment (discussed further in Chapter 5).

Scientism and Managerial Rationality

The temporary industry tries to control the discourse around temporary employment through the use of scientific discourse as a justification for pay rates and working conditions. Scientific language about "skills testing" and "job matching" is used to justify wage rates to temporary workers. In this way, unsatisfactory pay rates or working conditions are seen not as the direct product of the agency's actions, but as the result of a complex, scientific set of factors.

> We also marry the best of computerized testing ("QUIZ" Testing Software) with our analysis of your job requirements to create tests that duplicate tasks you need done. (pamphlet from a temporary agency)

> Your rate of pay for each assignment is determined by the specific skill level required for the job, so you know you will always be paid fairly. (pamphlet from a temporary agency)

Temporary workers don't always buy the scientific justifications, however. When we examine the experiences of temporary workers, we find that they fall far short of what the industry portrays.

> I think they have a set fee and then what they do is they kind of play with the temps and give them what they think will pay. I know they do that because you write down what's the lowest amount that you'll take. (Cindy Carson, thirty-eight-year-old white woman)

The assignment of pay rates and "matching" of temporary workers with jobs is far more haphazard than would be allowed by "scientific" standards. In fact, a fair amount of capriciousness and chance are involved in both setting pay rates and assigning jobs. Yet a scientific discourse helps to obfuscate this reality, decreasing the likelihood of resistance from temporary workers.

Closely related to scientific discourse is an ethic of managerial rationality put forth by the temporary agencies. Managerial rationality is a particular understanding of the employment relationship that considers the concerns of employees only insofar as they align with the goals of management (productivity, profit, compliance). All other concerns are subordinated to the goals of management.

> A temporary employee comes into the work environment and they don't have the social demands and mandates of the employee. OK, they come in, they sit down, and they go to work. They're doing eight hours of productivity. There's a higher productivity than a regular employee. (Charles Morton, fifty-three-year-old white man, agency owner/manager)

This orientation is not surprising, as the functions performed by temporary agencies largely overlap with personnel/human resource functions in companies, which historically are aligned more closely with management than workers (Kaufman 1993). Traditionally, underlying the field of human resources has been the notion that management alone is endowed with rationality while workers are hopelessly irrational (Kaufman 1993).

Managerial rationality is supported by two different types of appeals. First, the use of temporary workers in place of "permanent" workers is said to be a management tool that helps companies become both more efficient and more profitable in an age of global competition. This justification is used despite the fact that many of the functions that temporary workers perform cannot be sent "offshore."

> The business community has increasingly recognized that the use of temporary help is a supplement to permanent staffing and a strategic personnel management resource that can save money and increase productivity. . . . Temporary help is an effective way to solve staffing problems. A strong, stable core of full-time workers surrounded by a flexible ring of temporary employees is recognized as one solution to weathering economic fluctuations. (public relations material from the National Association of Temporary Services, 1992)

Second, temporary agencies espouse (without question) the notion that the use of temporary employees is gaining popularity as a method to reduce employer responsibility and liability.

> [It's because of] all the employer laws that they have here in the state of California. It's a very difficult state to be an employer. . . . You almost have to be degreed legally to deal with the employer mandates from federal and state. And then you throw in the unions on top of it. It's a very sophisticated responsibility. It's dangerous being an employer in the state of California. (Charles Morton, fifty-three-year-old white man, agency owner/manager)

These appeals support the asymmetrical relationship between the agency and its workers. The party of primary importance in this employment relationship is unquestionably the client, who uses rational management techniques to increase the viability of its enterprise. The agency and the worker are there to meet the needs of the client. Thus employment policies such as the following are difficult to challenge:

> Finish the assignment. When you accept an assignment, you have an obligation and a responsibility to finish it. (pamphlet from a temporary agency)

This is a courtesy that neither client companies nor agencies reciprocate, as is evidenced by numerous accounts of assignments cut short. Yet this asymmetrical relationship is institutionalized throughout the industry and is supported by employment law and sometimes even temporary workers' own understandings of their situation. Temporary workers sometimes internalize managerial rationality even when they are describing their difficulties in acquiring a full-time, permanent job. They display a certain amount of empathy for the client companies that are hiring them as temporaries rather than permanent workers.

> There will be no more jobs in the near future that you can spend twenty years at. Because companies, with the way the market is going, you're not gonna be able to do that. They're cutting back on health care, on benefits, and they're not gonna be able to do that. (Larry Landers, thirty-eight-year-old African American)

> A lot of companies don't want to hire the temp directly because that means if they have a temp agency all they have to do is call up the agency and say, "Gee we don't like her, get rid of her." So the temp

agency calls and says, "By the way, you're not going to work tomorrow." They don't have to worry about two weeks' notice. They don't have to worry about anything. So it gives them a little bit of an edge. (Cheryl Hansen, twenty-three-year-old white woman)

In identifying with the imperatives of business (that is, efficiency and profit generation), temporary workers are less likely to object to conditions of their employment that they find bothersome. Managerial rationality mutes any potential conflict between temporary workers and the agency or between temporary workers and the clients by helping temporary workers identify with the needs of management (both the agency and the client) for profit over their own needs for a steady job with decent pay and benefits.

The Desire to Work

Temporary help services agency representatives also use discourses about the desire to work as a way to control the definition of the situation in an attempt to shape temporary workers' perceptions to the benefit of the agency. The representatives often mention temporary workers who "want to work" versus those who do not. Those who want to work get the assignments, while those who do not want to work do not.

Attitude, attitude. The desire to want to work. We get people that come in the door. . . . How do you measure attitude and a desire to do what's necessary to get the opportunity? They're ready to go out to work when they come in the door. If they don't come in the door and they're not ready to go off to work, then what are they doing coming into our door? (Charles Morton, fifty-three-year-old white man, agency owner/manager)

These people call in for jobs. And they call and they call. And the temp agency calls them back and says, "Look we've got this job. It's not exactly what you were looking for." And they go, "I don't feel like working this week." Well, why did you sign up? (Manny Avila, twenty-eight-year-old Latino, agency placement manger)

The people they know, people who show the real desire to work, are the ones who get the jobs. (Bernice Katz, thirty-six-year-old white woman)

Therefore the implication is that if you do not have work, it is because you do not have the desire to work[18] or, even more important, you have not sufficiently demonstrated that desire to the agency. Demonstrating the desire to work becomes a critical aspect of temporary workers' lives and can involve being available for all types of assignments, being willing to take lower pay than desired, and being willing to change one's schedule at a moment's notice. In other words, the advertised "flexibility" that temporary employment offers temporary workers is sacrificed by those who "desire" to work. In fact, it is actually temporary workers rather than jobs, agencies, or clients who are flexible in temporary employment.[19] Flexibility of the temporary worker, which means accepting the inflexibility of agencies and clients, is the hallmark of the desire to work. When they attempt to demonstrate the desire to work, temporary workers put the interests of the agency and the clients above their own. Conflict is muted as temporary workers' needs are submerged and reframed in terms of their own work ethic. Proper demonstration of the work ethic *means* a minimum of conflict.

Even more dramatic are the times when temporary workers reported "going above and beyond the call of duty" because, in addition to demonstrating the desire to work, they are also fighting to shake off the stereotype of the lazy temp. These "supertemps" report working harder than "permanent" workers, working overtime for free, and taking on extra work in the office.[20] Such efforts to demonstrate a desire to work can result in an intensification of the work that temporaries do. Client companies get more work for their dollar; temporary agencies and the industry get good public relations from the extraordinary efforts of these temporary workers. Temporary workers themselves get nothing beyond the slightly better possibility of future assignments. While "supertemp" behavior was especially prominent for those temporary workers who hoped to land a full-time job through temping, other temporary workers were supertemps when they simply needed to maintain their work hours.

The Myth of the Full-time Job

The myth of the full-time job is one of the most powerful weapons in the temporary industry's arsenal and an attempt at discursive control that is aimed at temporary workers and the public. The myth portrays temporary employment as a "bridge to full-time employment," and the temporary agency as a labor market intermediary that benefits all parties: workers looking for jobs, companies looking for workers, government trying to keep unemployment low. Interestingly, in some portrayals by the industry, temporary workers are cast as secondary earners who prefer temporary work and are not really interested in full-time employment.[21] The myth of the full-time job, however, tells us that the industry is catching on to the fact that most temporary workers desire a "permanent" position.[22] Not surprisingly, then, most of the temporaries I interviewed desired a full-time job either in office work or in some other field. Many stated that they thought temporary work might be a good way to find that permanent job.

> I think it would be a great way to get into a place that you would normally never be able to get into off the street. And if you play your cards right, you show some kind of initiative on the job, you don't come in there to play around, then you might get a job that you wouldn't normally be able to get off the street. (Jean Masters, thirty-four-year-old African American)

> Well, I'm pretty good with dealing with the public and personnel, people, and keeping things going and uplifting. Maybe they could get me to do something else in their company that would pay more rather than stuffing envelopes or answering the phone. (Doug Larson, thirty-nine-year-old white man)

> Any position they walk into can turn into full time. If someone likes them, the way they work, their personality, the way they click with their other team members, they can be brought on full time. (Leanne Shearer, thirty-five-year-old white woman)

These statements echo the language of the temporary industry:

> You'll recall the story of Roger, the former musician assigned as a clerical temp to a record company who eventually worked his way up to vice president. When he first registered with the temporary service, Roger was more interested in paying the rent than in securing a permanent career. He quickly recognized, however, that being placed in a record company presented a rare opportunity to catapult himself to a position that he hadn't originally envisioned. (Fanning and Maniscalco 1993, 170–71)

> A company doesn't necessarily place an order with the hope of finding someone permanent; sometimes it just happens. . . . Often, the chemistry is right. (Lewis and Schuman 1988, 10)

According to temporary industry figures, approximately one-third of temporaries are *offered* "permanent" jobs from their assignments (National Association of Temporary Services 1992),[23] leaving two-thirds who do *not* get offers of employment. The figures the industry chooses to high-light are actually very poor information. One-third sounds like an astounding success considering all the assignments that are short-term with the employer having no intention of hiring. One must use a fair amount of caution in assessing this information, however. Currently no reliable aggregate-level data exist to tell us how frequently temporary workers actually move into full-time employment from their temporary assignments. Furthermore, the industry data fails to disclose what *types* of jobs are offered or how many temporaries actually accept the offers. Are the jobs offered "good jobs" that are desired by workers? My research can only suggest that in many cases, the jobs offered to temporary workers more often resemble the scut work they are doing as temporaries than the work they desire to do on a full-time basis. For example, a temporary worker is more likely to be offered a full-time filing job than one that allows him or her entry into a management training program. For this reason, many of the workers I interviewed turned down offers of employment through temporary agencies, as they were hoping to hold out for a better quality job offer.

> I was offered a job and I turned 'em down. It was the same thing I was doing. (Doug Larson, thirty-nine-year-old white man)

> And I was offered a lot of full-time positions from the temp jobs . . . things that I could do, but that was those jobs, I didn't want to. (Ellen Lanford, thirty-eight-year-old white woman)

> When I was working at [a hotel] they wanted to hire me permanently. And I didn't want to work there, and I especially didn't want to work in the catering department. (Albert Baxter, thirty-one-year-old white man)

The available data here prevent me from making any definitive statements about offers of full-time employment. There are organizations that strategically plan their use of temporary workers as a means of "test-driving" their new employees. In these cases, the experience of receiving offers and the types of jobs offered may be very different from what is described here. While some of my interview subjects did work in such environments, it would be more useful to take an in-depth or longitudinal look at an organization using temporaries in this way (see Smith 1998). Temporary workers initially hired as regular employees into low-skill jobs may or may not move rapidly up the job ladder.

Nevertheless, even for workers who found the job offer elusive, believing that their "dream job" is out there waiting to be discovered through temporary employment keeps them invested in temporary employment, so that they work hard on a job to which they might otherwise have little attachment. As a form of social control, the myth of the full-time job is an integral part of what keeps temporary workers from outright conflict with agencies and client companies. Again, this is not to say that there are no cases in which a temporary worker has gained access to an excellent job through temping. For instance, the host of a new television game show was "discovered" while she was working at the studio as a temporary. In fact, the effectiveness of the myth requires that workers find their "dream job" just often enough to perpetuate the myth, just as lottery organizers must publicize their grand prizewinner to keep the masses coming back.

Difference as Control

Traditionally, there have been three primary ways to address "difference" (primarily gender difference) as control: difference as a "divide-and-conquer" scheme to reduce working-class unity (Amott and Matthaei 1991; Kemp 1994), "doing difference" as a means to encourage subordinate behavior (West and Fenstermaker 1995), and using difference as discursive control to construct marginal jobs (Ward 1990). Temporary clerical work is no exception to workplace divisions by gender, class, and race, as it does not occur in isolation from larger social institutions. The increased uncertainty of temporary employment, however, can exacerbate existing cleavages. The temporary workers I spoke with talked a great deal about why they felt they were not given a particular assignment or opportunity. Reluctantly, some temporaries settled on their gender or race as an explanation for what they had experienced.

Cindy Carson asked her "supervisor" at the agency for a raise and was told it would not be possible to pay that much money for an assignment like hers. She was being paid seven dollars an hour. Shortly afterward, she overheard two other agency representatives recommending a male temporary at the same job location be given more than eight dollars an hour:

> I really thought it was sexual discrimination. I thought, "This is happening to me because I'm a woman." That's what I really thought.
> (Cindy Carson, thirty-eight-year-old white woman)

Ironically, some men felt that the agencies often favored women for a variety of temping assignments.

> At least in the entertainment field, a lot of the execs are males, and they want females in their office. And I think I wasn't even considered for jobs because of that. (Doug Larson, thirty-nine-year-old white man)

Others felt that a premium was placed on appearance or wearing the right clothes (also see Henson 1996). Having a neat and "professional" appearance is stressed in most of the literature I collected from temporary agencies. Henson (1996) recounts the difficulty he had with his agency because he did not possess the proper corporate attire, while I was told that I was placed on certain "prize" assignments because I had "that corporate look" (which in part came from a wardrobe collected from several years of working in a conservative corporate atmosphere in a middle-management position). This emphasis on "the look" takes on gendered, racialized, and class-based meanings as agencies, consciously or unconsciously, rely on these distinctions among temporary workers to determine placements. Had my experience prior to temping been in a lower-level service job or an entry-level clerical position, or had I been fresh out of high school or coming off a long stint of unemployment, I would not have had the clothes that helped to get me higher-paying assignments such as executive secretary or administrative assistant. Furthermore, if I had been temping as my primary source of income, I doubt that the instability of temporary employment would have allowed me to purchase the appropriate clothes.

My discussions with temporary agency personnel illustrate that temporary workers are not imagining the emphasis placed on appearance, gender, race, and class. In fact, the notion of "proper appearance" is imbued with race, gender, and class divisions. Regina Mason, a temporary agency representative, described what she finds clients desire most in a high-profile temporary:

> Nine out of ten times it's a little blond girl with light-colored eyes. Or somebody with an English accent. Nobody overweight. And if it's a person of color, she's gotta be drop-dead gorgeous. Not just pretty, [but] drop-dead gorgeous. (Regina Mason, forty-four-year-old Latina, agency branch manager)

Race, gender, and class intersect in Regina's description of the acceptable woman of color. Her statement assumes that any person of color hired would be a woman, and that there are special "look" requirements for women of color. Not only must the temporary give off the right class appearance, she must also be "drop-dead gorgeous," a standard not applied to white women applicants and certainly not to men. Interestingly, white women are expected only to be pleasant looking rather than "drop-dead gorgeous."[24] Another agency representative, Manny Avila, told me how an agency where he used to worked used ethnically based code words with their clients to signify certain types of female temporaries without having to use obviously discriminatory language. For instance, a client who asked for "no Marias" meant no Latinas, while "no Kims" meant no Asians. While most agencies I observed did not participate in such blatantly discriminatory behaviors, this extreme case reveals the extent to which race matters in temporary clerical employment. Temporary agency personnel recognize that even when they do not wish to comply with blatantly discriminatory requests, to not do so means running the risk of losing lucrative clients.

> Well, that's why there's clients that we won't work with you know. Because they'll specifically ask for something and you'll say over the phone, "I don't know if you can tell, but I'm a brown-skinned person, too." You just pass on the order. Or if you need the money, work on the order and swallow what you've gotta swallow. (Manny Avila, twenty-eight-year-old Latino, agency placement manager)

During the course of my research, I had a difficult time gaining access at one agency. The management was concerned that I was some sort of "spy" for the Equal Employment Opportunity Commission (EEOC) or another temporary agency. When I was finally granted an interview, one representative told me that clients ask for a particular gender or ethnicity in a clerical worker. She mentioned that this has been problematic because the EEOC seemed to be cracking down on temporary agencies. Afterward the same representative showed me the card that she reads from when clients make illegal requests. They tell them that they will send the best qualified candidate. When I asked what the clients think of that, she said some are OK, and some push it, and some get mad and want to order what they want to order. She says they try not to lose clients, but sometimes it happens no matter how nice she is (field notes).

Here, too, the representative acknowledged the tension between maintaining the law and maintaining a thriving business. In cases of discriminatory requests, clients may be able to push their demands because they provide the agency's income. The potential loss of a client is taken very seriously. Divisions among workers are worsened by this alignment of the interests of the temporary agency with the client, which may decrease collective action by temporary clerical workers, who are already physically separated from one another (Rogers 1995).

Those workers who can "do" race and class in such a way as to meet the "needs" of the agency and client will benefit materially. They get the assignments while others do not. Although the portrait I paint of temporary clerical employment is not highly favorable, the type of work (clerical) may represent a more desirable alternative to poor women and women of color—women whose occupational choices have been greatly limited to "backroom" service work (Glenn 1992). For these women, certain temporary clerical jobs are highly desirable. The competition among middle-class white women, poor white women, and women of color serves to dampen potential threats to managerial control.

"Doing" difference not only discourages workers from coming together, but it also encourages subordinate (that is, feminized) behavior. It quickly becomes apparent that the type of femininity one must "do" in temporary work is white, middle-class, heterosexual femininity. While certain "exceptions" are made, it is nearly impossible to "do" this brand of femininity if you are a woman of color (and not drop-dead gorgeous). For many workers, the consequences of the gender-, race-, and class-based organization of temporary work are lower-paid, back-office jobs; more sporadic jobs; or no job at all.

Men pose an especially interesting case in the feminized world of temporary clerical work. Their presence in female-dominated work has the potential to disrupt gender categories because men who are temporaries fail to live up to normative conceptions of masculinity by not having a "real job." Therefore they risk gender assessment.[25] One accommodation that underscores the gendered nature of temporary work is the popular construction of male temporaries as gay. On the popular television drama *NYPD Blue*, a steady stream of stereotypically defective female temporaries in the precinct is stemmed only by the arrival of a marginally competent male temporary who is obviously gay. This construction neither disrupts the essential nature of gender for the observer nor challenges the dominant/subordinate statuses of male/female. Male temporary workers, heterosexual and gay, were well aware of this construction. For example, Michael Glenn, an openly gay man, accepted and essentialized the construction of temporary workers as gay (and therefore more suited to the work!) with only minor reservations:

Temps usually are women or homosexual men. It's not to say that some heterosexual men don't make good temps, but I think it's harder to find. And then you get into the whole psychology of heterosexual men, I suppose. *Men Are from Mars* and all of that. But heterosexual men are not as great at being people people. . . . You have to be flexible. And there's more of a rigidity to a heterosexual male. And then again in the gradations, I would say there's more rigidity for a homosexual male than for a woman. (Michael Glenn, twenty-six-year-old Asian American)

Other discussions of male temporaries' masculinity highlight the gendered nature of the work as they struggle with maintaining masculinity in an organizational environment that requires "doing" femininity. The agencies employing the temporaries I interviewed demanded that their workers adopt a "pleasing" demeanor while on the client company's premises. Thus the proper enactment of gender was conflated with proper job performance and monitored by the temporary agency.

The extent to which deference was conflated with proper job performance is highlighted by the negative reactions of many male temporaries to these demands for subservience and its implicit threat to their sense of masculinity.[26]

It's a manly thing to be in charge. And men should want to be, supposedly in charge and delegating things. If you're a man and you're being delegated to, it somehow makes you less manly. You know what I'm saying? Whereas it seems to be OK for the person delegating to women. They seem to be OK with that relationship. And the women, maybe they're just projecting that to get by. It seems that they're more OK with that than men are. I guess I'm saying that it makes me feel less of the manly kind of qualities, like I'm in charge, you know. And men should be, like, takin' meetings and barking orders instead of just being subservient. (Harold Koenig, twenty-nine-year-old white man)

Henson (1996) discovered the required nature of deference when he refused to adopt a sufficiently submissive demeanor and was removed from an assignment despite adequate completion of the formal work. Several male temporary workers remarked to me that they had never anticipated being treated so poorly. Many felt a college degree would exempt them from such treatment, and few had regularly experienced the requirement to enact deference in other contexts.

The requirements of a temporary closely mesh with the elements of "emphasized femininity," as defined by R. Connell:

One form is defined around compliance with this subordination and is oriented to accommodating the interests and desires of men. I will call this, "emphasized femininity." Others are defined centrally by strategies of resistance or forms of non-compliance. (1987, 183)

Temporary workers are valued and rewarded for being accommodating and compliant, and are sanctioned when they do not comply with these expectations. In fact, the temporary industry uses gender as a marketing strategy by advertising the type of temporary worker who matches the construction of emphasized femininity. I found emphasized femininity embodied in the omnipresent industry poster of a smiling, young, attractive white woman. The message to employers is to expect smiling, docile, compliant workers.

The message to the temporary worker is that he or she must be extremely "cooperative" (in other words, submissive) to be considered for assignments. Two self-help books written by temporary agency owners and geared toward temporary workers repeatedly remind temporary workers to be cooperative and to go out of their way to please the agency:

Nevertheless, we have seen people get started on the wrong foot by adopting a negative attitude toward the entire process. There are any number of ways to express this negativity: poor dress, bad manners, or a general lack of responsiveness or cooperation. (Fanning and Maniscalco 1993, 97)

The attribute most frequently cited as a necessity for temporary workers is "flexibility." Despite all the discussion of flexibility in temporary employment arrangements, it is the temporary who must be flexible, a trait of emphasized femininity. Temporary clerical workers are duly rewarded for displaying emphasized femininity. In my interviews, I found that workers who were able to "do" gender in line with the expectations of emphasized femininity seem to obtain assignments more readily. The job of temporary worker is "feminized" (Ferguson 1984), and therefore, temporary workers learn to become subordinate in their employment relationship. Thus, behavior that is necessitated in the workplace helps to construct temporary work as gendered. Temporary clerical work is considered "natural" for women and "deviant" and constructed for men.

Gender and Constructing Marginal Jobs

Even though temporary agencies have become savvy enough to change their gender-laden monikers to appear more gender-neutral, the temporary industry still uses gendered notions about work to render the marginality of temporary jobs nonproblematic. Some industry proponents acknowledge that the image of the "bored housewife" (Lewis and Schuman 1988) as temporary worker is outdated. The primary purpose of their acknowledgment, however, is to assure critics as well as those who may want to try temping that it is a legitimate form of employment. While this would initially seem to contradict a gendered construction of temporary work, it actually contributes to it by maintaining the notion of women's employment as secondary.

The temporary industry constructs temporaries' (and women's) work as secondary through its emphasis on temporary employment as a "flexible" form of employment. Carefully couched in gender-neutral terms, the flexibility of temporary work is said to meet the needs of "parents" who wish to balance work and family. Yet many studies have shown that temporary employment is seldom as flexible as advertised.

Despite the gender-neutral language, most temporary workers are women (although there is now an increased number of men in temporary employment owing to the increase in both industrial and professional temping [Polivka 1996; Spalter-Roth et al. 1997]), and a significant majority of temporary clerical workers are women. While we know that by and large women still bear a disproportionate share of "family" responsibility, we also know that most temporaries, including women, are doing so out of necessity rather than a desire for flexibility (Polivka 1996). Without using gendered terms, the industry is framing women with children as a large portion of its workforce, although it is much more diverse than that. These people (women) are said to want flexibility to earn some money without the commitment of a "real job" while they maintain their primary responsibility of caregiver to their children. Temporaries become characterized as secondary wage earners, so that any problems associated with temporary employment (for instance, lack of health insurance benefits and job instability) are diminished in importance. In this way, criticism can be deflected by pointing to the voluntary portion of the temporary workforce—those who do not want a traditional job. This cleverly gender-neutral approach justifies and reasserts the stereotype of women workers as secondary wage earners.

The industry points to low participation rates in agencies' existing health plans as an indication that temporaries really do not need or want health insurance because they are likely covered by a spouse's plan. This was in no way the case for the temporary workers I interviewed.[27] Nearly all said they would like to have health insurance through their job. Of the two who had health insurance, one was on COBRA coverage from his previous employer, and one had purchased individual insurance. The remaining temporary clerical workers either had difficulty in meeting the somewhat stringent eligibility requirements for coverage through the agency or felt that they could not afford the coverage owing to the irregularity of their employment or to their share of the cost.

The gendered construction of temporary employment also takes on age-specific forms. Temporary workers are overrepresented in both the under-twenty-five age category and the over-fifty-five age category (Polivka 1996). The temporary industry increasingly uses images of college-aged summer employees, recent high school graduates, or grandparents supplementing Social Security payments to depict its workforce rather than showcasing middle-aged people who might have to rely on temporary wages to support a family. In fact, included in the materials sent to me by the National Association of Temporary Services were a number of pamphlets specifically addressing older and younger workers. Still heavily concentrated in the clerical field, the temporary industry most often depicts these younger and older workers as women. Again, the characterizations of workers employed by temporary agencies act to construct temporary workers as marginal workers whose work is supplemental to that of a male spouse, parents, or Social Security. Therefore the industry assuages any concerns that temporary employment might be a form of underemployment generating a host of social problems.

The increasing participation of men in temporary work potentially poses a problem for the temporary industry's constructions of temporary jobs as secondary. However, as with other men who cross over into "women's" work (see also Pringle 1988; Williams 1989, 1995), male temporaries risk their status as "real" (or at least heterosexual) men. In everyday practice, these violations of gender expectations are understood as reflections of the essential nature of the individual men and not the gendered organization of the work. The seeming contradiction of a male temporary clerical worker is resolved by their sexual orientation, their "drive," their "motivation," and their competence for (male) career success. In other words, no "self-respecting" man would accept a temporary clerical job because such jobs are thought to lack upward mobility.

I think men get a little less respect if they're temping. There's that expectation that they should be, like, career-oriented and, like, moving up in the world and being a businessman and moving himself forward in business. Where[as] women can do that, but it's not an expectation. And so I think . . . that's where that Kelly Girl image—that temporaries are women—is. I have noticed that there is a certain amount [of] looking down upon. I think that's true of temps in general. They're somewhat looked down upon. I think the men maybe more. (Albert Baxter, thirty-one-year-old white man)

Ironically, dead-end temporary clerical jobs are rarely seen as problematic for women. Their presence in temporary work is justified and naturalized by constructing all women as mothers (or in this case, parents) first and foremost, and as incidental wage earners second.

Good Cop/Bad Cop: Obscuring Control

Another way in which the agency and the client obscure their control is by insulating each other from blame. For example, the stated role of the agency is to fire or remove temporary workers from assignments if they are not meeting the requirements of the client in any way. The client needs only to call the agency and notify it that they would like the temporary replaced. The client does not have to deal with the unpleasantness of conveying any "shortcomings" directly to the worker. Conveniently, the agency is not required to give the temporary worker any justification for removal from the assignment. The agency can simply say that the client cut the assignment short, allowing the worker to feel that the agency has also lost potential income owing to an inconsiderate client. The agency representatives I spoke with preferred to be vague about reasons for dismissal because it caused them fewer problems with their temporaries. Under these arrangements, workers cannot know for sure whether the assignment was cut short or if they were actually replaced by another temporary from the same agency.

I just remember that's when a six-week assignment suddenly became a two-week assignment and nobody was apologizing about it. (Ludy Martinez, thirty-six-year-old Filipina)

Here, another worker struggles to find a reason for why she was let go from an assignment:

Well, essentially they let me go. . . . The assignment ended. Although I did call in sick one day, and I had been taking these lunches [the client expected her to work through lunch] and not charging them for it of course. And the thing is, I knew I was losing points because my boss was a total workaholic. I only saw him go to lunch two or three times. (Cindy Carson, thirty-eight-year-old white woman)

The temporary agency never did give Cindy a reason for her being removed from that assignment.

The "good cop/bad cop" scenario can also work in reverse, with the agency taking on the good cop role and the client taking on the bad cop role. For example, the agency can justify particular pay rates to the temporary by stating that the client will only pay so much money for that assignment, and the agency cannot afford to give any more to the temporary worker. Thus the good cop/bad cop scenario acts to secure cooperation from the temporary worker or to punish those who do not comply without the temporary worker being able to place blame or precisely locate the source of the power relationship.

They're very two-faced people. They have to be. It's their job to please you when they're on the phone with you by criticizing the client. And please the client when they're on the phone with them by criticizing you. (Michael Glenn, twenty-six-year-old white man)

The point here is not so much the extent to which these practices are maintained, but that they *can be* maintained *invisibly.* In a three-party employment relationship where the interests of the client and the agency are quite often closely aligned and very little justification is owed the worker, control can be hidden and distorted. These murky power relationships have important implications when we consider resistance in the next chapter.

TEMPORARY clerical workers find themselves subjected to an array of controls exerted by the temporary agency and the client company. Controls over temporary workers fall into three overlapping arenas, each of which is permeated with gendered and racialized understandings of "difference." Thus, gender and race intertwine with each arena of control to exert controls differently for different groups. Structural control includes greater divisions of labor among workers; however, racial and gender divisions are also exacerbated by the organization of temporary work. Interpersonal control takes on several forms, an important component of which is the requirement of temporary workers to "do" difference in a way that recreates their subordinate relationship to the agency and the client. The temporary industry attempts to employ discursive controls to align temporary workers' understandings in a way that benefits the industry and its clients and legitimizes temporary employment and its practices. By employing a gendered construction of temporary work as secondary employment that meets the flexibility needs of the workers, the industry thwarts any attempts to characterize the phenomenal growth of temporary employment as a social problem. At the same time, temporary agencies and their clients employ several methods by which they obscure controls as they are exerted.

Yet, these controls are not complete. Temporary workers do not always cooperate, nor do they always put the interests of the agency and clients above their own. In the next chapter, the variety of ways that temporary clerical workers respond to unfavorable working conditions is explored and the manner in which they employ resistance strategies with varying degrees of success is examined.

4   Resisting Temp-tation

Don found many of his temporary jobs boring. He told me that on one assignment he made stationery to pass the time:

> At one point I used Pagemaker and I designed this stationery because I lived in this new apartment. And then I just printed every single envelope through the laser printer and it was, like, three hundred envelopes. And if you hold up the stationery [the watermark] says the company's name! And phone calls, long-distance phone calls, that's important. Lots of long distance calls, yup. (Don Birch, 24-year-old white man)

In the previous chapter, we looked at the many intertwining, and sometimes contradictory, mechanisms of control over temporary workers. Despite the best efforts of temporary agencies and clients, however, temporary workers are far from passive. Temporaries resist many aspects of their work, including boredom, abuse, and lack of control over their assignment. Like Don, who fought boredom by making personal stationery, many other temporaries creatively attempt to cope with or even actively change their world in the face of enormous constraints. This chapter looks at how the organization of temporary clerical work shapes forms of resistance.

Conceptualizing resistance in the past has been difficult. Traditional definitions of resistance restricted to the demonstration of collective effort are too narrow, leaving many groups of workers mistakenly characterized as "passive." Underlying these notions is the understanding that some forms of resistance are superior or more "genuine" than others. Specifically, resistance that is collective, planned, highly visible, and aimed at social change is considered "real" resistance, while other activities are relegated to the dust bin of "reaction." In other words, "real" resistance evokes images of marching, banner-waving, chanting, and, on occasion, arson or the overturning of cars.

Much resistance, however, falls outside the boundaries of traditional resistance. The daily lives of workers are filled with resistance. To ignore the quotidian nature of resistance is to render these workers' struggles invisible. Specifically, much of women's resistance has been made invisible or illegitimate, resulting in stereotypical assumptions about women and their lack of potential as valuable union members. Resistance can include subtle forms like crying and using "female" problems to obtain breaks as well as obvious forms like sabotage and union organizing.[1] This understanding is implicit in the definition of *resistance* as

> . . . any individual or small-group act intended to mitigate claims by management on workers or to advance workers' claims against management. Worker resistance thus includes sabotage (Jermier 1988; Taylor and Walton 1971, 219), but it also *includes less destructive acts that have been referred to more generally as 'the withdrawal of cooperation"* or as part of the "effort bargain" (Edwards and Scullion 1982, 154; Wardell 1990). (Hodson 1995, 80; my italics)

Nevertheless, I must interject a word of caution here. If we understand "resistance" to mean merely coping behaviors attached to individuals, we cannot help but conclude that any form of nontraditional resistance is in vain. Instead, if we see resistance in the context of structural constraints and opportunities, we might begin to envision possibilities for social change (Romero 1992). Kanter's (1977) early work clearly demonstrates the ways in which organizations and their power structures elicit certain kinds of responses from individuals, depending on where they rest in the hierarchy. "Counterproductive" responses easily become conflated with gender in gender-homogeneous environments as actions are taken as evidence of "natural" gender traits rather than reactions shaped by existing power arrangements.

At the same time, we also must avoid the temptation to enlist a singular, "grand theory" of resistance to explain local practices, because "resistance is a condition and a consequence of particular knowledges and subjectivities" (Collins 1994, 29). These "knowledges and subjectivities are shaped, but not determined, by the organization of work as they are mediated by wider political, institutional, and economic factors" (Collins 1994, 96).

Because resistance is not a completely "objective" phenomenon, one person's resistance may be another person's compliance. Therefore, it is necessary to "tak[e] the word of the participants in assessing the significance of local resistance practices" (Jermier, Knights, and Nord 1994, 11). In searching for resistance, one must attend to the meaning of resistance as defined by those engaged in it. Simply taking what appears to be cooperation at face value can result in mistakenly assuming that control is complete. A domestic worker may be nodding and smiling and saying "Yes, ma'am" at the same time that he or she is "accidentally" pouring bleach on fine washables.

While researchers have opened up our understanding of resistance as a concept, it is still theoretically underdeveloped.[2] Most research in worker resistance enumerates or divulges kinds of resistance but does not systematically link these forms to the organization of the work being resisted. Therefore, while we have many colorful or entertaining examples of resistance, we cannot offer much in the way of prediction or explanation. Some research does make loose connections between types of resistance and constraints or types of work, but it does not self-consciously link agency to the organization of work. We therefore cannot address why one type of resistance is exercised here and another is exercised there. Instead of simply broadening our definition of resistance, we can link forms or repertoires of resistance to organizational/occupational/structural/political elements that promote certain forms of resistance.

We also can gain a clearer perspective on gender and resistance by attending to the organizational forces that shape resistance. Rather than being theorized, women's resistance has in effect simply been "added" to what we know. Researchers have observed that women's forms of resistance are frequently different from men's or "traditional" resistance. So why is women's resistance so different from or at the very least more varied than men's? Without carefully linking women's actions to the gendered organization of work, the answer comes dangerously close to essentializing and romanticizing women's resistance. Women's and men's paths of resistance appear to derive not from differential organizations of work but from outside social action.[3]

Because the organization of work is deeply gendered, women's repertoires of resistance have as much, if not more, to do with the organizational/structural/political situation of women than women's different ways of being. While others have echoed this sentiment, they have not made explicit connections to the organization of women's work. Occupational segregation means that women work in jobs that may have very different characteristics from the jobs that men hold, and that they experience a different organization of work from what men experience. The gendered organization of work ensures that opportunities for resistance are distributed unevenly across male- and female-dominated occupations. If forms of flexibility are gendered, and if worker control is gendered, then the same must be true for worker resistance.[4]

When work is organized differently for men and women, opportunities for resistance differ. If women are overrepresented in temporary employment, which affords certain opportunities for resistance, the resulting "gendered" forms of resistance may appear to be related to women's essential difference from men, but they are more likely a reflection of employment constraints and the essential difference between temporary and permanent employment. To the extent that women have experienced exclusion from labor unions,[5] they have been excluded from traditional forms of resistance that have become associated with men's resistance. There is nothing inherently male about organized labor resistance; rather, access to the power needed to participate in such resistance has been monopolized by men and denied to women.

Finally, a broad conception of resistance creates space to explore the contradictory nature of much resistance. Resistance in one realm may make workers complicit in their own subordination in another realm, elicit further attempts at managerial control (Collinson 1994), or reinforce damaging stereotypes (Rollins 1985).

Temporary Work and Resistance

While there may be debate about what is properly labeled "resistance," the ethnographic evidence of how temporary workers attempt to navigate their work lives is beginning to take shape. Gottfried (1994) illuminates some of the methods of resistance used by temporary workers but does not tie these forms of resistance to the specific organization of temporary work. Importantly, she makes a foundational link to debureaucratized jobs, the service sector, and what she calls "dual levels of control." The story with temporary clerical work gleaned from this research is more complicated than that, however, and resistance derives from the unique combination of the organizational elements of temporary employment *and* of clerical work. While we see that temporary workers' resistance does not fall within the traditional rubric, we do not get a clear sense of why these forms of resistance occur and not others. For instance, because temporary work separates temporary workers from one another, temporary workers from "regular" workers, and temporary workers from union workers, we would expect unionization for temporary workers to be unlikely at this time.[6]

Many of the attempts at control by agencies and clients are incomplete, unsuccessful, and even contested by temporary clerical workers. In the evidence that follows, I provide a framework for analyzing resistance that takes into account the unique aspects of temporary work that shape modes of resistance. Some of the difficulty in understanding resistance in temporary work arises because, at first glance, much of what temporary workers do in order to regain control of their work lives may go unnoticed. We hardly notice temporaries themselves, so it is not surprising that we do not notice their subtle forms of resistance. When we use traditional definitions of resistance, temporary workers seem even more passive.

Using the broader understanding, however, a rich picture of resistance in temporary work begins to emerge. Clearly, temporary clerical workers are not drones—they can see relationships of power at work, and they have a lot to say about these relationships.

Individual/Collective Resistance

Temporary work, by its very nature, constitutes temporary workers as *individuals*.[7] As we saw previously, many factors, including the division of labor and efforts at discursive control, help to individualize temporary workers and obscure their common interests. Temporary workers tend to be socially and sometimes physically isolated from other temporary workers both on the job and off.[8] Therefore, much of temporary workers' resistance tends to be individualistic rather than collective. Few of the people I interviewed were able to create relationships on the job either with other temporaries or permanent employees.

> Well, I got to the Christmas party and I realized that I just didn't know any of these people. I mean, I knew the woman who interviewed me, but that was it. (Katie Hallaway, sixty-year-old white woman)

> I very seldom have formed any kind of friendship relationship with the people I work with. (Albert Baxter, thirty-one-year-old white man)

> My paychecks are usually mailed to me. I don't see . . . too many other temps. . . . At work, I usually eat lunch by myself. (Leanne Sheerer, thirty-five-year-old white woman)

The temporaries I spoke with felt that the more rapid their movement from assignment to assignment, the more difficult it was to get to know others. Many believed that co-workers stayed away because they did not want to "invest" their time getting to know a temporary who was going to leave in a short time. While discussing her feelings of isolation, Carol reflects on the times that she, as a regular employee, worked with temporaries:

> I find that even as a permanent worker I created a distance between myself and temps, you know. It's like I don't want to get too close to them because you know they're leaving. (Carol Ketchum, twenty-nine-year-old white woman)

Cheryl explains her reluctance to form personal ties on temporary assignments:

> It's because you look at this place and say, "In six months I'm not gonna be here." And you just know that because that's your assignment. (Cheryl Hansen, twenty-three-year-old white woman)

Isolation fosters individualized resistance. Along with agencies' policies forbidding discussion of wage rates with co-workers, isolation can deny temporary workers the knowledge they need to frame their wage struggles collectively. Although many temporary workers articulate feelings of underpayment relative to "permanent" workers, they are reluctant to frame these feelings as anything more than a hunch owing to their isolation. At the same time, temporary agencies are busy "objectively" setting wage rates for each *individual* on each separate assignment. Wage rates, and by proxy temporary workers, are constituted as individualized phenomena.

Nevertheless, temporary workers do not always adhere to the rules set out for them by the temporary agency and its clients. For instance, in my interviews as well as in my personal experience, some temporary workers do discuss wages with other temporaries and with regular workers. One day, another temporary approached me about how I liked my temporary agency. I told her it was decent. She told me she felt she was not being paid as much as she could be. I told her I had heard some agencies, particularly those that place people in entertainment companies, paid less. She asked what I was usually paid on assignments, and when I told her usually eleven [dollars an hour], she was surprised and angry. I don't know all of her duties, but it seems we ought to be paid about the same. I felt badly, but she took the name of the agency I work through, stating that she would see what rate they would give her. She quickly added that she wouldn't let them know I told her. I felt relieved, since that's a temp no-no (field notes, 1994).

In this example, we both learned about pay rates among temporary workers; however, the other temporary's actions after our conversation likely remained individualized because of the potential loss to me. I do not know whether she ever went to my agency or if she got her pay raise. I can only assume that, because I was not reprimanded, she did not tell them about me.

Individualization is also fostered because temporary workers must compete with one another for assignments. The temporaries I interviewed expressed a keen sense of competition.

> They kind of make it seem competitive, like you have to be ready or you're going to lose this position. (Irene Pedersen, twenty-five-year-old white woman)

> You've got to be a presence because it's a little competitive. A lot of people are there out of work, and you've got to show a desire to work. (Bernice Katz, thirty-six-year-old white woman)

> I've noticed in certain entertainment companies that are considered pretty glamorous, a lot of temps will even offer to do personal chores just because they want to ingratiate themselves. And that makes it more difficult for other temps to say no. (Ludy Martinez, thirty-six-year-old Filipina)

The temporary agency further contributes to the isolation of the temporary worker through the use of "bad temp" stories. In the previous chapter, we saw how bad temp stories exerted control over individual workers. Here, however, bad temp stories serve to isolate temporaries from one another. Because no temporary worker wants to be seen as a "bad temp," that person tries to distance himself or herself from this model, and the stereotype of temporaries in general, thus unwittingly contributing to his or her own isolation. Many temporaries told me that employers or agencies told them bad temp stories early on in their relationship.

> The agencies don't really like it when you flake out that way and don't show up. They told me about these people. In fact, when I first signed up they warned me about this kind of thing. And I'm there, like, "No, people really do that?" They're like, "Yeah." They've had people just flake

out. They didn't feel like going to work that day, or had an audition that day. (Bernice Katz, thirty-six-year-old white woman)

I think [the client] expected a less competent person. . . . They definitely expected a less competent person from a temp agency. I think that's the stereotype. (Sarah Tilton, twenty-six-year-old white woman)

Temporary workers contribute to their own isolation not only when they seek to avoid the bad temp image related by agencies and clients, but also when they disparage other temporary workers as a group. For example, many of the people I interviewed made a point to say that they were not like "other temps." Temporary workers also told bad temp stories similar to those told by agencies and clients as a way of distancing themselves from a negative association. Therefore, rejecting identification as a temporary can be viewed as a form of resistance against stigmatizing labels, but one that, at the same time, reduces solidarity among temporaries.

Temporaries who compare themselves favorably with bad temps are successful in their resistance to internalizing the negative identity themselves; however, this does leave the broader stereotypes intact. These temporary workers are in effect stereotyping other temporaries and thus themselves. While this may not be in their best interest in the long run, it reassures their sense of self today. In addition, the bad temp stories coming from the agency or the client operate as a mechanism of social control, reinforcing temporaries' marginality and serving as a warning against poor-quality work and deviant behavior.

Temporary workers' efforts to distance themselves from the negative stereotype of the temporary do not stop with disparaging remarks. They also try to differentiate themselves through their actions. To show that they are not a "bad temp," many temporaries become the "supertemp," doing anything and everything possible to perform well above and beyond expectations. Temporaries hired to perform clerical work find themselves running a magazine or coordinating human resources functions. I found myself involved in trying to demonstrate that I was not "just a temp" by using my prior benefits administration experience in an assignment that required me to type and file. A man came in one day from [Deductible] Insurance Company. He was going to meet with my supervisor about the rerate of their health and dental plans and about their 401K. My supervisor asked me to see if he wanted any coffee or doughnuts. So I went in and inquired. After he said he would like some coffee, I went to the coffeepot, which was virtually right next to him, and poured him a cup. My supervisor had also asked that I "keep him company" while she finished up some other work. So I struck up a conversation. I told him that I used to work for Executive Life. We both got a chuckle out of that. He asked what I knew about 401K plans, and I told him a little, and that from what I could see this company was in danger of losing its qualification. We continued our talk until my supervisor arrived, and he was so impressed that he raved to her about how I was an unusual find for a temp. Reflecting on this, I realize that I wanted him to know that I was not really a temp (field notes, 1993).

That assignment lasted for three weeks, and I was asked to return on my winter break. From that day forward, I found myself being asked to work on benefits administration in addition to my typing and filing duties. I was glad to do it, as it increased my status in the office and alleviated some of the boredom I had experienced. In resisting both the identification as a temporary and the monotony of filing, I increased my value to the agency and the client. I became complicit in my own subordination as I made the agency look good to have hired such a wonderful temporary, and I performed more duties than agreed on for the wage I was being paid. At the same time, my resistance solidified the marginal position of temporary workers as I raised the stereotype if only so that I could reject it as it pertained to me.

If collective resistance or solidarity derives out of identification with one's job and not from opposition,[9] we can understand why temporary workers use individualistic resistance. Like other temporaries, I did not wish to identify with my job, so I did not enter into collective resistance to protect it.

Temporary workers and permanent workers are also seen as competitors. Some temporary workers and agents relayed stories of permanent workers who were threatened by the presence of temporaries in the organization.

> I was just a legal assistant there. I'm a pretty quick learner. The head of the legal assistant group, she felt threatened by me because I was some college know-it-all. It's really frustrating because you look at a job and you're just temping for it. You look at it and you go, "I could master this job really easy, and I know more than you do. I can do your job, too." But you don't tell that to people. (Cheryl Hansen, twenty-three-year-old white woman)

> Because people get threatened if you know more. . . . Sometimes we'll tell the temp, "Don't let them know that you know how to do all this

stuff. If it comes up, handle it, and you know just how to do it. Don't go out and say, 'I do this and this and this.'" (Manny Avila, twenty-eight-year-old Latino, agency placement manager)

It seems that temporary workers pose a latent threat of replacement for permanent workers, thus putting temporary and permanent workers at odds. The latent threat is exemplified in two examples taken from contemporary media. The first example is from a *Doonesbury* comic strip, wherein an executive is describing to a manager how he will cut operating expenditures by firing everyone and hiring temporaries. The manager expresses his admiration asking, "When do we start?" to which the executive replies, "We?"

The second example is from a commercial for Interim Temporary Services. A corporate controller is complaining to an executive that they cannot execute his plan of action on the budget they have. A human resources manager jumps in to say they could hire a temporary workforce through Interim. The controller complains about having to train them, and the manager replies that they are already trained. The controller still appears negative as the human resources manager flashes him a mischievous look and states, "You know they have temporary controllers, too."

In both of these examples, and in the stories related to me in the interviews, permanent workers are made to feel that their jobs may also become temporary if they're not careful. As discussed in the previous chapter, this latent threat acts as a mechanism of control over permanent workers and reduces the likelihood of collective action among temporary workers as well as between permanent workers and temporaries. Under no circumstances are permanent workers going to consider collective action as a group or with temporary workers for fear of being relegated to temporary status themselves. Security and opportunity are prerequisites for worker solidarity (Vallas 1991), and because the organization of temporary clerical work tends to foster insecurity, resistance in temporary work is usually (but not exclusively) individualistic rather than collective in nature.

Planned/Ad Hoc Resistance

Traditional conceptions of resistance generally contain a sense that resistance is something that is planned as well as being collective. Planned resistance gives the impression of rational behavior. Impromptu or ad hoc resistance, by comparison, can appear irrational. Rationality can be a label used to discount the legitimacy of impromptu acts of resistance (Clegg

1994). Thus unplanned acts of resistance can be framed as emotional acts of frustrated individuals (often women) rather than logical, well-planned responses to workplace injustices. Viewed in this way, even a seemingly "irrational" act like sabotage can be considered a rational, class-conscious act, as such action often involves planning and organization (Jermier 1988).

Because temporary work is often transitory, resistance is more likely to be ad hoc than planned. Frequent movement of temporary workers from assignment to assignment, and from agency to agency, and the uncertain duration of many assignments makes it difficult to plan ahead. Therefore we see how the structure of temporary work (as opposed to the irrational nature of temporaries themselves) frequently disallows planned resistance.

We cannot assume that unplanned resistance is not resistance, "proper" resistance, or nonrational resistance. Nor can we assume that temporary workers do not try to plan resistance. For instance, a temporary worker may plan to address her supervisor about her workload only to find that she has been moved to another assignment.

Ad hoc resistance is opportunistic in that temporary workers unexpectedly find ways to push back the walls of control from their work situation. Most acts of sabotage[10] reported in the interviews I conducted occurred in just such a fashion. Carol Ketchum felt that she was not considered for a permanent job opening because she was "a temp," even though she had already been doing the job for a month. When she heard someone else had been hired, she took action:

> I wondered . . . if they didn't like me or whatever. So I got back at them (this is an entertainment company) by stealing one of their screenplays. I showed them. (laughs) (Carol Ketchum, twenty-nine-year-old white woman)

Carol clearly realizes that there is no long-term damage from her one act of resistance; however, knowing she would soon be leaving, she felt that taking a screenplay would even the score.

On several occasions, Bernice Katz had an assignment end abruptly and was not informed by either the agency or the client so that she could seek work elsewhere. Bernice was resentful of the way she was treated:

> I had a little revenge with it, too, because they had these cabinets that you locked, and I had the key, you know. While I was there another employee had given it to me. And in it I stored things, my coffee cup, a couple of work tools. So I locked it and there I had the key with me. So they had to break their cabinet open. I was not gonna go all the way back

there just to give them their key back. They had made such a big deal about "Don't lose the key." I guess they had to break it. Which is fine with me. (Bernice Katz, thirty-six-year-old white woman)

Quitting assignments and walking off the job, although usually a last resort, were also usually unplanned, with one notable exception.[11] When Shari Jensen found one work situation particularly intolerable, she set out on a course to get fired from the assignment.

I said, "Do you expect me to continue to work like this without a raise?" [My supervisor] said, "Yes." I said, "OK." What I did, I wanted to get fired. I kept calling in sick every single day even though I didn't have anything. (Shari Jensen, thirty-three-year-old African American)

One problem that arises when temporary workers resist in an ad hoc fashion is that they risk reproducing stereotypes of temporary employees as flaky, irresponsible, and unpredictable. Such behavior can be used to justify both the marginal position of temporary workers and even greater social control of temporaries via the agency. "Flaky" behavior is one of the problems most frequently reported by temporary agency personnel.

We get flakes all the time. A lot of flakes. You'll meet with somebody and they need to work. They're telling you they need to work, they have no money to feed their kids or whatever. I got her working the following day, and the day after that she calls in sick, you know. I'm thinking, "There's something wrong here." They're not thinking properly, you know. (Manny Avila, twenty-eight-year-old Latino, agency placement manager)

These interviews provide some evidence that temporary workers' "flaky" behavior should at least be considered in the full context of temporary work, including the opportunities for and the constraints on more effective types of resistance. This is not to say that all flaky temporaries are simply resisting some aspect of their work, but it does shed light on simplistic interpretations of these actions as irresponsible and unwarranted. The very organization of temporary work often shapes workers' actions in a way that reproduces existing stereotypes about them.

These same actions can also reproduce gender stereotypes in female-dominated temporary clerical work. Women may be characterized as emotional and unpredictable when they engage in resistance or "flaky" behavior. The marginal employment position of women is justified by calling attention to the ease with which they leave a job. Women who leave assignments with little or no notice are thought not to need the work, but rather to be dilettantes in the labor market. Men in the same situation are seen simply as not being "real" men.

But these are not gendered responses; they are due to the organization of temporary clerical work, which *is* gendered. Male temporary clerical workers' resistance is no more planned than women's. In an all-women setting, we might mistake forms of resistance as stemming from women's culture or stylistic gender differences. The organization of work, however, can create what might appear to be gender differences in resistance. If quitting is a popular form of resistance among women, it may be due less to the gender of the worker and more to the opportunities for and the constraints on resistance in that workplace that just happens to be dominated by women.

Sometimes temporary workers are able to use planned forms of resistance that do not reproduce damaging stereotypes. Where they had too little work to keep them busy, temporaries found one of their greatest opportunities for planned resistance. Temporary workers sought control of their time in a way that created an image of a "hard-working temp." Temporaries could not control the workflow coming to them, since temporaries (especially on the shorter term assignments) typically do not possess enough organizationally specific knowledge to seek additional work tasks. They could, however, surreptitiously control the use of their time at the work site. So rather than sitting and staring at the wall, some temporaries did "their own" work, "cruised," or even slept at work.

> I realized that I tended to be real fast, and rather than slow myself down and socialize, I could work real fast and take a lot of breaks. I call it cruising. (Carol Ketchum, twenty-nine-year-old white woman)

> Very bored! I'm telling you . . . I used to sleep there. Yes, there's nothing to do. I always bring my book. When I get sick and tired of reading, I sleep. And I wake up and take the phone calls. Sometimes, OK, you're not supposed to make phone calls, but what am I gonna do with eight hours? OK, you can only read so much. After that, you sleep. You're going to wake up because it's not in your bed. OK. And then after that, you make some calls. (Shari Jensen, thirty-three-year-old African America)

In fact, most temporary workers I interviewed did report that at least occasionally it was necessary for them to "look busy" after repeated requests for additional work were to no avail.

I would have nothing to do, and I had to pretend to look busy. Even when I was doing receptionist work and when the phone didn't ring, I didn't have anything to do. And people were always bitching at me to look busy. And I'm, like, "There's nothing for me to do." (Marianne Wayne, twenty-six-year-old African American)

One common strategy, which I learned early on in my own experience temping, is to go to an assignment prepared with reading material or personal computer work to do in case there is not enough work to keep you busy.

I used to get around things like that by always bringing in, like, Xeroxed magazine articles or something. And I just looked like I was proofreading or something, and I would catch up on a lot of my own private reading. But I knew, again, blend in with the landscape, sort of feel it out. (Ludy Martinez, thirty-six-year-old Filipina)

Some temporary workers even take advantage of available office equipment to add to the authenticity of their reading materials. Ellen Lanford told me how she would bring in a magazine and spend time early in the morning copying the articles she wanted to read. She looked busy while at the copier, and while "working" with the papers on her desk. The fact that many assignments offered access to a computer created additional opportunities for resistance.

You just, well, it was easier if you had a computer in front of you because you could, like, do your own stuff, and at least you were looking busy. And you were doing things that mattered to you and not the company. (Albert Baxter, thirty-one-year-old white man)

There were times when somebody, another office worker, would say, "Listen, you really can't be reading." And so I'd put my book away, and I wouldn't read, and I would just do whatever. Sometimes I would play computer games if I felt I could get away with it. Depending on how much supervision I had, if I felt comfortable working on my own stuff. I just can't sit and not do anything. And oftentimes I would hide what I was doing under something associated with work. But I also felt responsible to the temp agency. . . . I didn't want anybody complaining about me back to the temp agency. (Ellen Lanford, thirty-eight-year-old white woman)

Because having to "look busy" on the job is a recurring scenario in temporary work (Henson 1996), this strategy is one of the few avenues of planned resistance. Particularly in this instance, there is no distinct line between resistance and self-preservation. Some temporary workers framed their actions as a way to get through the day without "going crazy," while others framed similar actions as a way to "fight back" against perceived injustices of the temporary situation.

While this type of resistance offered temporaries a measure of control over their work, it also helped to project the image of a hardworking temp. Through "looking busy" by doing their own work, temporary workers may be struggling against the feeling that their work is meaningless. Indeed, many (including myself) asked, "Why am I here?" when there was too little work to be done. The temporaries I spoke with managed to carve out a space of their own even though they did not challenge the overall structure of temporary work.

Still another planned form of resistance arises in temporaries' responses to social isolation at work. One way temporaries resist social isolation is by taking longer-term assignments when available. The temporaries I interviewed felt that at least part of their isolation came from the transitory nature of temporary work. Seeking out less transitory assignments (for instance, a duration of several months) was one effective way to combat social isolation. A longer assignment, however, while providing more of an opportunity to meet people, does not guarantee social integration.

> Basically, when you work long-term assignments, after a while everything gets to be yours so to speak. You know where you're going every day. You know, maybe you're working through the agency, but you're going through one agency, so that's all you have to deal with. (Jean Masters, thirty-four-year-old African American)

A second way I found that temporaries planned to reduce social isolation was by restricting their work to one or two agencies. Although turnover in the agencies or lack of available assignments can limit the effectiveness of this strategy, one woman got around the problem by "following" her representative to a new agency. Temporaries often work very hard at maintaining relationships with agency personnel. Frequent phone calls and "check-ins" help the agency get to know a temporary. This relationship work, a type of emotional labor explored earlier, often serves an economic purpose as well, as some temporaries feel that an agency is more likely to give them more work if they know them better.

> I do think that being known to them helps. I mean, there are temps who sign up with an agency and never call them again. . . . It doesn't work

that way. You've got to be a presence. When I went out of town, I sent them postcards and I was a presence, even when I'm not there. It helped. The people they know, the people who show the real desire to work, are the ones who get the jobs. (Bernice Katz, thirty-six-year-old white woman)

In a fashion similar to what Collinson (1994) calls "resistance through distance," some temporaries ironically sought out assignments that would isolate them from other employees to avoid negative social interaction. For those who used this strategy, "back-office" jobs such as filing cushioned them to some extent from the demands for emotional labor that are typically found in "front-office" assignments such as executive secretary or receptionist. For example, Shari preferred filing jobs to receptionist jobs, as filing jobs can often be done with minimal contact or supervision. After recounting a bad experience with a supervisor, Shari told me that she came to prefer filing assignments because everyone left her alone to do her own work:

> I like computer filing. That was my favorite because, you know, nobody told me what to do. I used to start there at 7 A.M. Nobody bothers you. (Shari Jensen, thirty-three-year-old African American)

Unfortunately for Shari and those like her who wish to decrease unwanted interaction in the workplace, back-office jobs usually pay less than front-office jobs. In addition, it is in the better-paying front-office jobs that we see racial and class segmentation within the temporary workforce. Front-office assignments are often reserved for "polished" or "professional" applicants—that is, attractive, white, middle-class women (see Rogers and Henson 1997). Those who do not fit this image, regardless of whether they have the "skills," are channeled into less visible positions (Glenn 1992).

Coping/Change Orientation

Much of temporary workers' resistance can be described as oriented toward coping with a negative work environment rather than attempting to effect change.[12] While this is certainly due in part to the individualization of temporary workers, other factors are important as well. The same organizational aspects of temporary employment, particularly frequent movement and uncertainty, that shape resistance as ad hoc more so than planned, also make resistance oriented toward social change more difficult to achieve than resistance in the form of coping.

In addition, the label "temporary" itself diffuses action that would potentially alter the social organization of temporary work to the benefit of temporary workers. In referring to situations they would like to change, many temporary workers concluded with the familiar phrase, "It's only temporary," even if they had been working as a temporary for more than a year or continued to experience the same problems at several agencies or on several assignments.

> I know that I'm just a temp there. I rationalize and know that I'm only there for the duration to do this job. (Doug Larson, thirty-nine-year-old white man)

> If it gets bad, it's like, it's like anything else. It's only temporary. (Ramona Geary, forty-eight-year-old white woman)

Here's what Ellen Lanford did when someone treated her poorly:

> I would just shut down, and I would do the work, and I would be in my own space in my head. I'd be writing my own story in my head. Because when someone treats me badly I know that they've got their own problems. . . . I mean, I'm a temp; I have nothing to do with any of their problems, and so I don't let that stuff bother me. (Ellen Lanford, thirty-eight-year-old white woman)

Ellen uses her status as a temporary to reject internalizing any poor treatment that occurs on an assignment. This also prevents her from engaging in other types of resistance, however. Other temporaries I spoke with felt they could tolerate the boredom because the job was "only temporary."

> You have to look at the duration of the time the assignment's for. You say, "Oh, it's for two weeks. I can deal with it." Or, "If they're going to want me for three months or more doing this, I think I better let somebody know now that it's a problem for me." (Michael Glenn, twenty-six-year-old Asian American)

> There's a task to be done, and you have to do it. And you do it. Big deal. I mean, it's not fun, but you're not there to have fun. I just did it. It passed. I got paid for it. (Doug Larson, thirty-nine-year-old white man)

Although each assignment may be temporary, for the worker, temporary work itself may be not-so-temporary and may go on long after a particular assignment has ended. Those temporaries who try to deal with boredom by reminding themselves that it's only temporary may find themselves moving from one boring job to the next and having to use the same rationalization again and again. In time, such rationalizations may lose some of their effectiveness.

> You can only answer the phone so many ways. You can only do so much filing. It's pretty much, even though it's in different locations and there's different players, it's pretty much the same thing everywhere you go. And that's just really it. I mean, everybody pays their bills the same. And A to Z is the same, 1 to 10, "Hi, how are you this is so-and-so company." It's just not that hard. That's what I find. (Cindy Carson, thirty-eight-year-old white woman)

While "it's only temporary" was a popular coping strategy for those I interviewed, temporary workers also spent a considerable amount of time in the related strategy of reminding themselves that they are not "just a temp."

> It's important to keep in mind why you're doing it, because if you're treated badly you can have something to hold onto and keep your self-esteem up. Try to be assertive if you're called "the temp" or if you're picked on. Try to be clear about what your skills are and keep your long-term goals in mind. (Carol Ketchum, twenty-nine-year-old white woman)

> I was happy to redefine in my mind that I was only there temporarily, and to let everyone know that I was only there temporarily . . . and let everyone know that that wasn't my life. (Irene Pedersen, twenty-five-year-old white woman)

This response works most easily for temporaries who have something "going on the side," but it can work in other cases as well. For example, temporaries set themselves apart from "just temps" by using skills that co-workers were not aware they possessed. Both Linda Mejia and Ludy Martinez surprised co-workers and supervisors with their ability to speak two or more languages. Cheryl Hansen and Jean Masters showed that they were capable of using complicated computer software from previous job experience and education. As a result, each of these women was given additional job duties that made her feel better about her work and herself because she was able to feel less like "a temp." In other words, these women were able to reject the negative stereotypes about temporary workers.

The "only temporary" viewpoint is also fostered by the agencies, as seen in the self-help books available on temporary employment.

> So if you can't stand your assignment, tell your service; but use your judgment. Make sure the situation really is intolerable, because you

don't want to get a reputation for "crying wolf." Also, services know that some temps try to extort higher rates from them by saying an assignment is awful. Save your SOS for serious situations. One of the best things about temping is knowing you won't be in a certain job forever— they do end! (Lewis and Schuman 1988, 55)

And again, it's important to remember that, no matter how bad things get, these situations are only temporary! (Fanning and Maniscalco 1993, 106)

Nevertheless, temporary workers tried and were sometimes successful in coping with undesirable aspects of their work situations. In the case of monotonous work, they reported shifting their interest from the tasks that they were performing to the objects on which they performed the task, or to other aspects of the work environment. In the Los Angeles entertainment industry, temporaries have a unique opportunity in this aspect. For example, one temporary worker who was filing motion picture studio memorabilia for four months took great interest in perusing the old pictures and scripts she was filing.

We were handling a lot of neat things, like original scripts and stills and things from some of these television shows like *Dr. Kildare*, *I Spy* with Bill Cosby. Oh, and *Get Smart*. We were handling the original scripts, and that was pretty exciting. (Bernice Katz, thirty-six-year-old white woman)

Another temporary described her favorite assignment as one in which the monotony was broken by watching celebrities come in and out of the offices at her work site.

Yeah, I still think that the movie company comes to mind. 'Cause I found it intriguing and interesting, and I had never been exposed to anything in the entertainment business. And I ran into Marilu Henner one day. That was good. (Carol Ketchum, twenty-nine-year-old white woman)

Even in nonentertainment companies, temporaries find some interest in their work to alleviate the monotony. For example, one woman who was doing transcriptions found interest in the content of the material:

It's like piecework. That's when I would make a game of it. You know, it's like sewing machine work. You sit there and you do it. You get paid by the hour. You take a break. You have to be able to do spelling. And you can get kind of interested in some of what you're doing. I was doing these transcriptions of death row inmates. And I was sitting there saying, "Oh my God!" Same thing with personal injury cases. But then the other stuff could be just incredibly dull. You just sort of get through. (Ludy Martinez, thirty-six-year-old Filipina)

Another temporary amused herself through her access to the personal affairs of her supervisor.

And you know, work is work. And I was privy to a lot of stuff, reading personal bills for so and so who gets a massage every day for two hours. And his financial transactions. He just sold five thousand shares of this and that. So to me all this stuff is fascinating. The good, the bad, the ugly, and in between. So I always found something to intrigue me about whatever dreg work. (Ellen Lanford, thirty-eight-year-old white woman)

Thus, finding some interest in one's work made it bearable for the short duration. In fact, several temporary workers told me that although their work was usually boring, it was *different* boring work each day or each week. Seeking a variety of work helped temporary workers cope with their boredom without challenging the tendency for many companies to assign the most monotonous work to temporaries.

Another popular coping method for temporaries was to co-opt the temporary worker stereotypes and use them to their advantage. I call this the "just a temp" strategy. When confronted with something they did not want to do (usually because it was not included in the job description given by the agency), some temporary workers feigned ignorance or helplessness, saying, "I don't know; I'm just a temp." It is important to distinguish these acts of resistance from situations in which temporary workers are truly incapable of performing a task because they do not have organizationally specific knowledge. For instance, I worked the reception desk as part of my duties as an executive secretary. I did not like to do reception work, so I was always sure to ask the agency if reception was included in my duties. In this case, I was initially told that I did not have to do reception. After a few days, however, they stuck me at the reception desk during lunch hours. One of the first calls was from a man who said gruffly, "Give me Bob." When I quickly glanced down at the company phone list and saw at least four Bobs, I asked him which Bob he wanted. He got really angry, as though I was supposed to know who he was. Then later someone asked for Chuck. I assumed he wanted the president, Charles, so I sent his call to the president's secretary. I was wrong again and she called back to let me know about it. What I did not know was that the president's son (also Charles) was in and out of the office over his summer break from law school. No one told me. That day I realized why I hated reception; you have to know the company (field notes, 1993).

Later on in that assignment, I found myself being very vocal about my temporary status to callers.[13] Once when a caller became extremely irate after being transferred to the wrong extension, I "accidentally" hung up on her as I tried to transfer her again. When she called back, I apologized profusely and told her I was just a temporary trying to figure out the system. Then I transferred her call to the correct extension.

In my conversations with temporary workers, I found they, too, "dropped" calls or confessed their temporary status as a way to resist abusive treatment. Such resistance had to be used sparingly at the risk of losing favor with the agency and reproducing the flaky temp stereotype.

> Yeah, I've hung up on people. What I do is I do it while putting them on hold or sending the call over. Especially to voice mail. That's one of the best inventions, voice mail. Then I tell 'em, "Oops, just a temp!" One time [the client] called the agency because of a complaint. I told the agency they never showed me how to use the phones right, which they really didn't, but I figured it out. That saved my butt that time, but I'm careful when I do it from now on. (Bernice Katz, thirty-six-year-old white woman)

When temporary workers told me about things they would like to see changed about their work, I asked them what could be done about it. Responses usually involved finding another agency or hoping to get out of temporary work altogether. Both of these responses are located closer to coping than to social change. A few individuals mentioned labor organizing as a possibility, but this was done in a joking matter, as if to indicate that the very notion of a union for temporaries was absurd. Negative aspects were not seen as things that could be changed; rather, they were a "natural" part of temporary employment or the employment arena today.

Other temporaries even closely identified with the cost-cutting objectives of management and spoke of their situation as if it were a "natural" phenomenon.

> A couple times I found myself doing budget analyses, and I'm not trained in budget, but I do it anyway. And that's when I just had to tell the boss I couldn't do it for him anymore because, you know, I'm not a CPA. But he was trying to save money. (Ludy Martinez, thirty-six-year-old Filipina)

Constraints on Resistance

In this section, I explore the constraints on resistance in temporary clerical work. Temporary workers, like other workers, often resist at their own peril. While sometimes their resistance is effective, their efforts can be thwarted more easily than resistance in permanent work situations owing to the way temporary work is structured.

As we have seen, the structure of power relations in temporary work is heavily weighted in favor of the temporary agencies. Agencies have more temporary workers than they can place in any one day, and their income comes not from the temporary workers but from their clients. This seems to leave little room for temporary workers to successfully redefine the value of their work through increased pay. Temporary workers regularly report "negotiations" over their wages, but reports of these negotiations leading to increases are rare and, more important, occur on an individual basis.

> I also learned about temporary agencies. They pay you, and they try to get you to do a temporary assignment for a really low amount. But I know more or less what the job is. They get paid quite a bit more. They have to pay you and make some money. I don't take nothing less than ten [dollars] an hour. Ten is low to take. So they try to get me . . . to work for nine dollars an hour. I said I won't do it for nine dollars; it's not worth my time. So [the assignment manager] got me ten. (Linda Mejia, thirty-one-year-old Latina)

Sometimes temporary workers are successful in increasing their pay rate on a given assignment. Mostly these increases fall in the range of fifty cents to a dollar per hour; however, one temporary reported having her hourly rate raised ten dollars per hour in situations where she was working in a foreign language. Unfortunately, her gains were more symbolic than real when the client company asked her to "fudge" on her timecards by not recording all the hours she worked in a foreign language. Pay increases give temporary workers a sense of accomplishment, but the gains are often transitory. Because temporary workers' rates can be determined from assignment to assignment, a one-dollar-an-hour increase might be short-lived. The next assignment could very possibly pay less. In fact, any work condition negotiated by a temporary is itself temporary and potentially subject to elimination in subsequent assignments.

Many temporary workers report that they will not work for less than a certain hourly wage. They often turn down assignments that pay less than their desired minimum amount unless they are in dire financial need (and many of them report being in dire financial need at least from time to time). Therefore, most temporaries that I interviewed who said they would not take less than a certain hourly wage have ended up taking the lower wage because of their financial situation. They expressed concern at taking such a low wage because they felt that temporary agencies would keep them at the low rate once they agreed to any assignment at the low rate.

> I've turned down a lot of assignments, but they still call me to see if I'll go. If I'm just bored or something I'll go, you know, just for something to do. But I don't make that a practice. Because once you start a practice, you know, take eight or nine [dollars an hour], they figure they can send you on that all the time. You get stuck taking that. (Larry Landers, thirty-eight-year-old African American)

Temporary workers must determine if they need the work badly enough to take the low rate and risk being excluded from higher rates in the future.

> It's definitely hard to go up wagewise while you're a temp. Your rate stays the same for a pretty long time. I guess that has to do with what you'll accept. Say, "No I won't take that if it's not for this much." But you can also only be so finicky when you have to work. (Albert Baxter, thirty-one-year-old white man)

While it appears that any gains temporary workers make are in danger of elimination by the agency in subsequent assignments, temporaries feel they are at risk of having their concessions solidified. Once again, the asymmetry of the temporary employment relationship is highlighted. Such uncertainty and structural lack of power makes it difficult for temporary workers to manage their financial situation.

Nevertheless, temporary workers are actively engaged in trying to revalue their work even if it is only for a short duration. These individualistic strategies show little promise for long-term revaluation of temporary work. Temporary workers are aware that they are competing with other temporaries who may take that lower wage and compromise the wages of all temporaries.

The organization of temporary work breeds competition between temporary workers, who, although they may struggle, struggle within a constrained environment. Yet if temporary agencies can capitalize on competition between temporary workers, temporary workers can attempt to capitalize on the sheer number of temporary agencies. This, of course, depends on the local temporary agency market. In Los Angeles, where this study was done, there are hundreds of offices for temporary workers. In such a context, temporaries report playing one temporary agency off against another in order to get better wages.

> I basically just told them that I wouldn't accept any jobs for that level and that I would just go elsewhere. I didn't work for that agency hardly any more after that. I worked for another one that kept me busy. (Linda Mejia, thirty-one-year-old Latina)

> My one temp counselor is quite the mother hen type, and she would beg and say, "Oh please, no, no, no. You can't go with that other agency. Hang up on them right now." I had one day in which two of these agencies were fighting over me for the same job. (Ellen Lanford, thirty-eight-year-old white woman)

Where fewer agencies exist, temporary workers are more constrained in their attempts to play agencies against one another. Some temporary workers, however, have used this tactic to their benefit. Temporary workers who benefit from such strategies are usually extremely overqualified for the job in question, and are usually considered among the temporary agency's "elite" workers. These are the people the agencies send out to new clients in order to make a good first impression. Given the premium placed on appearance and other ascribed characteristics over skill, opportunities for resistance are likely to be stratified by gender, race, and class in accordance with what traits or skills temporary agencies and clients value as well as in accordance with how agencies and clients identify groups as possessing or not possessing these valued traits and skills (Rogers and Henson 1997).

Despite some degree of elite status, these favored workers are not always successful in their struggles. Don Birch negotiated a dollar an hour increase for an assignment because of his elite status. When he received his paycheck, here's what happened:

> Yeah, well, they fucked me over. And I got so angry. This was the thing that sucked. The first time they paid me, like, ten dollars an hour. A couple months later, they asked me to go back. And I say, "OK, it's twelve bucks an hour." They say, "Yeah." So I write it in my Filofax. I worked for two and a half weeks, and I get the check later. They paid me ten dollars an hour! I call the office and say, "What the heck. You know I was budgeting for this amount of money. I would not have worked for this." And

it was the head of the agency who was there, like, "There must have been some error. I don't know who told it to you." I knew myself that she was the one who told me. You know, maybe it was a slip-up, but, no, she lied. She was dishing it off on someone else when I know she's smart enough to know she did it herself. Just whatever it took to get you in the job. (Don Birch, twenty-four-year-old white man)

Although the previous example is at the extreme, is does reflect the asymmetrical power relations in which temporaries try to negotiate and resist various aspects of their work. The constraints on resistance are largely due to temporary workers' marginal position in the workforce. Their relationship with the agencies is one of dependence: They must please the agency in order to continue to receive assignments. This often means tempering or foregoing one's resistance. Bernice was asked to take an assignment at a company where she had previously had a bad experience:

Oh, I said, put it this way. If they really needed someone and I didn't have a job that day. . . I mean, it's a job for the day. But it's not my first choice. . . . So I did it, and they were pleased with me. (Bernice Katz, thirty-six-year-old white woman)

Once Ludy Martinez complained about being overworked on an assignment. She told me about the agency's response:

They said, "If you're not *happy* on that assignment, well, we'll take you off and put somebody else on." And if I couldn't afford it, then I'd just stay there. But I noticed that most agencies, even when they knew I was being taken advantage of, they wouldn't go to bat for you. . . . They very often wimped out. They wanted to keep the accounts or whatever: "Just accommodate them." What does that mean, "accommodate them?" (Ludy Martinez, thirty-six-year-old Filipina)

Cindy Carson was angry when she learned she could not get her paycheck until the next day:

And I stomped out of the office. And I thought, "OK, I guess when this assignment ends that'll be the end of me." I figured I'd be canned or something just for expressing myself. I'm not sure. (Cindy Carson, thirty-eight-year-old white woman)

Indeed, temporary employees' perceptions of their position vis-à-vis the temporary agency are confirmed by my interviews with temporary agency personnel. The agency representatives I spoke with expressed an unwillingness to continue relationships with temporaries they considered "flaky" or bothersome. Joe Harcum, a branch manager, said that he is less likely to place someone who "won't work with him."

For some temporary workers, dependence appeared to be less of a factor. They actually felt empowered to resist, stating that they could leave their agency and use other agencies instead. In Los Angeles, the proliferation of agencies seems to offer some chance for temporaries to break the dependency relationship.

> And I said if she ever screamed at me, I'm out of there. And she did it once. And that's when I thought, I mean, you don't pay me enough. . . . I'm not permanent. So I left. (Linda Mejia, thirty-one-year-old Latina)

Linda was able to leave because of the relationships she had cultivated with several other temporary agencies in the area. She left the one agency and successfully found work through two others. As of the interview, she had not returned to the offending agency.

Other temporaries used the contacts made through the agency to gain a permanent job or additional temporary work. Once introduced to a client by the agency, the temporary worker directly contracts with the client company for subsequent assignments. Both temporary workers and clients are keenly aware that temporary agencies typically receive between a 50 and a 60 percent markup on their workers' wages (of course, not all of this is profit—agencies pay taxes, overhead, and so forth). The employer can pay a direct-hire temporary worker a greater hourly rate and still pay less than what they would for an agency temporary by eliminating the markup to the temporary agency. This particular strategy is explicitly prohibited by temporary agencies, yet a few temporary workers have reported success with this strategy.

> The one place that I was, I did do what I wasn't supposed to do, which was I gave her my résumé and said that I understand that you're looking for people. (Ellen Lanford, thirty-eight-year-old white woman)

Each mode of resistance is tempered by the organization of temporary work and the financial constraints each temporary faces.

Shari Jensen told me what happened after a particularly bad work experience. Although Shari supports herself, she shares an apartment with her mother and sister who also work. Breaking the relationship with one temporary agency did not pose a great financial threat to her even though she consequently went several weeks without finding work.

> I called the agency and told them what happened. So what, you're not gonna give me another assignment. Am I gonna die? No, I'm not gonna die. I will survive. So and after that, they never gave me another assignment. I don't care. I knew they were gonna do that, but I don't care. (Shari Jensen, thirty-three-year-old African American)

In addition, leaving one agency means greater reliance on other agencies (as many temporary workers use more than one agency) or cultivating relationships with new temporary agencies. Jean Masters initially fought a pay decrease, but eventually ended up taking the cut and going to a different agency:

> I went from seventeen to twelve [dollars an hour]. It was too hard to get a job that was even thirteen an hour then. And then they wanted to cut me down from that to eleven. I think I was getting, like, twelve. I know whatever it was that I fought it. In those cases with unemployment, if someone called you for an assignment you had to have a really good reason not to accept that assignment, otherwise unemployment will cut you off. So basically you had to accept the job. But when they wanted to go to that second pay cut, I fought it. You know, because if I accepted it, that means I'd have to accept jobs from now on at that pay scale. (Jean Masters, thirty-four-year-old African American)

While temporary workers manage to resist in a variety of ways, this resistance occurs within a context of constraint that includes the asymmetrical relationship between temporary workers, agencies, and clients; the availability of work at other agencies; and the temporary worker's financial situation. Although resistance occurs in a variety of ways, it is more likely to occur surreptitiously than overtly. Modes of resistance are shaped by the organization of temporary work and can have contradictory and unintended results. Nevertheless, temporary work should be described as a struggle rather than an exchange, as is the situation often portrayed in the industry literature.

This is not to suggest that all temporary workers should seek work without an agency, nor is it to suggest that agencies do not provide a service to temporary workers. What I do mean to illustrate is how the organization of temporary work has led to particular strategies for worker resistance that ultimately benefit the worker only in the short term, if at all.

TEMPORARY workers' resistance, just like temporary workers themselves, is often invisible. This invisibility is largely a byproduct of employing traditional conceptions of resistance to temporary employment. Using nontraditional conceptions of resistance, we can see that temporary workers do not passively accept their situation. Rather, like workers in other occupations dominated by women and people of color, temporary workers have fewer opportunities to enact more visible, collective resistance. These resistances are less a function of unique ways of doing and being than they are of the organization of work. Clerical work, for instance, does not have a long, success-filled history of unionization.

Although the organization of control in temporary work makes resistance difficult, it is not impossible. Temporary workers resist within a context of constraint that uniquely shapes these opportunities. While most resistance can be characterized as individualistic, ad hoc, and oriented toward coping, temporary workers have occasionally participated in collective, planned action. For now, we need to consider resistance in all its forms, constraints on that resistance, and the small victories that temporary workers achieve in their daily working lives.

5   Are We Not Temps?

Here's how Ludy Martinez responded when the temporary agency she worked for refused to raise her rate:

> Well, that's the only thing you have as a temp, the only advantage you had was to be connected to ten different temp agencies so that when one didn't treat you right, you'd go to another. Or you'd play them against each other. Being able to compare the different pay scales. And I in fact had a couple of agencies. One place I temped at had temps from, like, five different agencies there, and I can't remember if I was there longer than the others, but certain other temp agencies tried to woo me away from the one that I was at. And I couldn't remember if I had an ethical question about that. Just say, "How does this agency treat you?" Well then screw that. You know, and the rule was supposed to be you couldn't work at that company unless you had a separation period for, like, six months where you stopped temping and all that. And that was the time when I just threw that rule out the door because I said you have not earned that right from me, you know. And I was never called on the carpet for that either. But I just decided this is all a temp has. If one agency treats you badly, you have a right to accept a job even if you met these people because you were placed originally. I mean, that was the first time I felt really mercenary about it. And they didn't care because the turnover at their agency was so [bad]. I never got reprimanded for it. (Ludy Martinez, thirty-six-year-old Filipina)

The Missing Subject

Studies of work seem to fall into two categories with regard to workers' subjectivity. One perspective portrays workers as having very little will of their own,[1] as mindless drones with no ideas or opinions. They seem to be completely controlled by their circumstances. Workers appear oversocialized, their behavior easily predictable according to their role in the labor process. At times, it seems an almost fruitless inquiry to locate any knowledge that is not predetermined and scripted by the organization of work.

The second perspective, derived largely from the human relations school, focuses simply on job satisfaction and its effects on productivity.[2] These studies seem lost in a completely subjectivist orientation that fails to recognize very real constraints on human behavior.

Over time, more sophisticated analyses have emerged wherein identity and subjectivity are explored, even if they are undertheorized with regard to the organization of work.[3] Attending to workers' subjectivities helps us to understand how some workers may experience the very same work conditions as oppressive while other workers do not. For example, workers do not uniformly experience work routinization as oppressive (Leidner 1993).

Leidner (1993) also identifies a contradiction in workers being socialized to be themselves. She reveals one insurance agent's practice of reminding himself to act authentically by keeping visible in his car a note stating "Be Kevin." Implicit in the analysis is the notion that work routines are imposed on a worker's true self.[4] One might also want to investigate the problem of workers maintaining a secure identity, and the results of their efforts. Actions do not take place outside power relations, and the pursuit of a stable identity may itself be a means through which power relations are reproduced. The very notion of authenticity can help to reproduce power relations in routinized service work. Some service workers experience routinization as helpful because it protects important aspects of their identity. Thus the imperative to protect one's identity shapes workers' feelings and actions such that it diminishes resistance to managerial prerogatives.

This chapter explores temporary clerical workers' subjectivities and their role in challenging or reproducing power relations. Important questions remain about how temporary workers feel about their employment relationship. Several researchers, myself included, have demonstrated the exploitative structures of temporary employment, but do temporary workers actually *feel* exploited? How do temporary workers characterize their acts of resistance? Do temporary workers embrace the temporary industry's efforts to shape their understandings of the employment relationship?

More complicated are issues of identity. Given a work situation where social relationships are constantly in flux, what are temporary workers' struggles with identity? In trying to maintain a stable identity, temporary workers may help to reproduce the very power relations that constrain them. In other words, temporaries' subjectivities may contribute to the "outflanking" of their resistance.[5]

From existing studies we can already see a preoccupation of temporary workers with their identity. For instance, some temporaries tell a "cover story" to alleviate the stigma of temporary employment: Temporary workers are actors waiting to be discovered, entrepreneurs in the making, and just passing through on their way to the top.[6] Others proudly and self-consciously reject the hierarchical values from which the stigma derives; climbing the corporate ladder just gives them vertigo, so they take a first-floor job.

Whatever the case, these examples show temporary clerical workers trying to maintain a stable identity. Just how these attempts are intertwined with organizational power/knowledge relations and what their consequences are warrants investigation.[7]

I Temp, Therefore I Am Not

If the temporary workers I interviewed had one experience in common, it was the experience of being a "nonperson." One symptom of nonpersonhood in temporary clerical employment concerned naming practices. Many temporaries reported being referred to not by their name, but simply as "the temp." "Give it to the temp," "Oh, she's the temp," "Where's the temp?" I found this naming practice to be quite common. When I arrived at one assignment in particular, I found a letter with instructions left by the "permanent" secretary. The letter was addressed, "Dear temp." Many times, I was introduced to co-workers with the simple phrase "This is our temp."

These naming practices occur both for practical reasons, and because of temporary clerical workers' low status. Often they are not in a workplace long enough to have others learn their names, so they and others like them become "the temp." Co-workers' tendency to replace an individual's name with "temp" may also reflect asymmetrical naming practices with regard to social status. Subordinates must properly name their bosses (proper title, the correct name, no first names); however, bosses need not reciprocate and seldom show the same consideration or respect.[8]

What struck me in my observations as well as from the interviews was the extent to which the people around temporary workers did not find this practice troublesome, while at the same time most temporary workers seemed bothered by it. Being labeled "the temp" denied some temporary workers important aspects of their identity (Rogers 1995).

> And it didn't really matter if you were good at your job as a temp; you were still identified as a temp; you were going to be treated in that way. (Ludy Martinez, thirty-six-year-old Filipina)

> Sometimes you get in a situation where no matter what you do it's not good enough because of the fact you're a temp. Sometimes being just totally alienated because you're a temp. They're like, "Oh that's the temp." And the reputation of some temporaries have followed temps on down the road. So sometimes you have to override that stereotype. One strike already against you. But then you override the stereotype. (Larry Landers, thirty-eight-year-old African American)

As illustrated by Larry, most temporaries reported wanting to show that they were "better" than the temp label they were given. Because one's work is still a principle means of identity formation and maintenance in U.S. society, temporary workers not surprisingly appear to be overly preoccupied with, or fetishize, their identity. Certainly, the structure of temporary employment with its transitoriness and its construction of the temporary as a nonperson helps to place further emphasis on identity issues. Imagine starting a new job every day or every week: "The unpredictability and variability of social relations inevitably renders identity precarious or uncertain" (Sturdy 1992, 140). The following quote represents the feelings of many of the temporaries I interviewed.

> You have to know that you don't mind arriving in different clothes, meeting all different kinds of people. It's not safe. It's not comfortable a lot of times. If you're doing different things with different people in different environments. A lot of change. A lot of change. And that's difficult for a lot of people. (Doug Larson, thirty-nine-year-old white man)

Many temporary workers experience the unpredictability as problematic, not only for important practical reasons (scheduling, budgeting), but because constant flux presents a challenge to maintaining a stable identity.

However, we cannot simply predict temporary workers' subjectivity from the structure of temporary employment. Individuals' differential attempts at maintaining a stable identity can reproduce or challenge unequal relations in temporary employment. Some will identify with temporary agencies and corporate clients even as they experience the negative aspects of temporary employment. Others can draw on their experiences to unveil exploitative, if interdependent, relationships. Neither of these cases is without its contradictions.

Identity fetishism, an excessive preoccupation with identity, often results in temporary workers' attempting to gain a sense of competence through a variety of means. While earlier we saw how this results in work intensification, here the focus is on how it accomplished the individualization of temporaries as subjects, the result of which is often the reproduction of power relations.

Part of each "cover story" told by temporaries is the notion that they are not "just a temp." Rather, they are an artist, a teacher, a student, an actor, an upwardly mobile yet unrecognized talent, a professional who has been laid off. Temporary workers who invoke these cover stories are not lying; rather, they are rejecting the label of temp and its associated stigma.[9] The larger implication of these identity struggles is the individualization of temporaries. Temporaries do not feel or act as part of the group "temporaries" but feel attached to the groups they identify in their cover story. Changing the conditions of temporary employment is much less a priority for many temporaries than is getting out of temporary employment.

Still other temporaries asserted their individuality by emphasizing their upbringing as a differentiating factor between "real temporaries" and themselves.

> I was raised that way, sort of compulsive. Even though you're a temp, you don't blow it off. You know and usually, especially if I were working for people I respected I didn't want to do a shoddy job just because I know how important it is. And I have a good friend who is doing a temp stint right now for somebody in the entertainment business that's just a total whack-off. And she's an out-of-work producer right now, and she's just absolutely compulsive about doing a good job, and she's carrying the ball and he's a nitwit. You run into the same types. Just some of us were raised to believe in no matter what you're doing even if it's just for a few bucks, you just don't do a shoddy job. (Ellen Lanford, thirty-eight-year-old white woman)

These descriptions, although couched in highly individualistic terms, are imbued with class and racial understandings of what constitutes a good employee—that is, *not* a temp. Temporary employment relations value middle-class femininity and whiteness (Rogers and Henson 1997), but they do so in a way that grants those who can "do" white, middle-class femininity a reprieve from being classified as a temp. Successful "performance" of white, middle-class femininity does not result in one being praised for being a good temporary worker; rather, one is rewarded for *not* being just a temp. The pejorative label "temp" is reserved for those who, for whatever reason, do not "fit in" to the dominant corporate culture. As Ludy explains,

> I would see other temps coming in that also didn't have a clue and were usually also the ones who were not used to temping or sort of undereducated in a lot of ways. They did not have a clue either of how to behave and read signals or, um, what to do to even just look busy. And a lot of them would just sit there and say, "Well, nobody's given me anything to do." And they didn't know to ask for more work. And those were the ones that would sit there with *People* magazine and say, "Can I leave early?" because there's nothing to do [laughs]. But, yeah, there were probably a few that I realized proper screening would eliminate. You know sometimes they weren't educated enough, not really brought up to understand that they were working in the white corporate world and didn't really know how to blend in. You know you don't speak Black English on the phone; you know [you don't] chew gum; you know you don't interrupt. (Ludy Martinez, thirty-six-year-old Filipina)

Thus, socially constructed differences in class and race accomplish the further individualization of temporary workers. Those who can successfully identify as not temporary receive the added bonus of having confirmed for them their class or racial privilege. Although of Filipino descent, Ludy emphasizes her education and class standing in opposition to another "minority" group to whom she attributes a lack of education and communication skills.

Many temporary workers, the men in particular, felt stigmatized because temporary work was not seen as a "real job," which implies stable, full-time employment.[10] The notion that "real men have real jobs" is explained by Harold Koenig:

> Like they're thinkin', "Gee, what's the deal?" Shouldn't you be, I don't know, doing something else?" They never say that, but that's just me projecting that. More so now the older I get. I mean, it's like sort of fine if you're just out of school. They kind of expect you're doing this until

you get a regular job. It's like I get the feeling now that they're thinking, "Why? Why? I'm suspicious of you." (Harold Koenig, twenty-nine-year-old white man)

Harold and other men reported feelings that could be characterized as masculinity struggles. For those like Harold (white, with an upper-middle-class background), the masculinity struggles seemed most intense. Working in a "feminized" occupation (secretarial and temporary employment) seemed to threaten aspects of their masculine identity. Male temporaries felt that they were perceived by others as somehow defective and lacking in character because they were not in a position of power and were not on the fast track to one. Particularly troublesome was the sporadic nature of the work. As with part-time work, temporary work is seen as viable for women, whose work still is often constructed as secondary to men's. Similarly, women's location in contingent work arrangements is often "explained" by reference to their home and family duties regardless of whether they actually have these duties. Thus, there seems to be no legitimate reason for a man to be employed temporarily, especially in secretarial work, so the identity of male workers is questioned from the outset.

Most acutely felt by the heterosexual men among the workers I spoke with was the fear of being labeled "homosexual," as their logic dictated that a man in a feminine occupation was of questionable sexual orientation.[11] Both straight and gay men conflated sexuality and gender in their discussions of men in temporary employment. While most straight men felt the association of gay men with temporary work was problematic and stigmatizing, at least one gay man, Michael Glenn, had a different perception. Recall earlier how Michael characterized gay men as ideally suited to temporary work, second only to heterosexual women. By far the exception, Michael Glenn positively constructs temporary work as feminized to include gay men, whom he sees as feminized as well. Despite other problems he had with temporary employment, Michael was not troubled by this aspect of temporary work. But just as Ludy was able to confirm her class privilege at the expense of other temporaries, straight men who deride temporary employment as something beneath them, as women's work (or gay men's work), are able to confirm both their gender and sexual privilege over women and gay men at the same time that they reduce the likelihood of identification with them. While Michael Glenn's characterization of the gendered nature of temporary employment is not derisive, it *is* individualizing in that it does not "challenge the dominant/subordinate statuses of male/female" (Rogers and Henson 1997, 223). Heterosexual men still are conceived of as problematic in temporary employment, while women's and gay men's temporary employment is naturalized rather than considered in conjunction with the low pay, low status, and lack of power of temporary workers. Thus the problems associated with temporary employment are deemed problems only as they relate to *individual* workers, and in this case individual male workers. Solutions therefore are aimed at individuals escaping temporary employment rather than transforming power relations within temporary employment.

So stigmatizing is temporary employment that many temporaries go so far as to hide their temporary employment experience from potential permanent employers by rewriting their résumés, as did Larry Landers:

> I don't list a lot of temporary experience. I don't like to list a lot of my temp [work]. I maybe list skills-wise. But a lot of jobs don't like temp experience, because it shows instability. And you always want to project stability. Don't show them that you've been jumping from here to here to here. Don't want to show that. They frown on that. (Larry Landers, thirty-eight-year-old African American)

In their recognition of employers' dislike of the supposed instability of temporaries, these people once again deny their membership in the ranks of temporary workers. They again constitute themselves as individuals free from the stigmatizing label of temporary employment. The need to do so derives not only from identity fetishism but real material requirements for obtaining a secure position that might otherwise be denied were they to reveal their stint of temporary work.

Despite the fact that many of the temporaries I interviewed had been at it for more than a year,[12] and that many of them have recurring periods of temporary employment, no one actually identified himself or herself as a temporary worker. By its very definition, *temporary* is a condition that cannot be part of a solidified or stable identity. Collective identification, much less collective resistance, seems difficult at best when dealing with highly individualized subjects, a topic I investigate further at the end of this chapter.

Freedom

As seen in the previous chapter, the temporary industry and client companies try to influence temporaries' perceptions to their favor. Temporary employment is cast as an exchange relationship entered into by equal parties—the temporary and the client company are said to be "free" to "try out" each other. In fact, the temporary industry proclaims that temporary workers' freedom to leave a job is one of the greatest benefits of temporary employment. Appeals to freedom resonate with basic cultural values of agency in the United States, wherein individuals are seen as "free" to succeed or fail.[13]

> Temping is not bad. But when you take a permanent job you're locked in. You're locked into this personality, that personality. If they don't like you, you always have to have a backup plan. Like for me, if one agency doesn't work, I call all the agencies. If one doesn't work, another one will. (Larry Landers, thirty-eight-year-old African American)

> You get to see the whole dynamics of the company, and if you really want to work there or not. Because they treat you completely different. When you're a temp, you get all the shitty work. Excuse me. But you can always tell them, "Thank you very much, but I won't be back tomorrow." You get to see how everyone works, and you get to decide if you really want to work there or not. So temping allows me to, you know, kind of test the waters. (Doug Larson, thirty-nine-year-old white man)

> I think temping is the best. Because you just say, "No more; I'm out." You know, you don't have to put up with anything. No commitment. That's the best part about temping. (Shari Jensen, thirty-three-year-old African American)

Yet few temporaries ever question this "fact." First, individuals in the United States are not legally prohibited from leaving a job when they wish. Why should this differ for temporary workers? More important, the freedom appeal is devoid of any recognition of power relations that might constrain temporaries' opportunities to use this freedom. In fact, few temporaries report ever taking advantage of their newfound ability to leave, as this quote from Shari Jensen exemplifies:

> But now I ran out of unemployment; I have no choice, you know. That's why you go back to temping. But I like the no commitment, you know. I hated being a secretary. Because I don't like being told what to do. That's why I guess I like temping, because I don't have to put up with it. I can just pick up and go anytime. *But I'm not like that. I cannot do it. If I say yes, I cannot break it.* But you can always give them a week or something. That's good. And you know it's short-term, so you feel good. You

don't have to put up with it for a long time. (Shari Jensen, thirty-three-year-old African American; my italics)

Although the temporary workers I interviewed seldom took advantage of their loose employment affiliation, the possibility that they could do so was important to their understanding and appraisal of temporary employment. Despite the fact that many faced serious, material constraints on their ability to leave a temporary assignment, they did not feel locked into a situation that, if permanent, would feel oppressive to them. Temporary work provides an escape from some types of work pressure. Seeing temporary employment as an escape from the pressures of "permanent" work helps mute conflict because the negative aspects of temporary work are framed as a necessary trade-off to other types of work pressure.[14]

In reality, temporary workers are asked to commit to the duration of each assignment, somewhat reducing their freedom to leave a job willy-nilly. In fact, one agency I visited went as far as to have their temporary workers sign the following contract:

I, _____, understand that if I am ever employed by [Amanuensis Temporary Agency], it will be on a temporary, not permanent, basis. I therefore am never guaranteed continuous full or part time employment and my temporary association can be discontinued at any time with no notice or explanation necessary.

I understand that if I am employed by [Amanuensus Temporary Agency], I am committed to complete the agreed upon assignment term. If, for any reason, I am unable to complete the assignment, I will give [Amanuensis Temporary Agency], two (2) weeks written notice.

I also understand that if I do not report to work when scheduled, or fail to call to report off work before scheduled, my affiliation with [Amanuensis Temporary Agency] will be terminated immediately.

Those temporaries who exercise their freedom to leave are generally labeled as "flakes" by clients, agencies, and other temporaries. Just as there are pressures for "regular" workers to remain in a job, temporary workers experience pressures to remain in an assignment. Leaving an assignment prior to its completion is not looked upon kindly by temporary agencies and may result in work deprivation for the temporary. Nevertheless, it was important to many temporary workers I spoke with to characterize these pressures differently from the pressures associated with permanent employment.

On the one hand, I would like to have a permanent job. I would like to have the benefits. I'd like to have the security. I'd like to have a decent wage. But on the other hand, being a temp offers me the freedom to leave a job when I want. But you can also only be so finicky when you have to work. So, um, I would say frankly there's much more disadvantages to working temporary than there are working permanent, other than [the] freedom to not being tied down. I mean, to not have a complete commitment. That's the good thing, but not for everybody. For me it's good, but at the same time nobody has a commitment to you. They could let you go tomorrow and not tell you. So you have absolutely no security and no guarantees and no insurance and no benefits. (Albert Baxter, thirty-one-year-old white man)

Albert Baxter recognizes the limitations on his ability to leave a job, along with several other disadvantages of temporary employment. This does not, however, diminish the importance for him of being able to leave (at least in theory) an assignment to pursue other interests. In fact, he is reluctant to take on a permanent job:

If a permanent job came to me—[and] right now I'm not looking very hard for one, not at all really—then I'd have to consider it. And consider, like, a career. I mean, my planned career is just writing, period. I'm not gonna settle for anything else. And people say, "Here's this wonderful opportunity to become an insurance broker." And I say, "No I don't think so." (Albert Baxter, thirty-one-year-old white man)

It is important to remark that Albert Baxter is not representative of temporary workers because, unlike most, he would not prefer "permanent" employment (Polivka 1996). Among the workers who did not desire a permanent job, however, Albert's reasons were not uncommon. Albert does represent a small minority of people who do not want a traditional employment arrangement. This population of workers, while it does exist, is vastly overemphasized by the temporary industry. The "freedom" sought by a few is manipulated to appear as a desire of many and benefit to all, despite mounting evidence to the contrary.

Exploitation

Earlier we saw how some temporaries come to adopt the views of management by identifying with the cost-cutting imperatives of business and today's labor market. Yet if we re-examine the words of these temporaries, we find at least some ambivalence toward the temporary industry line. Apparently, efforts at discursive control are far from complete.

> You get in, like I said before. And I think that is the only reason people are doing it. And employers are reducing their overhead by hiring a lot more temps. It's working out for both, *but I think you'll see some type of revolt against temping in the next ten years. People won't be able to afford to do it. They want more than that.* Right now it's a stopgap measure for the people not working and for the companies strapped financially. (Doug Larson, thirty-nine-year-old white man; my italics)

Considering comments like this, we need to question whether efforts at discursive control are successful at all. Temporaries often reject industry discourses even as they invoke them, and they create a counterdiscourse out of lived experiences. One of the temporary workers I interviewed, Linda Mejia, told me that her extensive experience with a number of agencies helped her to know how they work, and what she could actually get from them if she pushed hard enough. But this knowledge does not come easily. In fact, this knowledge may be hidden intentionally from temporary workers. Agencies are well-served by making their actions (such as construction of pay rates and methods of work allocation) invisible. Temporary workers with less experience (as temporaries) feel mystified when confronted with the barriers to knowledge constructed by the temporary industry (for instance, prohibition of discussing pay rates, lack of reasons for assignment termination, client evaluation of the temporary's performance, and agency markups).

Ironically, increasing the extent and duration of temporary employment may help to reveal the exploitative nature of the temporary employment relationship, which relies on transitoriness both to control workers and to obfuscate that control. Thus, one of the contradictions of temporary work is that while it is a stream of "unfair" experiences designed to keep the worker in the dark, the longer the stream becomes, the more likely the worker is to develop a critical understanding of the organization of temporary work. Recall Doug Larson's account in which he feels taken advantage of because he is working for seven dollars an hour. These feelings gave rise to a budding sense of unfairness.

Doug believed that after his initial stint, he would be granted a pay increase, which never materialized. While he does not cast temporary employment as "exploitation" per se, he does question its fairness. Although Doug was unable to clearly articulate just what it was that bothered him about temporary employment, it seems obvious that he was upset about the failure of existing work structures to accommodate workers' needs for flexibility without workers bearing all the costs. And while Doug continually emphasized the need for the freedom inherent in temporary employment to pursue his acting career, he unfortunately did not find his ideal solution in temporary employment.[15]

In addition to Ludy Martinez's other temporary employment experiences, she temped for a friend in San Francisco. Because of Ludy's vast experience, her friend asked her to help size up the competition for temporary workers:

> I remember sitting down doing a little project for my friend Donna and comparing what a word processor was getting at different agencies because I'd been with so many of them. And I had to tell her, "You're on the low end." You know, this same job is posted over at this lady's agency and it's $11 an hour, and you're $9.50. That's ridiculous. And I remember going to certain agencies that I was registered with and, um, balking at going to certain places temping saying I've worked for another agency, and they paid me at least ten bucks and you're offering me eight. That's ridiculous. And they were, like, "Oh, you have an attitude." But I felt like I at least had to say that because they were saying, "Well, we pay whatever the market will bear." Well, what do you know about the *market*? (Ludy Martinez, thirty-six-year-old Filipina)

Ludy learned that pay scales are not as scientifically constructed as agencies claim them to be. In fact, Ludy questions the legitimacy of the very idea of market determination of wages. As she recounted this story to me, she laughed and emphasized the word *market* with disdain, as if to dispute its very meaning. Later, Ludy told me, "Temporaries definitely can be treated like a commodity. And even when they're treating you well, you know that they're treating you well as like a good business practice as opposed to actually having respect for you or caring about getting you a job." (Ludy Martinez, thirty-six-year-old Filipina)

Although Albert Baxter described feeling exploited and actually used the word *exploited*, he carefully qualified his expression of these feelings in terms of his "freedom" to choose:

> I know that I definitely do feel exploited. I don't like it, but it's also a position I've chosen to put myself in. And I can see that I can leave it. Whereas some other people cannot if they don't have the skills and ability. (Albert Baxter, thirty-one-year-old white man)

Once again, the construction of temporary employment as freedom from something else potentially obscures what might otherwise be understood as exploitative.

Recall Don Birch, the "elite" temporary with the Yale degree who thought he had successfully negotiated a dollar-an-hour increase for an assignment. When he received his paycheck, the increase was nowhere to be found. He told me that before this incident he realized that relations between temporaries and agencies were "inherently unequal"; however, this experience prompted him to characterize the temporary industry in the following way:

> It's fraught with problems and exploitation, and it's inherently an unequal, anti-labor exercise in which, you know, you don't get any benefits and you're exploited. You're just literally exploited. And it's a total step backwards. It's . . . very destructive for families and for people who are trying to plan and look longer-term. (Don Birch, twenty-four-year-old white man)

While most temporary workers did not describe their feelings as pointedly as Don, many characterized the structure of the economic relationship between temporaries and their agencies as "a rip off." Cindy Carson was upset when she learned that temporaries doing the same work earned a higher hourly wage than she:

> I got really angry with them recently. I mean, I'm not making that much money there, but then again the clerical positions don't make that much. But this is the first time that I've been doing temp work in my life that I feel like I'm getting ripped off. I never felt that way before. I felt like I was making an adequate wage. So I asked for a raise. . . . I thought I put it in a very diplomatic fashion. I said to this one woman who was always there handing out the checks, "Oh, can you find me a higher-paying assignment?" I thought that would be a way to say it. . . . And the next assignment they sent me on was two days, and I got fifty cents an hour more, which I was really happy about at the time, you know. Then . . . this office manager gets on the phone and says, "We have an assignment today; it pays seven dollars an hour. Do you want it?" She was really snippy with me, and I knew that this other lady had probably said to her that I wanted a raise. And I said, "OK, fine, I'll go there." And it was only supposed to be for a few weeks. So then I was there for three and a half months, and I just got really, really angry. I became more and more angry. (Cindy Carson, thirty-eight-year-old white woman)

Cindy's "raise" was short-lived, and her feelings of exploitation grew. When I asked her if there was anything she would change about temporary employment, she discussed the pay structure at length, citing profit margin and capriciousness as problems with the current system.

I would change the pay structure because I think it should be set. Like, I think they shouldn't be getting any more than like 25 percent of what you're making. Something like that maximum. And then the second thing would be some sort of system where if you're really having a problem that you can feel comfortable saying, "Well, they're saying this to me, and I'm really stressed out." . . . [There should be a system]where you won't lose the job. But, I mean, my main concern is the money, because I think it shouldn't be a barter system. Like, they're paying some people more to do the same job. . . . I'm really angry about that. I think it should be if you're superior then. OK, give you fifty cents an hour more or a dollar an hour more. But there shouldn't be this huge range. . . . They bill the company; that's another thing. That office manager told me how much they were charging for me. . . . It was really giving me the creeps. They were charging them $10.99, and I was getting $7. And I was *really* angry. Because I think they have a set fee. . . . We charge $10 for people to come empty trash cans, we charge $10.99 for filing, we charge $12 for phones. And then what they do is they kind of play with the temps and give them what they think will pay. When they ask you to write down the lowest you'll take, that's all you get (Cindy Carson, thirty-eight-year-old white woman)

Cindy's and the others' accounts of the exploitative nature of the temporary employment relationship exemplify the process through which any apparent consensus is broken: "When the self-defeating or self-denying nature of the practice is experienced most acutely, conflict occurs" (Sturdy 1992, 141). Discursive controls fail most dramatically when actual experiences sharply diverge from attempts to shape consciousness.

Knowing the Score

How, then, can we explain the lack of action in light of the awareness of exploitation articulated by so many of the temporary workers interviewed? Simply put, knowledge can be a double-edge sword.[16] In the scenarios depicted in this chapter, knowledge enabled temporary workers to perceive and articulate exploitative employment relations. Knowledge, however, can result in a type of organizational "outflanking" of temporary workers, which prevents them from resisting.[17] Specifically, knowing the high cost of resistance often prevents temporary workers from taking any action. For example, knowledge of the financial arrangement between agencies and clients makes temporary workers aware of the pecking order that places the client well above the worker. Clients, not workers, pay the temporary agency, and therefore, the loss of a client and any anticipated repeat business poses more of a threat to the success of the agency than the loss of a single, expendable temporary worker. This is particularly true in an area where competition among temporary agencies is high at the same time that unemployment is high. Thus, knowledge as well as ignorance can temper resistance.[18]

Contrary to popular theories that find temporaries acting impulsively and irrationally, temporary workers often weigh all the potential consequences of resistance. With the knowledge that temporary agencies have no obligation to their workers, Cindy Carson struggled with her decision to publicly express anger to her agency supervisor. Cindy was sure she would lose her job after she "stomped out of the office," but she did not. While she chose to express her anger in this case, Cindy remarks that in every other similar situation, she did nothing because of the knowledge of the tenuous nature of her position:

> But I got so desperate the past couple years that I just put up with it. It was awful, but I used to be very desperate. But when you're not desperate, I think you do the right thing. But when you're desperate you can't always. (Cindy Carson, thirty-eight-year-old white woman)

Cindy no longer characterizes herself as desperate, because she is only partially dependent on temporary employment for her income. She has had a relatively steady stint of part-time employment in the evenings, which she is able to supplement with temporary employment to provide an adequate, if not substantial, income.

One of the most savvy temporaries I interviewed, Ludy, expressed how a veiled threat from an agency prevented her from complaining about any problems in her assignments. Eventually, Ludy even refrained from mentioning clients' requests to alter her time cards, a practice that is clearly against agencies' policies. She understood that the small loss the agencies would experience from the alteration of her time card was insignificant when compared to the permanent loss of that client.

Thus, knowledge of the structure of interests in temporary clerical employment, while theoretically empowering, can also limit resistance when that knowledge also highlights the marginal status of individual workers in the temporary employment triad. Despite agencies' avowals that temporaries are valuable assets, clients and agencies are clearly the dominant parties in the transaction. Temporaries may be valuable assets, but they are aware that they often are replaceable valuable assets.

Similarly, knowledge of the individualization of temporary workers leads many temporary workers to conclude that resistance is futile.

> Obviously I wouldn't get involved in trying to change it. I mean, I'm getting out of this now. There are some things that would be nice to change, but I don't even know any other temps. I guess laws could be changed, but people are in and out of this business. (Jean Masters, thirty-four-year-old African American)

> Who is looking out for the temp's interest? The agency isn't looking out for the worker's interest. The business isn't looking out for the worker's interest. So I should start a temp union! I wouldn't want to organize that. Jimmy Hoffa of the temps. No, no, no. No one stays in one place. You all have your own thing going. No way. (Doug Larson, thirty-nine-year-old white man)

As we saw earlier, with few means of conducting collective resistance,[19] temporary workers inevitably emphasize leaving temporary employment over improving it. Many personal acts of resistance, including sabotage, do take place, but only a few attempts at collectively improving material conditions of employment ever surface. Most of temporaries' efforts at resistance are in the discursive realm, debunking temporary industry myths, shaking off stereotypes, and reaffirming one's identity often at the expense of other temporaries. In short, there is much evidence here to support the assertion that "resistance against perceivedly overwhelming odds tends to be through existential and symbolic gestures" (Clegg 1994, 294). Thus temporary workers' preoccupation with rejecting the stigma of temporary employment does not come from some inherent personal need, but rather is a byproduct of the highly asymmetrical power relations characteristic of temporary clerical employment. At the same time, this preoccupation can reproduce the very relations that prompted the preoccupation to begin with. Consequently, the knowledge of one's odds of success limits much resistance to the symbolic realm, where identity fetishism acts to individualize subjects.

ALTHOUGH many, but not necessarily all, temporary clerical workers feel exploited in their employment relationship, only a low incidence of collective resistance is evident. Temporary employment produces individuals who, in trying to secure a stable identity in opposition to the stigmatized "temp" identity, may help perpetuate the status quo. Their knowledge of the power imbalance in temporary employment outflanks their resistance before it begins. Gender, race, and class shoot through and surround individualized resistance when privileged positions are confirmed as a means of solidifying one's identity against and at the expense of the "other." How then, might temporary workers better their situation collectively?

These data show the challenges that potential organizers face with regard to the subjectivity of temporary workers. The data also demonstrate, however, the power of experience in revealing the asymmetries in temporary employment. Although most clerical temporaries seem too overwhelmed by their circumstances to take action themselves, if presented with realistic possibilities of successful labor organizing, they might be open to union membership. Few temporaries might lead, but many might follow.

Perhaps the struggle needs to be waged simultaneously on the symbolic and material fronts. To constitute temporary workers collectively instead of as individuals, organizers might reclaim the fluid identity of the "temp" and give it the dignity it lacks, providing temporary workers with the legitimacy to demand social justice. Reclaiming the fluid identity of "temp" may enable temporary workers to find a "solidarity in multiplicity"[20] to recognize their common plight despite their differences, real or constructed.

Because clients are the bread and butter of temporary agencies, their shared interests with the agency form a very powerful alliance against the interests of atomized temporary workers. Under current social, economic, and political conditions that favor the worldview put forth by the temporary industry (and business generally), waging direct battle over material improvements seems an arduous prospect. Nevertheless, the battle is brewing. DuRivage, Carré, and Tilly (1998) offer numerous suggestions to improve labor law, which currently makes organizing extremely difficult for contingent workers. Other innovative strategies under way include union-sponsored temporary worker centers to disperse important information; the Massachusetts Contingent Work Bill, an equal pay initiative; and geographical/occupational unionism to overcome some logistic difficulties of a fluid workforce (see also Carré 1998; Wial 1993). However successful these initiatives may be, if temporary workers continue to see temporary employment as something that is "only temporary," and if they continue to buy into the official discourse, we have to wonder if their problems will be only temporary.

6   Lawyers for Rent

One of the lawyers I interviewed told me a joke: "How many lawyers does it take to change a light bulb?" "How many?" I asked. "None," he replied. "Lawyers don't change."

Despite the implication of this joke, the law profession has experienced quite a few changes in the past twenty-five years. Rapid growth in the law profession, along with other changes such as the increase in salaried employment and advertising of legal services, has spurred continuing concern over the status of law professionals.[1] The term *law factory* is not an unfamiliar one to novice lawyers embarking on their first employment in large, bureaucratic, fast-paced metropolitan law firms.

Not the least of the changes in the law profession is women's increased participation. Lawyers are part of what are known as "the core professions"—doctors, lawyers, architects, and university teachers—because they offer market shelter and stringent gatekeeping for their members.[2] These historically male-dominated professions stand in contrast to what are known as "the semi-professions," usually female-dominated support positions, such as nurses. However, many of today's law and other professionals might object to a characterization that attributes such power to them and their profession. Indeed, many researchers have proffered various proletarianization or deprofessionalization theses, asserting a decline in the power and status of professionals through a loss of autonomy or incorporation into bureaucratic work structures.[3]

Notably, the increases in salaried employment and female participation traditionally have been associated with an occupation's decline in status. Typically, the decline in the occupation precedes women's entrance into a field as men abandon the occupation for better opportunities elsewhere

(Reskin and Roos 1990). Women's entrance into even a declining occupation finds them ghettoized into less prestigious, lower-paying subspecialties and in contingent employment.

In 1960, only 3.5 percent of lawyers in the United States were women; by 1980, that figure had risen to 15 percent (Sokoloff 1992). As of 1993, approximately 23 percent of U.S. lawyers were women (U.S. Bureau of the Census 1994). Although the profession itself may not be declining in status, it is becoming bifurcated into the elites and the rank-and-file (Freidson 1986). Portions of the law profession retain their high status and power, while more and more lawyers are employed in routine, less autonomous positions. Not surprisingly, women are overrepresented in the least autonomous, least prestigious, and least powerful positions in law, including part-time positions.[4]

A Temporary What?

Before detailing the work of temporary lawyers, I must reemphasize that owing to the difference in scale between the two groups of interviews, limited generalization can be drawn from the data on lawyers; however, these data do support some important, if tentative, conclusions. More important, the comparison of temporary work in these dissimilar occupations points toward areas for future research into occupational effects of temporary employment. The term *temporary professional* appears at first glance to be an oxymoron. Surely professionals cannot be disposable, as is implied by the moniker "temporary." Temporary employment seems antithetical to how we understand professional work—that is, extensive training and long-term commitment. Epstein et al. (1999) detail the degree to which long hours serve as "professional capital." Likewise, those working short hours (by standards in the law profession) are stigmatized. But as one attorney pointed out to me, the legal profession has a long history of "temporary" work in what is known as "overflow" work. Overflow work is simply one lawyer sending out his or her extra work to a professional contact who has the time and ability to complete the work. Obtaining such overflow work requires an adequate professional network, one that women often lack.[5] Historically, overflow work was predicated on strong networks among male attorneys. New (male) solo practitioners supported themselves with overflow work while they built their client base. In contrast, the temporary lawyers in this study obtain overflow work through an intermediary, the temporary agency, rather than an informal network.

The lawyers of today—that is, women—may not have access to that informal network.

Since the late 1980s, law firms have been cutting expenses and downsizing their staffs, resulting in unemployment or underemployment for many lawyers who would otherwise prefer to have full-time associate positions. In a *New York Times* article, several legal temporary agency managers and owners estimated that approximately 70 percent of their applicants would prefer full-time work (Mansnerus 1991). The agency managers with whom I spoke expressed no difficulty in obtaining qualified applicants, as economically difficult times have created an abundant supply of temporary lawyers.

Although the reluctance of law firms to hire attorneys into full-time positions is pushing both men and women out of traditional work arrangements, there is good reason to suspect that temporary attorneys may be disproportionately female if temporary employment for lawyers represents a sort of occupational ghetto. Indeed, data from this study give some support for women's overrepresentation.[6]

As with temporary employment in general, women may be overrepresented in the ranks of temporary lawyers.[7] While only 22.9 percent of lawyers in the United States are women (U.S. Bureau of the Census 1994), 52 percent of the temporary lawyers working through one agency I examined are women. The overrepresentation of women in the lower status strata of an occupation as well as the pay differential by gender is symptomatic of queuing, a process through which worker and employer preferences combine to create occupational segregation.[8] Thus the overrepresentation of women in the temporary employment of lawyers represents occupational ghettoization of women within the law profession.

Pay rates for temporary lawyers tend to fall between thirty-five and fifty dollars per hour but can be as low as twenty five dollars or as high as seventy-five to one hundred dollars for highly specialized, experienced attorneys on the best assignments. Typically, the agency bills at a rate 20 to 30 percent above what is paid to the temporary attorney, and the firm for which the work is done bills its client between one hundred and three hundred dollars per hour for the temporary attorney.

Temporary agencies for lawyers work in much the same way as temporary agencies for clerical or industrial workers. Lawyers submit their credentials to the agency, which maintains them on file as requests for assistance from law firms or individual lawyers come in. The agency selects an appropriate person and connects the lawyer with the client firm. Sometimes work is done at the client's work site; at other times the lawyer simply receives files to work on at home or in an independent office. In either case, the client firm pays the temporary agency, which in turn pays the temporary attorney. Temporary lawyers are not only cheaper by the hour than permanent lawyers, but they also save the hiring firm the cost of office space, staff support, and malpractice insurance. Like temporary clerical staff, temporary attorneys represent a saving of benefits expenses for the client company.

Although temporary attorneys are paid a lower hourly rate than associates, they are often paid for all hours worked whereas associates habitually may work 15 hour days for their high but fixed salary. Even so, work is often sporadic, leaving a temporary attorney's monthly compensation well below the earnings of full-time associates, especially if one considers the lack of health insurance and other benefits. The manager of the agency through which I obtained my access reported having many more applicants than she could possibly place, a dilemma she shares with her counterparts in other agencies.

Temporary attorney assignments include court appearances, status conferences, depositions, research, writing, law and motion, litigation, and projects. The least taxing assignments are the one-day court appearances, often involving minimal preparation and little more than an obligatory "Good-morning-your-honor," followed by a short status of the case. Temporary attorneys typically receive assignments working for a busy, small to medium-size law office, or for overloaded solo practitioners. Temporary attorneys also are contracted to provide expertise in an area that a particular firm might be lacking, although most attorneys I interviewed were called in for overload situations. According to the agencies, overload situations are the bulk of the work they receive. Assignments range in duration from several hours for depositions and appearances to several weeks, months, or even a year or more for larger projects and litigation.

Gender and Law: The Feminization of Temporary Work

Studies that herald women's dramatic advancement in the professions by citing their increased numbers or the increased rate of growth may be grossly overstating these changes (Sokoloff 1992). The fact remains that women are underrepresented in the professions, and that *within* the professions, they are situated in the least well-paid, least prestigious areas. For example, within the legal profession, women tend to be concentrated in family law rather than in the more lucrative specialty of corporate law, and they are underrepresented in litigation and as partners (Epstein 1993). In 1990, the median weekly earnings of male lawyers overall was $1,178, while for females it was $875 (Andersen 1993).

The law profession is gendered in other ways as well. For example, the practice of law rests on appropriate expressions of masculinity and femininity. Litigation is identified with hypermasculinity, as is made evident in the term "Rambo litigators" (Pierce 1995). Solo practice has traditionally been difficult for women because of the long hours and the needed connections to local political networks. In contrast to women, men in solo practices typically are relieved of all home-bound responsibilities, giving them the time to devote to building a practice, including time spent developing the necessary networks (Seron 1996).

Although women find themselves in the least well-paid and least prestigious areas within an occupation, the occupation itself usually represents a more desirable choice, in terms of money and prestige, than traditionally "female" occupations (Reskin and Roos 1990; Sokoloff 1992). This assertion was borne out by my research. Several of the women interviewed compared their temporary employment in relatively favorable terms with other options they perceived to be available to them.

> I think that most attorneys will agree that you can't earn a great living just doing this kind of work. You have to supplement it, but it depends on what a good living is. What I earn is great for a schoolteacher, who would think it's a fine salary. So it depends on what people think of as a good salary. (Diane Kraft, thirty-nine-year-old white woman; married with two children)

> I thought I would go to law school so that I could make enough income to support my singing habit. I always intended to work part time because you can make as much part time as you could in most jobs full time, especially waitressing or something like that that most singers do. . . . I like the little extra income, but it's a little. Especially when you're looking at somebody that's making $175 or $225 an hour and I scrub around for $50. (Kelly Bower, thirty-three-year-old white woman; married with no children)

While the women held traditionally "female" jobs as a reference point for their decision to work as a contract attorney, men were more likely to place their choice in the context of temporary work versus no work, where the income from contract work was perceived as a better alternative than having no income at all. Hence, while economics plays a vital role in moving individuals into temporary employment, that move is experienced by individuals in the context of their perceived work alternatives—alternatives constructed in part by the historical segregation of women into less prestigious occupations.

But the feminization of temporary lawyering goes beyond women's overrepresentation and their reasons for "choosing" temporary employment. The very notion of a temporary job is itself a gendered construction. From Rosie the Riveter of World War II to today's immigrant women textile workers, women's work is constructed as temporary and as supplementary to a male "permanent" income. At the same time, women's work historically has been constructed as temporary, and temporary work historically has been constructed as women's work. In fact, it was only in the late 1960s that Kelly Services dropped the moniker of "Kelly Girls" in favor of the more politically correct, gender-neutral name. But what happens when temporary work, historically identified with women, enters into the traditionally male domain of law?

While conducting this research it became readily apparent that there is a certain stigma associated with temporary employment for lawyers. In fact, one agency has gone as far as to directly address that stigma in its advertisement:

> If you're skeptical about temporary attorneys [we] understand. After all, with any other temporary attorney service, your concern would be justified. (agency advertisement 1993)

I asked each of the attorneys I spoke with how she or he thinks others in the profession would characterize contract attorneys. Most were keenly aware of the existing negative stereotypes, and some mentioned having experienced prejudice outright. This stigma appears to be related to the dominant sentiment in some sectors of the legal field stating that anyone who works less than full time, which in some cases may be fifteen hours a day anyway, is seen as uncommitted.[9]

In congruence with these sentiments, temporary legal jobs are further characterized in a derogatory (and gendered) manner as "mommy jobs," while the people who do them, especially the men, might be seen as "flaky," "peculiar," or "soft." Even though they did not characterize themselves as "flakes," the lawyers I interviewed were certain that others would perceive them that way, marginalizing them within the profession. Of interest for gender-stratification theory is that many of these negative images of temporary lawyers derive from gender ideologies that characterize women as "uncommitted" and "soft" at the same time that they devalue women's domestic labor.

We know that organizations (and jobs) are not gender-neutral (Acker 1990). In the case of temporary work, the "universal" worker is actually a gendered worker, and female at that. Hence the stigmatized identity is a gendered identity that seems to contribute to men's stronger distaste for temporary work. Although this stigmatized "feminine" identity acts to marginalize both men and women temporary attorneys individually, if women truly are overrepresented in temporary law, the stigmatized identity reinforces women's marginality, as a group, within the legal profession.

Indeed, the terms *temporary* and *professional* seem incongruous. Characterizing temporary professionals in gendered terms, however, partially resolves the incongruity when temporary lawyers are characterized as "soft" and "uncommitted"—terms usually reserved for women workers.

I think in the profession we're generally regarded as lightweights. I don't think they think we're serious. (Veronica Clarke, forty-six-year-old white woman; married with two children)

I think that they're thought of as soft. (Alice Lederer, 40-year-old white woman, married, three children)

Furthermore, temporary law jobs are most often characterized as "mommy jobs."

Maybe for women, you know, we have a male-dominated society always . . . and lawyers! It's like, "Oh, you want to be with the kids? It's a mommy job." That's OK. (Diane Kraft, thirty-nine-year-old white woman; married with two children)

So not only is temporary law conceived of as women's work, but a particular type of women's work—a "mommy's" work. Women who work as temporary lawyers are assumed to have children (many, but not all, do) and, as such, a lesser commitment to their profession.

Law is a sexist profession, and those people have made hours issues, flex time, temping, and the like into women's issues. Women are fed up from not making it in the partnerships track time and time again. The assholes at the top look down on anyone who has anything going except law. You must eat, breathe, and sleep law. They assume that women are the ones who will want to have a life in addition to law, so they use this theory to keep women out of higher positions. You know, the glass-ceiling thing. (Don Harkins, vice president of Legal Eagles, phone interview, 1993)

Men who work as temporary attorneys pose a special problem. Their presence in temporary law potentially disrupts the gendered construction of both law and temporary work. However, most of the individuals interviewed accommodated the disruption by finding fault with the individual men. Men who work as temporary attorneys are seen as "flakes" or unable to face the challenge of "real law," just as male temporary clerical workers are viewed as less than real men. Real men in the law profession practice *real* law, not *temporary* law. Real law, in other words, means a full-time, fast-paced, overworked, highly paid, male attorney.

I think there's an attitude that people who are working with the firm are doing it for peculiar reasons. And that somehow law is not the dominating, consuming passion that it is for the lawyers who work full-time and have an office. It's often a secondary concern. Children come first or some other career comes first or maybe writing or some other activity comes first. As a result people might not be seen as all that experienced or they might not be all that familiar with the developments in the law. (Robert Andersen, forty-one-year-old white man; unmarried with no children)

Thus, at least part of what constitutes a "real job," which theoretically men must have and women seldom desire, is the notion that it must be at least full time and permanent.

While men who are temporary attorneys are seen as problematic, women temporary attorneys are "naturalized," as temporary employment is seen as the logical mechanism for combining work and family demands. In this understanding, work and family are seen as competing demands that only women have, which must be resolved individually rather than by changing the structure of work relations. Men's presence in temporary law, rather than challenging the gendered organization of law or temporary employment, helps to reproduce these conditions, especially when we consider how the male attorneys I interviewed explained their reasons for working temporarily. None of the men interviewed mentioned family responsibilities as a reason for working temporarily, nor is men's parental status ever addressed in relation to men's temporary employment by the women or the men I spoke with. Whether men consider family responsibilities or if they simply do not see family responsibilities as a socially acceptable reason for men to temp is difficult to ascertain. Regardless of whether they are in fact working temporarily to accommodate family responsibilities, the male lawyers I spoke with framed their work situation as related to personal or professional goals, not to family.

Deskilled and Devalued?

Temporary attorneys perform the full range of tasks within the law profession; they are not paralegals. Most temporary attorneys, however, reported being assigned to the more routine, "boilerplate" activities, or what the agency manager calls "worker bee" assignments. Worker bee assignments involve much the same type of work that brand-new lawyers do on entrance into their first law job: extensive file work with little autonomy and no supervisory responsibilities. Nevertheless, most of the attorneys on file at the agency at which I conducted my interviews were not freshly out of law school. Karen, the agency manager, told me they preferred experienced attorneys, even though the work being assigned didn't necessarily require experience.

Also prevalent were short court appearances necessitated by California's "fast-track" system that allows for fewer postponements of court dates. At each of these court dates, the presence of an attorney is required. Often these appearances are seen as a nuisance by the lawyer handling the case. If an attorney has conflicting responsibilities, a substitute may be sent; however, that person must be a member of the bar. The result has been an increased need for these substitutes (temporary attorneys) who are called in for what are essentially perfunctory court appearances. One lawyer I interviewed called this type of work "good-morning-your-honor" appearances. Typically, the temporary attorney is provided with minimal information regarding the case, appears briefly in court, and returns paperwork to the client company.

Certainly, prior to the existence of the fast-track system and temporaries, attorneys had to perform these routine appearances, but they were a small part of any one attorney's repertoire. In larger firms, however, women attorneys traditionally were assigned this kind of work, which was known not to be of help in terms of building a career (Seron 1996). Using a temporary agency, much of this work now can be shifted onto temporaries. Some of the lawyers I spoke with mentioned that these appearances formed the majority of their work. Therefore, the shorter, less complicated assignments represent a fragmentation of the work process, with temporary attorneys concentrated in the lower-skilled tasks within the profession. Not surprisingly, the lawyers I interviewed gleaned little sense of completion or satisfaction from this type of assignment.

I end up doing court appearances and depositions. I'm stuck doing these sorts of daily things. And most of it's not that interesting. It's not interesting at all for me. (Diane Kraft, thirty-nine-year-old white woman; married with two children)

The only thing I don't like about it is that you don't really get involved in the case and with the client so you don't really get to feel like it's yours or you don't get to care about it that much. I mean, I don't even know what happened with the case. And then there were some status conferences. There wasn't any really good substantive motions or anything that I had to appear on. So, I mean, it's not really good work. It's more just kind of the general mundane things that people don't want to spend money to go send somebody to go do. (Rebecca Lamarca, thirty-five-year-old white woman; unmarried with no children)

You don't see things through or have any continuity. Here I'm brought in for a very specific purpose, which is to do one thing. Whereas when you're with the firm you'd be charged with all aspects of the client's representation, see the whole thing through, all the way from the drafting of the claim through the motions to the trial. Whereas now, I just might see a little sliver of that. I'm hired to do a motion and I'll do that motion, but I'll never even meet the client. (George Westin, fifty-four-year-old white man; married with two children)

A lot of times, going to court is a big nothing. You go to court, you expect to get up and make whatever statement you're going to make, and depending on how the court is run you might only be there for all of five minutes. But you still need to make an appearance. And so a lot of attorneys feel that it's a big waste of time. But somebody needs to do it, and a contract attorney such as I am, I'm willing to do it. (Veronica Clarke, forty-six-year-old white woman; married with two children)

It should not be surprising that most of these statements came from women lawyers. The more fragmented assignments such as one-day appearances were characterized as "women's work" because of the association of one-day appearances with flexible employment. Indeed, many but not all of the women used the flexibility of one-day appearances to manage work and family conflict. In the interviews, the men generally expressed a strong distaste for such appearances and an unwillingness to take them, although a few did, particularly when pressed with financial obligations. However, none of the men cited flexibility or family in relation to one-day appearances.

Much of the research concerning gender and skill has developed around the manufacturing, clerical, and service sectors. A comparison of the work process within these sectors with that of professional work should be conducted with several caveats in mind. The professions in general are highly skilled in the sense that membership in them requires long, intense periods of training and provides work that is complex in comparison to much of the work in other sectors. Furthermore, professional associations have substantial power to resist trends that they perceive as "de-professionalizing." Finally, temporary lawyers are paid a high wage in comparison to receptionists, waitpersons, or textile workers. However, changes occurring within the law profession such as the employment of lawyers in bureaucratic organizations and the rise in temporary employment offer some support for the idea that the profession is experiencing, at least in part, some degree of deskilling.

While much of the work is deskilled (relative to other work in the profession), some of the work done by temporary attorneys does fall into highly specialized niches. In fact, the agency manager I spoke with anticipates further expansion of this type of work:

> The trend is in the direction of expertise. So the more specialized the attorney, the more likely they are going to get work through us. And credentials are important, too. [Applicants need] top credentials, and [it's also good] if they have a niche or an area of specialization.

Thus temporary attorneys can be found in complex and nonroutine brief writing, research, and litigation, as well as in the "worker bee" assignments.[10] For example, Jerry often turns down the lower-paying, routine assignments:

> Typically, it's drafting stuff, ghost-authoring things for lawyers who are too busy, or it's a research project. I try to decline stuff that's, like, twenty dollars an hour, because you are just in and then out of there. If it's longer, then I can get into it and figure out a way to help the attorney who is involved and his client. . . . But lawyers are really craftsmen. They're like architects who are working with the court. The job is not designed to be phenomenally interesting 100 percent of the time,

because a lot of what you're doing is very rigorous and very technical. (Jerry Archer, thirty-year-old white man; married with two children)

Robert, who has his own practice in addition to the temporary work, has his fiancée do most of the copying and filing while she works at home preparing to take the bar exam. Her unpaid work leaves him free to handle the "select" cases:

> My circumstances are that I'm getting a select type of work and kind of the cream of the crop. . . . It's very desirable work. It's the long projects, and it's the interesting research and writing. It's more high exposure. It's for established firms or solo practitioners who, when they see the writing and the product, are likely to call again for that type of work. It's good exposure for experience for trials or arbitration. So it's really the desirable work and it's often on cases . . . [that] are amongst the best in the lawyer's office. (Robert Andersen, forty-one-year-old white man; unmarried with no children)

As expected, the more complex and challenging assignments paid more than the one-day appearances or the more mundane assignments. Unlike the situation in temporary clerical work, the highly skilled work of temporary attorneys is not devalued but, rather, is seen as highly skilled and remunerated as such.

Temporary legal work may be relatively simplistic and thus less fulfilling on the whole; however, there do exist assignments that resemble the complexity and autonomy of traditional legal work, at reduced but competitive rates. This research suggests that male attorneys "prefer" and receive these better temporary assignments.

Control and Resistance

Issues surrounding control and resistance in temporary law take on a very different character than they do in temporary clerical work. Compared with other occupations, attorneys have significantly more autonomy; however, their work life is not without controls or accountability. Temporary employment in law may represent reduced control for law firms that can no longer wield the partnership carrot over some of its attorneys. Similarly, because much of the work is done off-site, firms lose opportunities to monitor temporary lawyers' work or demeanor.

Certainly, the attorneys in this study reported a heightened feeling of control. Even when the work was more fragmented, both the women and men I spoke with report an increased sense of control and empowerment that comes from temporary lawyering. Many, particularly those who had worked in large, bureaucratic "law factories" prior to temping, described feeling that their careers had gotten out of their control, that the hours and conditions of work felt oppressive, or that they had no personal life until they started working as a temporary.

> I really didn't want to work for a big firm anymore. I was working sixty to seventy hours a week. And it wasn't worth it, driving downtown, and it wasn't worth it. (Diane Kraft, thirty-nine-year-old white woman; married with two children)

> I was just burnt out. I had spent five years working very hard as an attorney. The combination of long hours, a world that's sort of a harsh world, the practice of law. (Joshua Humphrey, thirty-three-year-old white man; married with no children)

Traditionally, a greater division of labor brings greater control over workers and their work processes. While there is a greater division of labor with temporary law, it does not necessarily translate to enhanced managerial control. The three-party employment relationship *potentially* increases employers' control over temporary attorneys; however, these controls were seldom invoked.

In fact, many temporary lawyers felt that temporary employment relaxed bureaucratic managerial control over them as it reduced the practice of law to a more contractual relationship. Absent the "partnership carrot," many temporary attorneys felt they were free to simply practice law without complicating social factors, including demands for masculinized emotional labor. This sentiment was particularly strong for those whose prior work was in large and prestigious bureaucratic law firms. For these individuals especially, temporary employment seemed to loosen both the bureaucratic and the interpersonal controls they found distasteful in their previous work environments. Ostensibly, this type of employment relationship would rely most heavily on responsible autonomy as a means to control. In fact, many temporary attorneys spoke of their allegiance to the profession, the practice of law, the intellectual challenge of law, or the values of law. Temporary attorneys cite these reasons for performing well on their jobs.

Interestingly, the espousal of responsible autonomy by temporary lawyers was intermingled with their attempts at rejecting the stigma associated with nonstandard employment. One could make a case that the stigma of temporary employment unintentionally acts as a control mechanism, prompting attorneys to assert their professionalism and direct their energies toward the requirements of the hiring firm without the aid of bureaucratic or interpersonal controls found in many large law firms. This is not to say that the use of temporary attorneys did not augment control over law associates in the hiring firms. This is an important issue to consider, but one that cannot be explored fully based on this research. Nevertheless, the majority of temporary attorneys interviewed did feel a sense of increased control over their work lives.

When indicating that temporary employment provided them with a heightened sense of control, temporary attorneys usually mentioned either control over the selection of work or control over the hours of work. This heightened sense of control over selection of their work needs to be considered with caution, based on my observation of the placement agency. There are limits to the attorneys' freedom to select work. Like temporary clerical workers, temporary attorneys who rejected assignments too often were labeled "difficult," and the agency therefore gave them lower priority for future assignments. Consequently, one's financial situation could tightly constrain one's feelings of control over the selection of work.

Control over one's hours of work seemed to be more valued than control over the selection of work. Nearly every temporary attorney I interviewed spoke about regaining control over his or her work time.

> I get to work at home, my hours. I have a lot more control over the work I take in. It's very flexible. (Robert Andersen, forty-one-year-old white man; unmarried with no children)

> It was horrible. Their philosophy was to work everybody to death, you know. We worked every weekend. We worked till seven every night. (Kelly Bower, thirty-three-year-old white woman; married with no children)

> I don't need permission from anybody to take an extra vacation day. And I have enough control over my schedule so I can do it. So I don't need anybody's permission or worry that I've only got "x" amount of vacation days to do so. I have an unlimited amount of vacation days really. As long as my work is done, I don't think they care because they're not paying me for vacations. When I'm not working, I don't get paid. (Charles O'Donnell, thirty-year-old white man; unmarried with no children)

I can stay here until two o'clock in the morning or five o'clock in the morning if I have to. And it's *my* choice. Which is different than being in a large firm and having somebody come up to you at eight o'clock at night and say, "Oh, by the way, I need you to handle this for me tomorrow." It's something that's in your control. (Alice Lederer, forty-year-old white woman; married with three children)

Not surprisingly, the reasons attorneys indicated they needed control over their hours divided rather clearly, although not exclusively, along gender lines. Generally, the men interviewed tended to state that they desired flexible hours in order to pursue other interests such as travel, writing, or another career even though some of them had children. Not one male attorney spoke in terms of the interrelations between his family and work life as having an influence on their decision to work as a contract attorney. While the small number of interviews makes it impossible to generalize these findings, in light of other research into family and work, the men's accounts are not atypical. There may very well be men who are using temporary employment in law to help balance their work and family lives; in fact, some of the men interviewed may have been reluctant to identify themselves in this way. The intertwining of masculinity with the practice of law, however, discourages men (and women) from attending to more traditionally "feminine" pursuits such as those relating to the family. As we shall see, temporary lawyering carries significant and deeply gendered stigma.

The women I interviewed couched their need for flexible hours in terms of incorporating family responsibilities, regardless of whether they currently had children or other dependent family members. One woman indicated that she sought flexibility in *anticipation* of having children in the future.

It was worth getting good grades and doing all the things you need to do to get into a big firm because I thought that my part-time opportunities would be better coming from [a big law firm] than coming from some little dinkle-bop firm. I wouldn't be able to go part time. (Kelly Bower, thirty-three-year-old white woman; married with no children)

Women lawyers and other professionals often report having difficulty managing home and work demands in a male-dominated field. Many avoid discussing their family life in the workplace for fear it will be taken as a sign of their lack of commitment to the job (Pierce 1995). According to the women interviewed, temporary law allows them to maintain a law career while incorporating family responsibilities—something that most lawyers (both men and women) are unable to do. The comparatively lower pay is seen as a fair exchange for flexibility.

> I win because I'm happy with fifty [dollars] an hour for my flexibility. . . . I pay for that. And I'm happy to have that, so I'm happy. (Kelly Bower, thirty-three-year-old white woman; married with no children)

Like many of the men, some women did indicate that they are using temporary work to pursue a solo practice, supplementing their clients with temporary assignments. In each case, however, the mention of family responsibilities was interwoven in the discussion of their professional goals.

> My family is my priority. They come first. My daughter, when she gets out of school, or [when] my husband comes home, I don't want to have my ear tied to a telephone and be baby-sitting clients. In that sense I want to have a certain quality of life, if you will, with my family and be able to spend time with them. Not just quality time, but time, period. And I know how easy it is to get kind of dragged into the mill of working so many hours that you don't pay any attention to your family. And I don't want that to happen. My daughter needs me, she's four years old, and I want that family life. I don't want to sacrifice my family for my practice. I know plenty of women that do, that put in a lot more hours. But I think it's at the expense of their child and their husband. (Sharon Frank, twenty-six-year-old, white woman; married with one child)

> I decided about a year and a half ago to open up my own practice. . . . For me, like a lot of people, the change comes through when you have a family. When you have kids and you realize that you see them in the daylight once a week, it's really not enough. (Alice Lederer, forty-year-old white woman; married with three children)

In Alice's case, she was as much forced out of her old job as she was making a conscious choice to change lifestyles:

> When this two-year-old child came to live with us, my managing partner sat down with me and said, "You know, Alice, you and Ed have very independent lives. You're both career-oriented. You can't do this." And I said, "Well, I appreciate your concern, but, number one, this is none of your business, and, number two, this is a biological grandson." . . . I think it was really downhill from there. There was one partner in particular who treated me all of a sudden like I was sainted, but not equal.

He'd say, "Let me talk to Alice first so she can go home because, you know, she's a mother." I'm sure from their perspective they saw someone who was perhaps less committed. (Alice Lederer, forty-year-old white woman; married with three children)

Typically, solo practice has been male-dominated partly because of time constraints placed on women by their family responsibilities. Temporary work appears to represent a way into a different sort of solo practice for the women in this study—a solo practice without the extra hours spent developing one's own clientele.

It may be that the women and men I interviewed are simply talking in socially acceptable terms about their work and family lives: the men by not acknowledging the existence of a family life, and the women by claiming sole responsibility for family life. I interviewed many of the attorneys in their homes, however, and was able to make some observations about their home life in addition to what was discussed in the interview. Of those women with male partners, my observations confirmed that, in most cases, the women were indeed solely responsible, or nearly so, for family duties even when children were not present in their relationship. In other words, the gender order at home remained intact. There was one exception in the case of Veronica, whose husband was significantly involved in childcare and household duties. In fact, when I arrived, Veronica's husband was just finishing vacuuming the living room. Both attribute his household involvement to her long battle with a serious illness, obviously an atypical situation. Veronica nevertheless describes her reasons for working temporarily as related to her family responsibilities:

I also feel like my husband still needs some of my time, and I have two children and they have some problems that need attention. And I don't want to neglect them. I felt like for a long time that was one of my big frustrations with working full time before. Some of the problems, I was concerned about them, but I wasn't here to be able to do anything about them. And so now I feel like if I need to talk to somebody at school about my children I can do that. I can call up during the day, and I'm not taking time away from an employer. (Veronica Clarke, forty-six-year-old white woman; married with two children)

While professional women represent a comparatively advantaged class and can afford to "buy off" much of their gender-assigned housework, childcare, and eldercare, the women I interviewed still reported pressures from second-shift duties (Hochschild 1989) even if on a more symbolic level. Most had purchased household help, and none with children was the sole caretaker of those children; however, several women described a certain pressure to personally see to certain household or family duties. For example, one woman struggled over picking up her children from daycare. Toward the end of the interview, she told me what her ideal situation would be:

> If I could have what I wanted now, I would have my own little practice in Santa Monica near where my son goes to school. You know, so my kid could walk to my office. (Diane Kraft, thirty-nine-year-old white woman; married with two children)

While walking me to my car, she returned to the topic of her son and brought up some issues that appeared to bother her about her days at the downtown law firm. Her friend who does not work outside the home made some comments that made her feel guilty, like she's a "bad mom." This friend occasionally used to pick up Diane's son from daycare and take him home with her until Diane got home. Her friend has stated, "Poor Jake. He looked so sad that he had to stay until six that I just brought him home and fed him" (field notes, 1993).

While this may seem to be a rather inconsequential task, it took on great importance in Diane's life. With her new work schedule, Diane was able to pick up her son from daycare on time each day. Certainly the work lives of many lawyers prohibit even minimal involvement in family responsibilities; therefore, we cannot discount the importance of even a small task in "balancing" work and family. Starting with absolutely no ability to be involved and suddenly being able to take on duties others routinely perform is a dramatic change. The symbolic weight of such changes should not be trivialized.

In contrast to temporary clerical workers, these lawyers truly do find flexibility in temporary employment. Flexibility is not a myth here. Social class aids in allowing for flexibility, because each of the women with children had partners with considerable incomes. They could afford to buy out of some domestic labor, and they did not have to worry about health insurance, which typically was provided through their partner. Not all of the lawyers in the study had a partner with health insurance; however, in these cases, they were more able than temporary clerical workers to purchase an individual plan.

While some overlap exists in men's and women's reasons for taking temporary legal work, the reasons are deeply gendered, so much so that women without children and men with children are unlikely to form exceptions. This is not to say that the potential to break these gendered divisions does not exist within temporary law. As of this writing, however, the overlap was not significant enough to characterize temporary work as a means to diminish traditional gendered divisions of household labor.

There is very little indication from my conversations that temporary lawyers engaged in acts of resistance except for their resistance to the stigmatized label of "temporary." In fact, temporary employment was itself framed as a means of resistance to factors outside of the temporary employment relationship. Temporary employment was characterized as an assertion of one's right to time off or to "have a life." Compared with the manner in which these individuals were required to work as associates, partners, or even solo practitioners, temporary employment is easily understood as a mode of resistance to ideologically dominant forms of employment in the field of law.

Yet in resisting the stigma of temporary work, attorneys fail to challenge the negative aspects of temporary employment such as its lower pay and status. Once again, if "it's only temporary" there is no need to change it.

Are We Not Temps?

While temporary clerical workers tend to identify themselves as anything but clerical workers or temporaries, temporary attorneys identify themselves first and foremost as lawyers. They may identify themselves as lawyers specializing in a particular area of law, but seldom do they identify themselves by any other means. Parents, men and women alike, did not perceive their identity as primarily deriving from parenthood, nor did those with outside interests (such as social work or opera singing) use these pursuits as their primary identification. Despite the fluidity of temporary employment, temporary lawyers had little difficulty constructing a stable identity as "lawyer."

Professionalism and managerialism construct temporary employment for lawyers as a relationship of equals for the most part. When discussing any problems they encountered on the job, temporary lawyers often responded with metaphors of "choice" and the language of contractual relationships. Virtually absent was any sense of injustice in the pay structure of temporary law. Most of the attorneys interviewed felt that one could simply choose not to accept a low rate of pay. Furthermore, Robert, who was among the highest paid, explained his position by his unwillingness to accept a low rate of pay:

> [I don't do those], I suppose, because my rates are just not competitive. I'm not gonna set aside a morning for the rate that they'll charge. (Robert Andersen, forty-one-year-old white man; unmarried with no children)

Even for the women attorneys who "do" temporary employment, their presence in the situation is explained largely as a result of individual choices. Even Alice, who had been "pushed out" of her law firm after adopting a child, framed her use of temporary employment as a choice freely made. In fact, when faced with the alternative of being an "employee," many of these attorneys said they "chose" temporary employment.

> I think that most attorneys have strong personalities, and you know you're just not that grateful as an employee. So that's why there's this. We want to make our own decisions. (Alice Lederer, forty-year-old white woman; married with three children)

In fact, for many of the attorneys, the term *employee* took on a derogatory meaning. Identifying as an employee rather than a professional was undesirable. As temporary workers, these lawyers felt less like employees and more like solo practitioners. Thus one's identification as a lawyer, a professional before all else, along with a highly individualistic orientation toward choice, shaped these lawyers' characterizations of temporary employment in nonexploitative terms. In fact, one might say that they characterized temporary employment simply as a benign contractual relationship, and with good reason. Even at the lower pay rates, working part time could supply a substantial income relative to what clerical temporaries can earn full time or part time. In the mid-range, with full-time hours, temporary attorneys could conceivably earn an income comparable to "regular" attorneys.

Networking: The Road to Nowhere

For a host of reasons ranging from intentional exclusion to the sexualization of after-hours drinks, women in law[11] have a more difficult time than men in forming and maintaining professional networks. Yet strong networks with potential clients and other lawyers are what is needed if one wants to become a solo practitioner.

Recall that a kind of temporary work known as overflow work existed in the law profession previous to the advent of temporary agencies. Traditionally, attorneys arranged for personal or professional contacts to handle their extra workload. While it is not necessary to have an extensive network of clients to obtain overflow work, a lawyer must at the very least be well-networked within the legal community. Traditionally, many lawyers wishing to begin a solo practice have used overflow networks to get their practice up and running while they develop their own network of clients.

In addition, would-be solo practitioners must spend many hours developing clientele, including time spent on the golf course, at dinner, or at other social events.[12] Contrary to what some may believe, the hours for solo practitioners are not flexible. In fact, one might characterize solo practice as hostile to parents who have even minimal household responsibilities.

Without access to inclusion in overflow or client networks, attorneys must turn to another source to obtain work. In this case, the legal temporary agency can be seen as an ersatz professional network, distributing "overflow" work to attorneys whose only connection to the client or their attorney is through a relatively impersonal intermediary. Temporary employment might represent a way into solo practice with flexibility because the temporary agency takes care of linking the client company to the attorney.

In the interviews I conducted, many attorneys expressed a lack of connection with these overflow networks. Temporary work was, in fact, described as a means to overcome deficiencies in one's professional networks.

> And I expect that with enough appearances I'll build up maybe a network of law firms that I can use as contacts. If I need them for a particular reference, I can use them. Or I can refer clients to them. Or possibly they might want to hire me on as an associate. (Veronica Clarke, forty-six-year-old white woman; married with two children)

This disconnectedness was especially strong for women. The men I interviewed consistently referred to a network from which potential work might be derived either now or in the future. For them, the use of the temporary agency was framed as a supplement to their existing network, not as a means to develop it. The women, however, made fewer references to having such a network and displayed greater reliance on the temporary agency for work. Although three of the women found work from sources other than the agency, all of the attorneys who relied solely on the agency to obtain work were women.

Women were also more likely to make reference to their lack of a network in acquiring work, whether it was to start their own practice or simply to maintain enough part-time hours to bring in what they considered an adequate income. The women were more likely to characterize the temporary agency as a substitute for strong professional networks.

Although some of the people I interviewed believed the temporary agency to be providing a substitute network that would aid in future client acquisition, there is evidence that this perception might be too optimistic. The ability to develop a network through this type of work depends on the nature of the assignments acquired through the agency. The more fragmented and removed the assignment from traditional legal practice, the less likely it will develop into a network contact. As noted earlier, women were somewhat more likely than men to be given and to accept the more fragmented assignments because of their presumed need for a certain type of flexibility. As such, the possibility for women to develop a network through temporary work is less real than it is for men. The following arrangement is typical of the individuals I interviewed:

> I haven't met any of the attorneys that I've worked for. I haven't met [the agency manager] face to face. I just talk to her on the phone. So I've done a lot of my business over the phone. That's kind of a down side of it, but I don't consider it a disadvantage. (Veronica Clarke, forty-six-year-old white woman; married with two children)

Several of the attorneys interviewed actually stated that they did not think temporary work was an effective means of developing professional networks.

> I don't think this is the best way to get ahead in the law world, you know what I mean. I don't think this is the way to impress potential employers or for that matter to obtain clients. I mean, you can't get clients working with different law firms. That's just not the way to do it. So I don't think it's good for somebody who wants to develop their own practice or to become a partner in a law firm. (Joshua Humphrey, thirty-three-year-old white man; married with no children)

> You don't establish a permanent relationship. You may not be developing your skills as an attorney. I wouldn't say that anyone doing contract work is interested in a career path. It's pretty much a given that if you're

doing that, you're not on a career path. And I don't know how some future employers would look at it as good experience or bad experience. If you did want to get back onto a career path and you've been a contract attorney for a year or two, I don't know what kind of credit you get for that. (Charles O'Donnell, thirty-year old white man; unmarried with no children)

Interestingly, some of these people were the same individuals who indicated that they initially sought out temporary work believing they could develop a network.

I thought it would be a good way to get some courtroom exposure on cases so that my name and my face wouldn't fade in front of the judges. . . . But Lawyers-R-Us is really a small portion of my business now. I've had to go out and find other means of getting that exposure. The short term, the small stuff doesn't get you lifelong clients. . . . It helps pay the bills until you get going. (Alice Lederer, forty-year-old white woman; married with three children)

To the extent that temporary work can substitute for a network at all, it would not be through these simple assignments. The "plum" assignments, like those given to Robert, seem to provide the only serious opportunity for network development. Ironically, Robert seemed to already have an extensive network prior to beginning his solo practice. He was not counting on temporary work to augment his network, but that was in fact what was happening. If Karen, the agency manager, is correct in her prediction that the quality of the assignments is increasing with time, then opportunities for networking should likewise increase if the client company has the opportunity to interact with the temporary attorney.

Considering the limited use of temporary assignments in providing a suitable substitute for professional networks, it appears that temporary work may be part of a vicious cycle that prevents disconnected groups (in this case, women) from being integrated into male-dominated professional networks. In this way, women's overrepresentation as professional temporaries can be characterized as a form of ghettoization resulting from women's increased participation in the occupation of law.

TEMPORARY professional work appears to be less exploitative than temporary clerical or industrial work considering its relatively high rate of pay and the professional standing and affiliations of its participants. Yet, when viewed in the context of the legal profession, temporary lawyers share some concerns with less privileged types of work as both labor process analyses and gendered analyses have demonstrated. Temporary legal work, in providing some measure of control over one's work and hours, also provides less prestige, less financial remuneration, and even less interesting work when compared to traditional legal work.

In this light, women's overrepresentation in, and differential experiences with temporary legal work becomes troublesome. If temporary legal work were simply one of a number of equally well-regarded options, women's overrepresentation within that group would not be problematic. Occupations are stratified internally, however, and it is women who continue to occupy the lower ranks. With temporary employment increasing in all sectors of the labor force, the opportunity for women's continual marginalization within occupations increases. As seen here, temporary agencies are not always a good substitute for professional networks, and can help reproduce women's outsider status.

Therefore some important questions arise. If, as we have seen, professionals' dissatisfaction with traditional work arrangements leads them to seek new types of work arrangements, what are the consequences and whom do they benefit or penalize? Do new work arrangements ease, worsen, or simply disguise inequalities? Future studies are needed to uncover the similarities and differences between law and other professions where temporary work has become accepted, such as accounting, engineering, computer science, and even medicine. One thing is certain, temporary work appears to meet some needs these professionals were unable to satisfy through traditional work arrangements. However, it does not do so without its own costs to the individual, or without the potential for perpetuating inequality.

In the next chapter, I will more explicitly draw out comparisons between temporary clerical workers and temporary attorneys.

7   A Temporary Job:

Is It the 'Temporary" or the 'Job'?

The caliber of attorneys available has risen so much. We have such top-caliber people who are doing work through [us]. I can't possibly place them all, but I try to get them as much work as possible and it has nothing to do with how good they are because they are all [that good]. (Karen Berger, legal agency manager)

The biggest problem . . . in our industry is having quality, skilled, dependable employees. We get all walks of life that come through that door. Unfortunately, most of the temporary services get entry-level people. We have a terrible time with the young ones—a good percentage of them are illiterate. Along with that, they're unskilled. If they come in and they're not properly dressed, and they're sloppy and you can smell them walking through the door, someone did a bad job in training these individuals. (Charles Morton, clerical agency owner/ manager)

It's hard to believe both of these quotes refer to temporary workers, but what they demonstrate is how, in many ways, the temporary employment phenomenon is a study in contrasts. These agency managers clearly do not value their potential workforce in the same way. There must certainly be other differences between temporary legal work and temporary clerical work. Unfortunately, until now, most research on temporary employment has assumed that observations about temporary employment were due solely to the temporary aspect of the employment relationship. While this may be true, it is impossible to substantiate without extensive comparative work. A comparative agenda will bring a greater understanding of temporary employment. By examining two vastly different occupations, clerical work and law, I have begun to unveil which aspects of the employment relationship are due to the temporary nature of the work rather than simply to occupational characteristics. Both the organizational dynamics of temporary employment and the occupationally specific labor markets of these two occupations, clerical work and law, frame the experiences, opportunities, and constraints for these two very different groups of temporary workers.

In this examination of temporary clerical workers and temporary lawyers, we find both similarities and differences of experience. Workers, depending on their gender, race, class, age, and occupation, experience temporary work in different ways. This is not to say that these attributes determine one's experience, but that temporary work is shaped by and shapes these relations. Nevertheless, there exists something about temporary employment that fundamentally reshapes the employment relationship. Even between two very disparate occupations such as clerical work and law, we find some similarities in the operation of temporary employment relations. Given the continued vitality of the temporary help supply industry and its expansion into every occupational arena, further research across occupations and organizational settings is a must.

Although we cannot say for certain that any similarities are due, and due solely, to the temporary nature of the work, the evidence suggests they may be. Together with a structural analysis of the employment relationship, these ethnographic data point toward a clearer picture of temporary employment relationships than that seen in prior research.

Overview of Comparisons

Temporary lawyers and temporary clerical workers represent a diverse group of individuals. They are "temping" for a variety of reasons, have varying backgrounds, and work temporarily for varying periods of time. One thing that is certain about both groups of temporaries is that although we can identify certain tendencies, no ideal-typical temporary exists. They are a heterogeneous group.

Yet differences do exist between temporary lawyers and temporary clerical workers. Most obvious are the differences in cultural and human capital. Lawyers enter into temporary employment with more education and their professional status.[1] Clerical temporaries carry less cultural and human capital, and they enter into an occupation in which even "permanent" jobs can be considered marginalized. Changes in technology and an increasing rationalization of work has resulted in truncated job ladders and an overall degrading of clerical work as an occupation.[2] Temporary employment is bound up with this overall process.

The norm for clerical temporaries seemed to be that they were working involuntarily in temporary employment—that they were not seeking flexibility. Most hoped to gain a "permanent" full-time job. In contrast, the attorneys held temporary jobs by choice, whether it was to escape the politics of the big law firm or to spend more time with the family. Not only did we have more flexibility seekers, but we actually had more flexibility finders among temporary attorneys. Obviously, temporary clerical workers and temporary attorneys enter into temporary employment under tremendously disparate conditions. These conditions shape their experiences of temporary employment.

In general, the attorneys did not use temporary employment as a means to secure a permanent position. They acknowledged that temporary employment was not an entrée into the firm. A more common sentiment was the feeling of "burnout" or even a legitimation crisis (Habermas 1975). Working a "regular" law job, which has come to be defined as being an employee in a law firm, large or small, held little attraction for those I spoke with. Many felt that routes to success, defined largely as partnership, were blocked by changes in the profession, including extensive downsizing.

In contrast, temporary clerical workers did not express feelings of burnout or legitimation crisis in reference to a full-time permanent job. They expressed frustration at the lack of opportunity for traditional employment. Rather than flee the confines of a traditional employment relationship, they sought the security of it. Legitimation crisis as well as work flexibility may be luxuries of the professional class.

Skill and Temporary Employment

We have seen a tendency toward deskilling for both temporary clerical work and temporary lawyering. Temporary clerical workers are likely to be assigned the least desirable, most monotonous work in the office. Temporary lawyers also tend to be assigned the least demanding type of work, especially when it involves one-day appearances or "boilerplate" tasks. Lawyers and clerical workers both routinely lament the lack of challenge provided by their temporary assignments. To some extent, deskilling appears related to the organization of work as temporary; that is, temporary workers (lawyers or clerical workers) are designated the least desirable work. Whether a conscious strategy or an uncalculated result of co-workers' actions, temporary employment represents a way to further divide work.

In clerical work, however, we also see a tendency toward devaluing of work that is actually highly skilled. Temporary clerical workers have been shown to perform a wide variety of tasks that more closely resemble autonomous, even managerial work. Unfortunately for the worker, these "extra" tasks go unremunerated and are often performed "voluntarily" in hopes of procuring a permanent position. Thus, like much of women's work, the work of temporary clerical workers is devalued as well as deskilled.

Temporary attorneys do not seem to have a corresponding devaluing of their work. Attorneys are generally not hired for a one-day appearance only to end up writing briefs or litigating a case. There is a more direct relation between what they are hired to do and what they actually do. So while relatively low-skill, even stigmatized, legal work exists for temporary attorneys, higher-skill work assignments are recognized and remunerated as such. In fact, these assignments and the workers who do them take on an entrepreneurial air largely owing to the long history of overflow work in the law profession. To be a freelance attorney is to be a solo practitioner and to be accorded the full status of the profession.

To be a temporary clerical worker does not accord one entrepreneurial status. In fact, it calls into question fundamental aspects of one's identity and personality. There is not the same history of entrepreneurialism in clerical work as in the law profession.[3] Who ever heard of a freelance secretary? Certainly they exist; however, they have not been institutionalized. Clerical work, specifically secretarial work, is highly personalized. Thus the notion of a freelance secretary seems a contradiction in terms. A freelance secretary could not possibly provide the highly personalized services that have come to be expected of secretaries. Finally, clerical workers do not have the power of a profession to inhibit the devaluing of their work. There is also little help from the power of collective bargaining owing to historically low rates of unionization in the clerical sector.

Gender also plays a part in whether the work of temporaries is devalued. Clerical work is a female-dominated field, while law is male-dominated. Worker gender affects perceptions of the skills needed to perform a job. Therefore clerical work is more apt to be subject to skill devaluing while law, both as male-dominated and as a profession, is less so. Lawyers have the power to define their work as skilled on an ideological level, regardless of the actual material skill content of their job. Thus even boiler-plate law is accorded a relatively high skill level, and lawyers' ability to define their work as skilled has implications for how further devaluation may occur through the organization of temporary work. Having a powerful ideological component of skill, greater educational requirements, and professional associations may help to forestall potential devaluing effects of temporary employment.

Occupational factors are important for understanding the relationship between temporary employment and skill. Relative to their "permanent" counterparts, temporary clerical workers and temporary attorneys experience some deskilling. While the tasks of both legal work and clerical work can be more finely divided through temporary employment, the power of the profession shapes skill for temporary attorneys. In fact, the work of some temporary attorneys may even require a higher level of skill than do many regular law jobs.[4]

Stigma

Both temporary clerical workers and temporary attorneys are stigmatized as temporaries. Because temporaries do not have traditional work arrangements, they are not seen as having a "real job"—a full-time, year-round, and ongoing job. Our entrenched belief in meritocracy in the United States renders those without a "real job" (or any job) responsible for their condition. Witness the recent and ongoing debates about welfare reform. We make assumptions regarding individuals' abilities and personal character, arriving at the conclusion that if someone was competent (hardworking, mature, and so on), he or she would desire and indeed would have a "real job." Co-workers and managers alike assume that something is wrong with a person who works temporarily. This is evidenced most acutely in the common appellation of temporary clerical workers as "flakes." To a lesser extent, temporary lawyers were also suspected of being flakes. With clerical workers, one was considered a flake until proven otherwise.

Recall the stories of temporary clerical workers taking on far more responsibility than originally expected. Temporary clerical workers work very hard to shed the stigma associated with temporary employment even if they do not wish permanent employment with the client company. In cases where the temporary does desire permanent employment with a client company, it is difficult to unravel the extent to which one's "supertemp" behavior is motivated by the rejection of stigma or the desire to land a job. Most likely these two factors are intertwined, in that a temporary must successfully reject the stigma associated with his or her temporary status before becoming a viable job candidate at the client company.

There is some room in clerical work for those who do not want a traditional job because of both a long history of part-time clerical work and women's overrepresentation in clerical work (which assumes a homogenous population of childbearing women). For lawyers, however, it is assumed that no one, at least not a *real* lawyer, would *want* a nontraditional job. The implication for the temporary lawyers I interviewed was that they were somehow less committed or less serious about their profession because of their employment arrangement. "Flakiness" per se was less of a concern.

The practice of law and contingent work arrangements are characterized as antithetical. Those who combine the two are not "real lawyers," with the extremely rare exception of the "specialist." This is slightly different from clerical temporary workers, who are said to not have a real job. They are not accused of not being a *real* secretary or *real* clerk, whereas lawyers emphasize the profession's incompatibility with nontraditional employment relations.

Perhaps all of this is merely splitting hairs. Temporary clerical workers and temporary attorneys are stigmatized somewhat differently, but both groups are stigmatized nonetheless. In both cases, the stigma arises from the contingent nature of the individual's employment situation; however, in some cases, male clerical temporaries derive additional stigma from being male in a female-dominated occupation.

Control and Resistance

Control over temporary clerical workers takes a very different form from control over temporary attorneys, yet similarities do exist. In both cases, control is potentially tightened through the temporary employment relationship. The intermediary, the temporary agency, can act as a buffer between the temporary and the client, shielding the client from criticism as well as legal and moral responsibility for workplace events, as is the case when the duration of an assignment is unexpectedly shortened. The buffer reduces temporary workers' power in the workplace, allowing them fewer options and thus increasing control over them. In a similar vein, the agency acts as an additional means of surveillance over the temporary worker. Both the agency's rules and procedures as well as the client's are enforced over the temporary worker. As many interview subjects noted, being a temporary worker is like having two bosses to satisfy.

While every temporary clerical worker reported having to answer to two bosses, the system of dual controls is less applicable to lawyers. In fact, many of the attorneys interviewed experienced a heightened sense of personal control over their work, or at least their work schedule. Dual control over lawyers may be more likely when attorneys physically work inside the client's office. Even in these situations, the agency's control over the attorney is limited to nontechnical matters when the agency manager does not hold a law degree. Nevertheless, the agency can still exercise control in making sure the attorney complies with basic work rules. Notably, there are few reports of agencies invoking the various control mechanisms available to them where lawyers were concerned. While some of the same controls used for clerical workers seemingly are potentially applicable to the lawyers, they seldom are used. Nevertheless, the very existence of such control mechanisms and the possibility of their use can in itself be a mechanism of control.

Why the difference in actual versus potential control over lawyers and clerical workers? One answer might lie in the agencies' perceptions of workers' characters. Although temporary, the attorneys in this study still had the discursive power of the profession behind them. "Professionalism" of attorneys is assumed by the temporary agencies, while the same behavior is not expected of clerical workers. Agencies tended to rely on responsible autonomy to control professionals so that more direct controls, immediately applied to clerical workers, were held in reserve for attorneys. Only those attorneys who proved themselves not to be "professional" were subjected to these control mechanisms. In contrast, clerical workers had to prove themselves to be "professional" before certain controls would be relaxed in favor of responsible autonomy.

In law, control also may be loosened in some areas because of the lack of a partnership carrot. Temporary attorneys largely do not expect upward mobility through their current employment relationship; therefore, certain controls that guide an attorney's behavior on the partnership track would have little effect for temporary lawyers. They are not as attached to the firm as law associates; however, there does not exist the same dependency relationship as between clerical workers and their agencies. The greater availability of alternatives (that is, traditional overflow work and solo practice) creates an atmosphere in which direct controls are applied only sparingly. With no long-term promises of upward mobility, temporary attorneys experience a sort of limited freedom from office politics and pressures. While both women and men reported feeling a sense of freedom from office politics, women often specified office gender politics in addition to general office politics.

Perhaps another reason I heard so little about resistance against aspects of temporary employment from the lawyers I spoke with is the fact that the employment relationship is less asymmetrical for attorneys than for clerical workers. Furthermore, lawyers' subjective experience of temporary employment is typically one of a market exchange between equals. While I did not uncover an enormous amount of data to bear out my suspicion that temporary agency personnel also construct the relationship as one between equals, the following does seem to lend some support to the idea.

> These are good people, the best and brightest, real professionals. They are breaking out of the old tradition of seventy to eighty hours a week. They are still excited about the profession; they just don't want it to be everything in their lives. (Don Harkins, vice president of Legal Eagles, phone interview, 1993)

The Gendering of Temporary Employment

One of the most striking aspects of this look into the temporary employment phenomenon is the way that both temporary clerical work and temporary law are gendered. Because both are considered "female" undertakings, women's overrepresentation in temporary employment is naturalized rather than problematized. Explicitly and implicitly, temporary workers and agency representatives labeled temporary work as "women's work." The ideal characteristics of a temporary clerical worker correspond with white, middle-class femininity. Employers were sometimes reluctant to hire male temporaries, particularly for the more "visible" positions that required one to "do" gender. For many reasons, men are seen as inappropriate for such positions. But is it the temporary nature of the job that creates these unwritten job "requirements" or the job itself?

Much of what is feminized in temporary clerical work derives from the fact that clerical work is female-dominated. Requirements for a particular type of sociability, sexualized interactions, and demands for performance of domestic duties on the job have all been noted as part of secretarial work in general. Such demands, however, are intensified for temporary clerical workers (Rogers and Henson 1997). Their marginal status makes resistance to the feminization of their work more difficult. Mobility of temporary workers makes the immediate realization of such "feminine" qualities imperative if one is to maintain a steady stream of work assignments. White, middle-class femininity is part of what is transacted when a client "purchases" a temporary. If feminine qualities are a plus in permanent clerical work, they seem to be a necessity if one is to be successful in temporary clerical work.

But what of men in temporary clerical employment?[5] How is this anomaly dealt with in the workplace? Male clerical temporaries are perceived and labeled as "defective men." Often this takes the form of questioning their sexual orientation, for men in U.S. society who fall furthest from the cultural ideal embodied in hegemonic masculinity are called to task in a manner that often concerns one's sexuality. Recall that some of the men I interviewed were openly gay, and Michael Glenn even characterized his sexual orientation as advantageous. Although he, too, essentializes sexuality and conflates sexual orientation with gender, he is unique in his positive framing of his alternative masculinity.

In other instances, male clerical temporaries are seen as lacking the proper, "normal" masculine motivation to succeed. Male temporary clerical workers do not hold the requisite masculine "real job"—that is, one that is not temporary, but full time, and one that is not female-dominated but male-dominated. Something must be wrong with these men, but what? The presence of men of color in temporary clerical work poses less of a problem for observers, because their race supposedly offers an explanation as to "what is wrong." Men of color, by virtue of their race, cannot meet the expectations of hegemonic masculinity. Their presence in temporary work, therefore, is not problematized. It is assumed to reflect a deeper reality of their orientation to work. When a white man who is not extraordinarily young is encountered in temporary clerical work, those around him express disbelief at his employment situation. They assume he must have something going on the side to take a job that is so obviously beneath him. Indeed, with temporary workers, most co-workers lack the information to know that a job would be inappropriate for any temporary. Therefore, their disbelief must be based on readily observable criteria—that is, he is white and a man. No such assumptions are made about men of color.

Although I did not document any glass-escalator effect (Williams 1992) in my research, because of the methods used I cannot conclude that it does not exist in temporary clerical work. Rather, the tendency for observers to assume white males must have something going on the side is indicative that there might in fact be a glass escalator in operation. On the other hand, few clerical temporaries, male or female, were able to use temporary employment to find their "dream job." Only longitudinal data would settle the question. We need to consider that although men in temporary work face gender assessment, this gender assessment may very well work to the advantage of some as individuals try to resolve the seeming contradiction of a white, male temporary clerical worker. Straight white men's presence in temporary clerical work is problematized, as is their presence in other traditionally female-dominated employment such as elementary school teaching (Williams 1992) and nursing (Diamond 1992). The idea that individuals may try to resolve the seeming contradiction by moving these men into "appropriate" positions is a reasonable one to believe. Nevertheless, it seems that temporary clerical work is gendered owing to both its clerical and its temporary nature.

Temporary law is also gendered, although in a different manner than is temporary clerical work. The understanding of women temporary lawyers as seeking flexibility necessary to effectively combine work and family seems to accurately reflect at least a segment of the lawyers interviewed. In temporary clerical work, however, very few women used temporary employment as a means to flexibility. In fact, most found it to be quite inflexible. Temporary lawyering is more flexible than temporary clerical work in part because it provides much greater hourly remuneration. Even at the low end of the pay scale, one can bring in a substantial income working twenty hours per week, while many clerical workers cannot make ends meet even on a full week's pay. In addition, unlike law associates, temporary lawyers are paid for each hour they work. One attorney even joked that he thought he might make more per hour worked as a temporary than when he was an associate putting in endless unpaid evening and weekend hours. A full-time temporary lawyer could conceivably make as much as a regular associate.

The labor process also is important to understand the flexibility of temporary law. Unlike temporary clerical work, many assignments can be worked on at home.[6] This is not to say that much clerical work cannot be done at home; however, much of what constitutes clerical work, such as filing and answering telephones, must be done in the office, and we find that such routine work is quite often what temporaries are hired to do. Law, as an elite profession, affords its practitioners greater autonomy (although many contend less so than in years past) than clerical work. While the professions are not without their control mechanisms, these center more on "responsible autonomy" gleaned from specialized education and professional socialization than on direct supervision. Because of the professional nature of the occupation, temporary lawyers are trusted to work unsupervised, whereas temporary clerical workers are not. Thus temporary clerical work does not afford the same flexibility of location as temporary law.

One-day appearances require the attorney to be present at a specified time; however, these typically last only half a day and require no more commitment than for the time allotted. The long-term, in-house assignments typically offer the least flexibility; nevertheless, temporary lawyers in these positions seem to have more leeway to negotiate flexibility than do associates who are expected to devote their lives to the firm. Because temporary law jobs are characterized as "mommy jobs," individuals in these positions often are expected to desire some sort of flexibility.

Like temporary clerical workers, temporary lawyers are considered "defective" in some manner. This is true, however, for both men and women temporary lawyers. The field of law is male-dominated and highly masculinized. It is organized around the "disembodied universal worker" who is responsibility- and child-free (Acker 1990). *He* is expected to have a female partner who cares for the domestic realm, leaving him free to devote his life to the practice. Men who do not have this arrangement are less likely to make partner than men who do (Hagan and Kay 1995). Women are, by definition, excluded from this arrangement even if they do not have a male partner or children. Their assumed capacity and will to reproduce or join a heterosexual union places them outside the possibility of becoming the disembodied universal worker.

Yet men and women temporary lawyers are stigmatized differently. As mentioned, women temporary lawyers are characterized as "mommies." In law, to be a mommy is not to be a lawyer. The "mommy" role always overshadows the "lawyer." In temporary clerical work, women's dual role is naturalized through the rhetoric of flexibility (although most do not seek flexibility but a full-time job), thus the juxtaposition of *temporary* with *clerical worker* does not appear contradictory. In temporary law, however, women's dual role is a significant reason that many of the women seek temporary employment. Contrary to temporary clerical work, the juxtaposition of *temporary* with *lawyer* is incongruous. To be temporary is not to be a lawyer. Female or male, a lawyer who is temporary is therefore not a "real" lawyer. Whereas female temporary lawyers are understood as mommies, male temporaries are looked on as defective men and consequently defective lawyers[7] unless they are able to successfully couch their employment in terms of entrepreneurialism—something that clerical temporaries find difficult to do (who ever heard of a freelance filer?).

Therefore, in temporary law, feminization derives largely from the fact that the position is temporary, unlike clerical employment, in which feminization likely derives from the fact that the position is both clerical and temporary. Law is a very masculine pursuit, while temporary law is highly feminized.

What does it mean for an occupation to be feminized? At the most basic level, it means that there is a preponderance of women in the occupation (or substratum of the occupation). Going deeper, we find that feminized occupations have a variety of characteristics in common: low status, deskilling (either ideologically or materially), and relative lack of power. By this definition, both temporary clerical work and a certain strain of temporary law can be said to be feminized. Yet clerical work, temporary or not, is already feminized. Clerical workers routinely report low status, deskilled work, and a relative lack of power. Even so, temporary work intensifies feminization for clerical workers. Status is further decreased, additional deskilling occurs, and power declines and organizational controls are increased over temporary clerical workers. By comparison, "regular" clerical workers might seem a rather privileged bunch to temporaries who seek full-time positions.

Few people would contend that law has become feminized, even though pockets within law are more female-dominated than others. Law is a relatively high status, highly skilled[8] (ideologically or materially), powerful position. Temporary law jobs are, in comparison to traditional law jobs, lower status, lower skilled, and less powerful. Temporary lawyers are marginalized vis-à-vis *other lawyers*. Yet there is no doubt that they still enjoy a privileged position over most other workers. The power of the profession combined with the marginality of temporary employment creates a relatively lower-status substratum within the occupation of law. This is not unlike ghettoization, in which women are more greatly represented in the lower-paid, lower-prestige areas within an occupation. Usually these ghettos are subfields within an occupation; however, temporary law provides a ghetto simply by work status. Therefore, this research provides evidence that temporary employment is an additional means of reproducing gender (and probably racial) inequality in the workplace. Whether this applies to all occupations remains to be seen; however, ghettoization in such disparate occupations as clerical work and law supports the notion that there is something about the temporary employment relationship that perpetuates inequalities. Let us not forget that just as all part-time jobs are not the same, neither are all temporary jobs the same. As with part-time jobs, "good" job traits tend to be bundled in temporary employment (see Tilly 1996 for a description within part-time work). Nevertheless, both good and bad temporary jobs share some elements of the labor process that are cause for concern over and above how they affect *individual* workers.

Subjectivity

Temporary lawyers are much less often referred to as "temps" than are clerical workers. In fact, the term *contract attorney* typically is used by agencies and attorneys. Resistance on the part of attorneys generally occurs at an ideological level through a rejection of what they often termed "the rat race," or by asserting an entrepreneurial motivation for their work, particularly for the men. Unlike clerical workers, however, lawyers did not seem to struggle as much with the maintenance of a stable identity. As mentioned in the previous chapter, they seemed to draw their identity from their profession, with the "temporary" status only secondary to their status as an attorney. Nevertheless, only when combined with the gendered understanding of nonstandard work, and particularly temporary work, did identity become a source of concern. Both men and women sought to reject the stigmatized feminine status of "temporary" lawyer.

Nor did temporary lawyers experience temporary employment as exploitative. In fact, most felt the rates paid were "fair" and dependent on what one was willing to accept. In contrast, for clerical workers, there is much less talk of rejecting dominant ideologies about hard work and more talk about the financial exigencies of their situation. Temporary work was seldom, if ever, experienced as a relationship between equals among those I interviewed. Without professional status behind them, temporary clerical workers found it difficult to maintain a stable identity in the face of being temporarily employed and the lack of stability that comes with it. In fact, the need to maintain this stable identity is in part what helps to reproduce some of the conditions of their inequality. For lawyers, a similar thing happens with the stable identity of "attorney," which may act to diminish their concern with the comparatively lower pay and prestige of temporary lawyers. In both cases, individuals' needs to maintain a stable identity deriving from employment status aids in the maintenance of a two-tier employment system of temporary and permanent workers.

It's Only Temporary?

While most people in the United States live under the conditions of employment-at-will, temporary employment further institutionalizes these arrangements. And while most workers no longer depend on having employment for life, even the traditional core of protected workers feel increasingly insecure with each new bout of downsizing, right-sizing, and re-engineering. If so-called permanent workers feel insecure, what is to be said of temporary workers?

Temporary work codifies insecurity into an employment system with explicit nonresponsibility and legal ambiguity; it is permeated and supported by individualistic, meritocratic ideologies that serve to mystify power relations. A third party, the temporary agency, plays a significant part in the structure of these relationships and the experiences of the workers.[9] There is nothing that says the third party must be a for-profit enterprise rather than a labor union or worker cooperative, or that any such organization must operate nearly free from constraint. Today the increases in contingent employment that initially appeared to many as a natural phenomenon have been revealed, if not accepted, largely as socially constructed. Rises in temporary employment have been shown to be employer-driven rather than due to an increasing desire for flexibility on the part of employees (Golden and Appelbaum 1992), and the temporary help services industry increasingly has been shown as an active party in constructing and ensuring its own success (Gonos 1997).

Temporary and Standard Work

What exactly are the unique effects of temporary employment? Theoretically, the addition of a third party who is paid by the client but who pays the worker realigns power in ever-greater favor of the employer (client/temporary agency). Workers now have two bosses, one of whom is paid to provide a service to the other. The essence of that service is a compliant worker who can do the job without encumbering the company with the myriad liabilities/responsibilities that go along with the traditional employment relationship. Thus temporary employment potentially increases some kinds of control exerted over temporary workers. Avenues for effective resistance are thwarted because the deck is stacked in favor of the employers.

Empirically observed effects of temporary work, however, do not always mesh with what is expected theoretically when we group all workers together. Variability among occupations necessarily affects any particular manifestation of temporary employment. Lawyers have several different but well-established methods of having a career in law, including working as an employee and various degrees of self-employment. Some aspects of temporary employment for lawyers can be found to different degrees in other modes of law work. Employment of clerical workers is more homogenous, in that clerical workers almost always are employed by an organization. Thus temporary employment represents a disjuncture between traditional forms of clerical employment and the increasing contingency of those workers.

Additionally, the prestige of any occupation can moderate or exacerbate any negative effects of temporary work. At least in the case of lawyers, temporary employment does not seem to significantly increase control over lawyers. In fact, in some instances, lawyers feel that they are the ones who are more in control. Lawyers are still placed in the position of "expert" over the temporary agency placement counselor unless that person also happens to be an attorney. Opportunity for interference by the agency personnel is limited, resulting in a relationship that more closely mirrors the job-matching services portrayed by the temporary industry as their modus operandi. Nevertheless, the structure of temporary employment leaves even temporary lawyers vulnerable to the pressures of this three-party relationship. Professional status places lawyers in a better position relative to that of clerical workers; however, lawyers, too, must please clients and agencies alike if they require a steady stream of assignments.

While temporary employment relies on the deskilling of many law jobs, temporary attorneys are still considered to have the skills of a lawyer. The deskilling that takes place in temporary law parallels that in clerical work; however, law's system of bestowing credentials and prestige distinguish it from clerical work, which can be described as truly monotonous.

Relative to temporary clerical work, temporary law is still privileged work. Relative to other law jobs, much temporary law is deskilled, although prime temporary assignments do exist. As with temporary clerical work, temporary law work is not typically a foot in the door to a better job.

The relative nature of clerical work and law is exemplified in discussions of flexibility. Class differences between the two groups crystallize especially with regard to flexibility. Only in temporary law can individuals reasonably expect to find flexibility, because lawyering pays enough to allow one to work fewer hours. In addition, if married, the partners of temporary attorneys tend also to be well-paid professionals. For the attorneys seeking better work/family integration, temporary employment seems a reasonable solution even though in most cases the gender division of labor in the home remains intact.

Clerical temporary workers seldom make enough in absolute terms to afford any sense of flexibility for family or otherwise. This is borne out by the fact that most of the clerical workers I spoke with, married or not, parents or not, attempt to maintain a full-time workweek out of necessity. The flexibility that professionals can find is often misattributed to all temporaries.

Temporary clerical workers' refrain of frustration, despair, alienation, and outrage can be best understood as a result of problems associated with both clerical work in general and clerical temporaries' relatively powerless position in the temporary employment triangle. Client companies, not temporary clerical workers, are prized by and pandered to by agencies, sometimes even when their requests are well over the line legally. But some of what temporary clerical workers experience is certainly part and parcel of what it means to be in a highly feminized occupation located increasingly on the margins of "good" work.

Just as Chris Tilly (1996) found good and bad part-time jobs, in examining temporary clerical work, I have found good and bad temporary jobs. There are far more "good" temporary jobs in law, and a few do exist for clerical workers. Neither of these types of temporary jobs, however, measures up in comparison to permanent counterparts within occupations. Considering that temporary work has stretched to all fields, one cannot, based on this research, assume that the same applies to all occupations in which temporary work operates. Temporary computer programmers, accountants, or executives may have vastly different experiences with temporary employment. In fact, some of these temporary workers may hold a privileged status over their permanent counterparts as experts, consultants, or troubleshooters. Either way, this is a question for empirical investigation.

Inequalitites

Many workers have never experienced employment security, the loss of which we bemoan in newspapers, documentaries, and books. White women, people of color, and the poor have always worked on the margins. Embedded in existing institutional inequalities, temporary work arises from inequality and at the same time is a mechanism of its reproduction. In many ways, temporary work relies on the secondary status of white women and people of color. Some men, some whites, and some middle-class individuals are being swept out with the tide of temporary employment. Does the recent focus on contingent employment and the corresponding sense of urgency merely reflect the fact that temporary employment has finally moved on to affect traditionally less marginal workers? Does temporary work only attract the public (or even the academic) eye when whites, men, and the middle class finally feel the sting? Future studies should be carried out with gender, class, and racial inequalities as explicit dimensions of analysis.

Understanding the embeddedness of temporary employment in existing relations of inequality leads one to conclude that neither the problems of inequality nor the problems of temporary employment can be solved in isolation. The suggestions that follow are focused on temporary employment, but it should not be misconstrued that solving the problems of temporary employment can be done without paying simultaneous attention to the many dimensions of inequality, including race, class, gender, age, and sexuality, in all facets of society.

Improving Temporary Employment

Temporary employment as a social problem does not exist in isolation from other social problems. Rather, it is connected to them in complex ways. Employers reportedly seek out the use of temporary help for many reasons, ranging from reducing benefits costs and unemployment compensation claims to union avoidance. Temporary employment as it is structured now is unregulated as an industry. The temporary industry has lobbied arduously and successfully to keep itself unencumbered by regulation. For example, in New Jersey, the temporary help supply industry sought classification as employers in order to avoid regulation as an employment agency (see Gonos 1997).

In practice, employers and temporary workers have found many employment laws lose their efficacy in the temporary employment relationship (Carnevale, Jennings, and Eisenmann 1998). For example, temporary workers who are sexually harassed have a difficult time reporting such incidents for fear of work deprivation (Rogers and Henson 1997). Proving retaliation through work deprivation in an employment relationship where no duty to provide work exists and no reason for dismissal is needed becomes nearly impossible. Existing labor law impedes collective bargaining rights for contingent workers (DuRivage, Carré, and Tilly 1998).

On an ideological level, contending with the desire for business to reduce its costs through temporary employment is difficult. At least with regard to benefit costs, two strategies toward reducing incentives to hire temporary workers are offered. First, in the United States, health and other benefits are largely tied to employment. Core employment offers a generous range of benefits, while marginal employment offers few, if any. One's marginal status is intensified through this system. If one is low-paid or in sporadic work, one can expect not to have health and other benefits. As a result of low pay, these are the very individuals who are least likely to be able to purchase their own health care or who can least afford to take time off without pay. Uncoupling work benefits from employment, although an unpopular solution, would help the marginally employed by providing them with benefits and partially reducing employer incentives to create marginal jobs.

Slowing or reversing the creation of marginal jobs helps temporary workers in more than the obvious ways. The creation of "good" jobs helps to empower workers vis-à-vis their employers. The institutionalization of temporary employment (along with other factors) has aided in all workers' feelings of expendability. The stories related in this book consistently reflect a lack of power on the part of clerical temporary workers. An economy with fewer temporary jobs and more permanent jobs gives potential temporary workers greater latitude in their job search and a greater ability to assert their rights in the temporary employment situation should they find themselves working temporarily. Under such circumstances, temporary jobs could be truly temporary.

Gender and racial inequality support and are supported by the system of temporary employment. With some groups of workers more valued over others, there exists a ready-made group of marginal workers whose placement in temporary employment is justified and naturalized with covert and sometimes overt ideologies about their abilities and suitability for certain types of work. In temporary employment, these ideologies are intertwined with a customer service orientation that sweeps inequality under the rug in the name of pleasing the client. This exists because temporary placement is a business, and human beings are brokered to clients. One cannot minimize the importance of understanding that temporary agencies' first alliance is and must be to their clients because of the organization of temporary employment. To interrupt this dynamic, one would have to change the very structure of temporary employment. But how do we realign the interests of workers, agencies, and clients without creating an equally troublesome relationship?

To expect temporary workers to become the clients by paying temporary agencies for placing them in work assignments seems unreasonable. Such an arrangement would only foster competition among temporaries, while still creating incentives to place people on a basis other than their job qualifications.

Worker-owned temporary agencies would be the most obvious means to align the interests of the agency with the interests of the workers: They would be one and the same. These agencies would be successful only to the extent that all workers were worker-owners. As soon as worker-owners were to hire on another tier of workers to supplement their labor supply, they would simply be reproducing the temporary employment relationship as it exists today. However, these efforts are potentially thwarted by temporary clerical workers' frequent denial of occupational identity and their desire to leave temporary employment as quickly as possible.

Alternatively, labor organizations might take over the functions of temporary agencies by re-instituting a "hiring hall" system.[10] Temporary workers' benefits could be paid out of a fee collected for temporary workers' services. Under current conditions, this fee (or markup) goes toward overhead and profit for temporary agencies. Under the hiring hall system, the markup would be shared by the temporary workers in the form of health benefits, vacation, and unemployment pay. This new three-party arrangement would significantly realign power relations in favor of the workers. Problems between temporary workers and clients could be resolved more judiciously, with the worker having the support of the union. With the profit motive removed for the temporary agency, clients have less influence in employment matters. Temporary workers could be guaranteed due process and de facto protection under the law. The Communication Workers of America in Cincinnati is one successful example.[11]

Although some unions are heading in this direction, there are many reasons to suspect that hiring halls will not be re-instituted on a widespread basis, at least not in the short run. First, unionization rates in the United States remain notoriously low, while temporary employment is proceeding most rapidly in areas that historically have had low rates of unionization (Polivka 1996). Second, at least in the professions, unions will run into competition from some professional associations that have taken up the task of job referral. Arguably, professionals are less in need of union protection than are clerical workers, who would greatly benefit from union representation just as the unions would benefit from greater organizing of these workers. Unions should maintain and even increase their organizing efforts even as they seek necessary revisions to labor law.

Union hiring halls would be in competition with nonunion temporary agencies.[12] Given some employers' hostility to the labor movement, it might be difficult to break into the placement business. Clients may simply choose nonunion agencies over union-run hiring halls. Finally, I have learned from informal discussions with union members and representatives that there might be some resistance to hiring halls. With temporary employees having been used to undermine union strength and solidarity, it is not surprising that some would be wary of the union's involvement in anything resembling a temporary agency. Union participation in temporary employment may be perceived as acquiescence to contingent employment and a change in an agenda that currently highlights the importance of "good jobs." Nevertheless, with unions in charge of the temporary service, temporary jobs could be created as "good jobs" or, at the very least, better jobs. Individuals working as temporaries would ostensibly be employed full time (albeit at a variety of assignments and job sites) if they so desired. With comparable benefits, job security, and due process, temporary employment would not confer secondary status. Flexibility, for those who desire it, would be more attainable for those not in professional occupations.

Yet tackling the problem of temporary employment cannot end with reducing temporary employment or realigning interests. The problems of temporary employment are intertwined with societal inequalities. We must act to reduce these inequalities at the same time that we try to improve or reduce temporary employment. Attacks on affirmative action must be rebuffed while new programs for reducing inequality should be initiated. Increasing inequality in the workplace will only serve to increase inequality in temporary employment.

The lingering societal notion that women's work is secondary still plays a part in constructing marginal temporary jobs. Despite changes to gender-neutral agency names, the public perception remains that temporary employment is largely a voluntary undertaking by women seeking flexibility to better integrate work and home responsibilities. To this group, the temporary industry has added students who seek gas money and senior citizens who seek something to fill their time. While these individuals do exist, by far the dominant mode of temporary employment is involuntary. Even if all temporary professionals were voluntary, their numbers would not surpass those of involuntary temps in clerical and light industrial work. Educating the public and policymakers about the facts regarding temporary employment is a necessary prerequisite to any of the other changes suggested.

While one goal may be the reduction of temporary employment, specifically involuntary temporary employment, maintaining its availability for the small segment of the workforce that desires temporary employment is important. The elimination of temporary employment for those individuals may be as detrimental as involuntary temporary employment is for many workers. To say that someone is a voluntary temporary worker, however, is not to say that this person find no problems with his or her employment relationship. To the contrary, these workers find many of the same problems as involuntary temporaries and would also benefit from the changes I have just recommended. In addition, it would benefit the group of workers who seek flexibility to develop truly flexible employment relationships (recall that temporary employment is not necessarily flexible, especially for clerical workers) that do not marginalize workers. One should not have to pay for flexibility with health care, lower pay, deskilled work, or poor treatment.

Regulation of the Temporary Help Services Industry

Although unpopular with business and the temporary industry, the recommendation for greater regulation of the temporary industry cannot be discarded. Given the issues raised in this book, regulation of either the temporary industry or client use of temporaries could be used to

- prevent the use of temporary workers in union-busting
- prohibit pay differentials based solely on temporary status
- consider affirmative action implications of temporary workforces
- prevent/reduce unjust treatment of temporary workers

- provide workers with an independent avenue of recourse for unjust treatment
- limit the use of "permanent temporaries"
- promote the use of temporary employment as a path to permanent employment
- reduce discriminatory practices in placement
- specify means for handling disputes
- give agencies better recourse for dealing with unethical clients
- provide the basis for greater organizing of temporary workers by unions
- coordinate employment benefits under multiple agency use

As regulation is a political process, any and certainly all of these regulatory goals would require lengthy battles against a growing and lucrative industry. Introduction of regulations is feared by the industry, as it may reduce the business opportunity that is temporary employment. In the long run, perhaps business, and certainly workers, may best be served by placing any remaining temporary work in the hands of a different party. The loss of temporary agencies as we know them would not prevent businesses from seeking flexibility through other means. In fact, businesses already make choices about whether they will use restrictive or enabling forms of flexibility for their workers (Smith 1993). Temporary employment does not prohibit the higher-skill, higher-pay, greater-power approach of enabling flexibility per se. Short of the temporary industry reinventing itself toward these ends, regulation seems necessary.

The 1997 United Parcel Service (UPS) strike brought contingency issues into the public eye. Chief among workers' complaints was the secondary status of part-time workers. Part-time workers at UPS, like many temporaries, receive lower hourly wages than their full-time counterparts despite performing the same work as employees under standard arrangements. While UPS part-time workers did receive a benefits package, they also faced barriers to promotion and transition to full-time status. Surprisingly, the public was largely supportive of the strikers. The Teamsters emphasized that part-time UPS workers were not "school kids" trying to earn an extra buck. We saw workers with bills to pay and children to raise being paid less simply because they were designated as part-time. In fact, there exists a group of part-time workers at UPS who consistently worked full-time hours yet continued to be classified as part time. These workers clearly do not "choose" these work conditions.

With the UPS strike, the public got a jarring glimpse of the growing contingent workforce, which is a result of employer strategies to increase earnings. As we saw with UPS, it is not only struggling companies that use contingent workers. Even successful companies are using contingent employment to cut their costs and reduce their liabilities. Temporary employment needs to be understood, investigated, discussed, and handled as a social problem. Only then can we begin to construct effective policies to deal with the complexities involved.

This study provides a small glimpse of part of the temporary industry as it pertains to clerical workers and attorneys. While temporary employment in clerical work and law may be feminized, this is not necessarily so in every occupation. Engineering and computer programming stand out as two potentially contravening occupations. Whether and to what extent this is true needs to be uncovered empirically. Occupational characteristics such as the availability of alternative employment relations in addition to temporary work, occupational prestige, and skill level as well as the gendering of the occupation affect how temporary employment re-organizes work processes, realigns power, and influences subjective experiences of temporary employment. Therefore, we should recognize that both the organization of work *as temporary* and the labor market positions of various groups of workers explain the dynamics of temporary work.

Future comparative study on temporary work in different occupations should attend to distinctions in occupational status, gender and racial/ethnic composition of the occupation, the historical existence of alternative modes of non-standard employment in the occupation, technical and organizational changes in the occupation, the extent of temporary employment in the occupation, and the legal status of temporarily employed individuals in the occupation. These and other factors will aid in further unraveling the relationship between temporary employment and occupational characteristics toward the end of understanding the effects of temporary employment for workers. We may then be able to point to a cluster of factors which, when coupled with temporary employment, makes this form of non-standard employment a step backward for workers. Policy decisions can then be tailored with the recognition of the diversity within temporary employment arrangements.

This research provides a basis for comparison and a guide to the kinds of questions and issues relevant to many temporary workers. Perhaps additional research will uncover other issues not addressed here. Perhaps the issues pertinent to temporary clerical workers and temporary attorneys are theirs alone. Either way, any investigation of temporary employment should seek to understand experience as linked to the structure of temporary employment and the effects of occupational characteristics and structures on the power dynamics of temporary employment. Given the findings of this research, I would be surprised to find that it's only temporary.

Notes

1 Gender, Occupations, and Temporary Employment

1. My discussion of temporary employment is limited to those workers who use a temporary agency to find work. There are at least as many direct-hire temporaries; however, their employment relationship is significantly different because there is no mediary in the form of a temporary agency.

2. There is a great deal of disagreement over which workers should be classified as contingent. Estimates range from 2.2 percent (Polivka 1996) to 30 percent (Belous 1989b). In the first estimate, workers are only classified as contingent if their work was expected to be of limited duration. In this way, some temporary workers would not be considered contingent. The second estimate, however, relies on categories of workers (for example, temporaries, part-time workers). For a detailed discussion, see Polivka (1996).

3. The designation of "involuntary" simply means that the individual would prefer to have a traditional employment arrangement but cannot find a "regular" job.

4. See Henson and Rogers (1999) for material on masculinity in temporary clerical work.

5. As Robin Leidner (1993) reminds us, many analysts look only at machinery in the classic sense of factory machinery. This leaves out the growing number of interactive service jobs in which few workers use any machinery at all, save a cash register. Here my choice of the term "machinery" is for the sake of convenience and not to imply that service work cannot be analyzed in a similar manner. In fact, the analysis does include technology traditionally conceived as machinery as well as other materials.

6. Heidi Gottfried (1994) is the exception here. She does follow this approach in her analysis of control mechanisms faced by temporary workers.

7. Los Angeles provided a site of heavily concentrated use of temporary workers. Interviews in Pennsylvania were not in an urban setting and were used as a check on my site selection. I found that while local labor market conditions differed, temporary employment in Pennsylvania was described as similar to temporary employment in Los Angeles.

8. These are attorneys who obtain work through a temporary agency rather than those who find "overflow work" or extra work from colleagues who are too busy. They are not simply independent contractors. I selected this type of law because of its similar structure to temporary clerical work. In both cases, the agency is a mediating presence through which

work is obtained. There are, however, some technical differences between the two temporary occupations. At the time of this research, the attorneys were not always considered employees of the agency in the same way as clerical workers were. Attorneys were sometimes considered independent contractors in relation to the agency, meaning that the agency did not withhold or pay taxes on their behalf. However, the relationships among the three parties (worker, client company, and agency) were very similar.

9. It is likely that temporary attorneys felt less obligated than clerical workers to provide me access. As the analysis demonstrates, the relationship between the temporary and the agency is quite different for lawyers and clerical workers. In addition, the difference in status between the attorneys and me was much different from that of the clerical workers and me. It made me uncomfortable to think that there might be an element of coercion in my access to temporary clerical workers. Therefore, I took special care to ensure that the interviewees truly understood the voluntary and confidential nature of the study. Alternatively, temporary clerical workers as relatively powerless actors in the temporary employment relationship may have been motivated by the opportunity to talk with someone they perceived as having more power, while lawyers were less likely to see me, a graduate student at the time, as more powerful.

10. The lack of nonwhite lawyer interviews may simply reflect the current racial composition of the law profession. At the time this study began in 1993, only 2.7 percent of lawyers were black, and only 2.1 percent were Hispanic (U.S. Bureau of the Census 1994). Because the case files I worked with did not contain any information with regard to race and ethnicity, I cannot be certain that I am not missing some important data. I cannot, however, overstate the importance of race and ethnicity in the issue of temporary employment. It has been shown that African Americans are overrepresented in contingent employment in general (see Belous 1989b); therefore, future studies should seek to incorporate race and ethnicity to provide an empirical analysis of its interconnections with professional temporary work. We cannot assume simple additive models of gender/race stratification.

11. Names of individuals, companies, and places have been changed to ensure confidentiality.

2 Deskilled and Devalued

1. Numerous examples of temporaries' routine office work can be found in Henson (1996, chap. 4).

2. This point is well-made throughout Mills (1951), Braverman (1974), Crompton and Jones (1984), Machung (1984), and Hartmann et. al (1986), although each varies in adherence to a strict "proletarianization" thesis.

3. See Feldberg and Glenn's (1987) account of this point of view.

4. Glenn (1992) discusses racial stratification among women in a variety of jobs in addition to clerical work.

5. We can all recall a secretary without whom the office would cease to function. Yet the skills that make her or him indispensable are seldom recognized or rewarded as such.

6. Steinberg (1992) provides a detailed evaluation of the many ways in which gender bias enters job evaluation systems that result in a lack of recognition of skills in female-dominated jobs.

7. See both Acker (1990) and West (1990) for a wider range of examples.

8. Although the tendency for men to do so is not homogeneous. Depending on the organization of interests in any given occupation in a historical period, men may work to define certain jobs as skilled in order to keep pay from declining and leading to female substitution (Milkman 1987).

9. For more detailed examples of the application of the Babbage principle, see Braverman (1974, pp. 79–83).

10. Compensation is not simply equivalent to the hourly wage, although temporary workers do typically earn lower hourly wages than their permanent counterparts (Callaghan and Hartmann 1991). Compensation includes material and nonmaterial benefits such as sick time, paid vacation, health and life insurance, job training, and consideration for promotion.

11. In actuality, most temporary agencies have a policy regarding the situation in which a client requests more highly skilled work than was ordered. In these cases, agencies request that temporaries report the situation so that their pay and the agency's fee can be adjusted. While aware of the policy, few of the interview subjects reported requesting a pay increase from their agency. They either felt uncomfortable making such a request, or they felt it would not be well received either by the agency or the client.

12. For an interesting discussion of the skills-matching process from the perspective of agency placement counselors, see Ofstead (1998). Ofstead emphasizes the rationalizing influence that temporary agencies claim to have on the recruitment process, and then finds that her data contradict a purely rationalistic view. Seen from the temporary workers' perspective, recruitment seems even less rational than reported in Ofstead's research.

13. Why the temporary industry might want to promote this particular construction of its testing procedures is discussed further in following section on control. I address how agencies might reap control over workers by defending placements and pay rates as the results of rationalized procedures. However, I do not address the possibly larger benefit that agencies gain from promoting rationalized testing to their clients. A discussion of the failure of these ideologies to convince many temporaries follows in Chapter 4, which deals with resistance.

14. Some agencies have begun recently to heavily promote their computer training resources. Because many agencies consider their training packages to be proprietary information, I have been unable to follow up on the more recent developments. At the time of this research, I had better access to try the training software. Because the interview data were also collected at the same time, I cannot reasonably assess the current state of temporary industry training packages.

15. These statements apply to "involuntary" temporaries—that is, temporary workers who would prefer traditional employment. Recent research shows that most temporary workers are in fact involuntary.

16. The expression of temporary work as a strategy to get a "really good job" seems to be predominantly emphasized by men in the study and is likely wrapped up in the relationship between masculinity and work. This is discussed at length later in the book.

17. The industry does promote the use of temporaries as a "test drive" of new employees. Because I sought individuals who were currently temping, I would have missed individuals who successfully completed a probationary period as a temporary employee before becoming a "permanent" worker. What this means is not that temporary workers never access internal labor markets, but that when they do they are usually aware of the arrangement ahead of time. They are much less likely to happen upon a road into the company by chance.

18. See Cappelli et al. (1997) for an overview.

3 Out of Control

1. I make the switch to "management" from capital with the recognition that these are not by and large the same entities. However, using the term *management* is more reflective of the situation at hand. The problem of incorporating management into Marx's dualistic employment structure is not a new one.

2. A variety of understandings of control build on Braverman (1974), including Edwards (1979), Burawoy (1979), Friedman (1977), and Ward (1990).

3. Scientific management and the division of labor are incorporated under Edwards's (1979) definition of technical control.

4. Burawoy (1979) shows us how workers' playing the game generates consent with managerial prerogatives. Resistance is deflected laterally at other workers rather than at management.

5. See Friedman (1977) for an elaboration on the concept of responsible autonomy.

6. Feminist literature on worker control is replete with examples of gendered forms of controls and resistance. See Ong (1987) and Ward (1990).

7. Adler (1993), Cockburn (1985), Acker (1990), and Smith (1994) all contribute to the gendered understanding of skill and control.

8. See Edwards (1979) for a full description of how forms of control map to different labor markets.

9. How this seeming opposition of interests translates into opportunities for resistance is somewhat developed by Gottfried (1994); nevertheless, it is an important question to which I return in Chapter 4.

10. Several writers have commented about the potential effects of increasing employment contingency on labor organizing. Among them are Parker (1993) and DuRivage, Carré, and Tilly (1998).

11. For a complete description of how social isolation occurs and is experienced by temporary workers, see Rogers (1995).

12. The problems of organizing temporary workers do not stop with these logistical difficulties. A host of legal and other issues come into play. For a fuller discussion, see DuRivage, Carré, and Tilly (1998).

13. On one temporary assignment I worked in a personnel department for several weeks. During those weeks, the department received numerous phone calls, mailings, and personal visits from local temporary agencies soliciting their business. The agency through which I worked even brought the personnel manager flowers and candy.

14. These experiences are expected to vary by local labor market conditions. At the time of the study, unemployment in Los Angeles was quite high.

15. See Edwards (1979, pp. 23–36).

16. Without talking to the agency representative who made this remark, I have no way to confirm Ludy's interpretation of the remark as threatening. However, the significance of this data lies not in whether the agent intended the threat but in how the temporary worker received the communication in a context of insecurity. Her actions that followed were based on what someone in her relatively powerless position would do when faced with a threat coming from her source of income.

17. Like domestic workers, temporary workers can use friendship to manipulate their employers into honoring certain requests. The degree of success is highly variable.

18. This is not unlike what we hear in today's political climate, which is hostile to welfare and unemployment compensation. Those who derive income from social welfare programs are cast as not wanting to work—if they wanted to work, they would be working.

19. See Martella (1991), Negrey (1993), and Henson (1996) for further evidence of the inflexibility of temporary work for temporary workers.

20. Of course, the level of work described is filtered through the perceptions of the temporary workers. The more concrete evidence of working harder is that temporaries report taking shorter lunches, taking fewer breaks, and participating very little in office socializing.

21. Sometimes the industry constructs temporary workers as secondary wage earners to draw attention away from the social implications of involuntary temporary employment. At the same time, they cast themselves as providing access to good full-time jobs. Which characterization is invoked depends on the audience and the issue at hand. When the industry is under attack for its lack of health insurance coverage for workers, it can invoke the secondary wage earner image.

22. The extent of involuntary temporary employment is increasingly well-documented (Parker 1994; Callaghan and Hartmann 1991; Polivka 1996).

23. Approximately one-fifth of the temporary workers I interviewed were offered jobs through the temporary agency. Of those, only two accepted the jobs offered to them. Of those two, one was laid off a year later and the other quit after six months because of an abusive boss. Because many of my interviewees were working as temporaries at the time of this research, my figures may underestimate the "temp-to-perm" trajectory. More systematic data is needed to support both the temporary industry's and my estimates of workers who move from temporary to permanent work. Future research should also explore the temporary work experiences of those who successfully made this leap. See Smith (1998) for a very different look at the temp-to-perm phenomenon.

24. "Drop-dead gorgeous" is certainly constructed in line with culturally dominant definitions of beauty, or "white beauty," which marginalizes most women of color.

25. See the discussion concerning gender assessment in Rogers and Henson (1997).

26. Pierce (1995) provides numerous examples of male paralegals' strategies for bolstering their masculinity in the face of performing female-typed work.

27. See Hipple and Stewart (1996) for a discussion of benefits and contingent employment.

4 Resisting Temp-tation

1. Ong (1987) details how women factory workers invoke female problems and claim spirit possessions in order to get time away from their machines. For other examples, see Bookman and Morgan (1988), Romero (1992), and Ward (1990).

2. Randy Hodson (1994) has offered a typology that parallels Edwards's (1979) work on control mechanisms and links resistance to the organization of work. His four types of resistance are "deflecting abuse, regulating the amount and intensity of work, defending autonomy, and expanding worker control through worker participation schemes" (80).

3. I feel it necessary to remark here that many feminists writing on resistance do not actually think of resistance in an essentialized manner; however, omitting connections to the gendered organization of work, which shapes women's and men's resistance, leaves the work open to this, albeit incorrect, interpretation.

4. Smith (1993) details gendered forms of flexibility, and Ong (1987) discusses gendered forms of labor control, including housing arrangements and control of sexuality.

5. Of course, men and labor unions did not always work to exclude women from jobs. Sometimes it was in their best interest to fight with women. See Milkman (1987) for a thorough exploration of times when men and unions fought with or against women.

6. See DuRivage, Carré, and Tilly (1998) for an in-depth exploration of the difficulties in organizing temporary workers.

7. This is similar to how Burawoy (1979) conceptualized shop-floor games constituting workers as individuals.

8. Rogers (1995) provides a discussion of the feeling of isolation among temporaries. One notable exception to such isolation is when a "temp force" is hired.

9. Hodson's (1997) study of organizational ethnographies demonstrates the importance of good relationships among workers as a prerequisite for effective resistance.

10. I am concerned that portraying some acts of resistance would reveal temporaries' "secrets" and bring closer supervision. I must reemphasize that all acts of resistance must be placed in the context of workers' struggles to negotiate within rather restricted boundaries.

11. Cornfield (1985) notes that quitting is a common form of resistance in the peripheral sector; therefore, it is not surprising to find quitting common among temporary workers.

12. Some might disagree with applying the label "resistance" to all of the acts I include here. By placing them on a continuum, one end of which is labeled "coping," I allow for differences in the intensity of resistance. If workers at least attempt to exert some control over their situation, I am satisfied to label it as a coping form of resistance. Recall that others have even characterized quitting as resistance.

13. "Accidentally" hanging up on callers turned out to be a rather popular form of resistance

5 Are We Not Temps?

1. Perhaps as a result, Braverman's (1974) focus rested more on the organization of work than workers' subjective experiences of that work. Not surprisingly, then, consequent labor process studies frequently have been accused of reducing all human action to the effects of or responses to capitalist social structures.

2. Jermier (1994, p. 4) emphasizes that studies of work have "reduced the subjectivity of workers to statements of job satisfaction or dissatisfaction."

3. See Burawoy (1979), Cockburn (1983), and Knights and Willmott (1989).

4. In negotiating the precarious path between action and structure, there is still the danger of resorting to an essentialist understanding of "human nature" (Sturdy 1992). In his study of the restaurant industry, Sosteric (1996) details the lack of conflictual relationships between management and workers, and then demonstrates how socialization of new employees urged them to "be themselves." Why must one be socialized to be oneself unless that self is in the process of partially being constructed by the organization? Curiously, the individualizing tendency of this seeming contradiction is left unquestioned.

5. Clegg (1994) provides an in-depth explanation of the relationship between identity, knowledge, and outflanking of resistance.

6. See Pierce (1995) for a similar phenomenon among male paralegals.

7. Although I approach this understanding in prior work that details forms of alienation and their resistance in temporary employment (Rogers 1995), I fall short of the mark with an implicit essentialist understanding of temporary workers' subjectivity. Temporary work is conceived of as something that alienates workers from their "true" creative selves. Although underdeveloped, this work does consider the ways in which temporary workers' efforts to resist alienation can have the unintended consequence of reproducing exploitative power relations.

8. See Judith Rollins (1985) for examples of asymmetrical naming practices between domestic workers and their employers. The naming practice not only derives from inequality, but it signals and reproduces it as well.

9. Henson (1996) notes the occurrence of these practices as well; however, what is at issue here is not the existence of these practices but their meanings and effects.

10. Of course, here part of the connotation of "real job" is due to the clerical/secretarial aspect of these temporary jobs. This theme is taken up in the next two chapters when we consider temporary attorneys in order to unravel the extent to which the stigma derives from temporary employment versus clerical employment.

11. More examples are found in Rogers and Henson (1997).

12. Cohany (1996) tells us that nearly one-fourth of temporary workers had spent more than one year as a temp. Her interpretation is that temporary tenure is quite low. That is true when compared with other workers; however, I must disagree that the figure is not worth noting, especially if we consider that patterns of temporary employment indicate discontinuous periods of temping interspersed with other types of employment. What is striking is the tendency, even for individuals who have temped longer than one year, to characterize their situation as temporary.

13. See Leidner (1993) for a discussion of this type of appeal to insurance agents.

14. Sturdy (1994) describes how the "shifting" of clerical work reduces some kinds of work pressure but mutes conflict, resulting in an "outflanking" of worker resistance.

15. Chris Tilly (1996) notes the problem of involuntary full-time employment: people who would prefer part-time employment but must work full-time.

16. Clegg (1994) provides a host of additional examples.

17. This phenomenon is also very similar to what Tiano (1994) refers to as alienation for maquiladora workers. Some of the women in Tiano's study very clearly articulated a consciousness of opposition but did not enact resistance because they felt they were powerless to have any effect.

18. While Gottfried (1994) reserves the phrase "learning the score" for the many acts of socialization on behalf of the agency attempting to secure cooperation from new temporary workers, "knowing the score" suggests a more oppositional perception derived from direct experience of unequal relations rather than socialization.

19. See DuRivage, Carré, and Tilly (1998).

20. This term is used by Teresa DeLaurentis in Donaldson (1992) to describe her feminist vision of women's solidarity at the intersections of difference.

6 Lawyers for Rent

1. Anleau (1992), Hagan and Kay (1995), and Spangler (1986), all to varying degrees, discuss the status of the law profession.

2. Freidson (1986) and Sokoloff (1992) both provide definitions of professions and professionals.

3. A multitude of researchers weigh in on this topic, including Anleau (1992), Derber (1982), Mills (1951), and Oppenheimer (1973).

4. Most recently, Epstein et al. (1999) provide a thorough look at part-time attorneys, also known as "time deviants." Not surprisingly, women comprise the bulk of part-time attorneys. See also Epstein (1993), Hagan and Kay (1995), and Pierce (1995) for more on women's marginalization in law.

5. Epstein (1993), Hagan and Kay (1995), Pierce (1995), and Seron (1996) all mention women's difficult access to male-dominated professional networks.

6. The temporary lawyer workforce was disproportionately female at the agency I used. Indications from other agencies I spoke with informally suggest the same. However, it has not been possible to determine the degree to which this finding can be generalized, and no national data are available.

7. Again, I must caution the reader in generalizing from my small sample here. Nevertheless, all indications are that women can be found disproportionately in temporary law positions, just as they are in part-time law positions. Reports from agency owners, although not systematic, seem to bear this out. There are also good theoretical reasons to suspect women's overrepresentation here.

8. Queueing theory is discussed in Reskin and Roos (1990), Strober (1984), and Thurow (1975). Reskin and Roos (1990) provide a multitude of in-depth occupational studies.

9. Epstein et al. (1999) discuss problems that part-time attorneys have with others' perceptions of their commitment. They note that men's commitment was less likely to be questioned than women's, although some part-time men were doubly stigmatized for violating gender and time expectations.

10. The "juicier" assignments were more likely to be done by the men in this group; however, two of the women interviewed occasionally got this type of work. Notably, these two women did not have children. Nevertheless, the bulk of the women's work tended to be deskilled. The trend seems to be gender bifurcation with some overlap, but because of the small, nonrandom sample, I caution making generalizations.

11. The gendered nature of professional networks is not unique to law. Women in many occupations experience the same problems. For a full discussion, see Campbell (1988).

12. Seron (1996) discusses in detail the time requirements of networking for solo practitioners.

7 A Temporary Job: Is it the "Temporary" or the "Job"?

1. Certainly not all clerical temporaries have less education than lawyers. Clerical temporaries are themselves a diverse group, and there may exist some who have extensive education but for whatever reason are working as clerical temporaries. Ellen Lanford, for example, has two master's degrees. She is an exception in this regard. As a group, clerical workers have less education than attorneys.

2. For more on the state of clerical work, see Braverman (1974), Glenn and Feldberg (1979), Greenbaum (1995), and Hartmann (1986).

3. That is not to say that individuals do not work directly for an organization on a temporary basis. Indeed, there are at least as many direct-hire temporaries as agency temporaries. The point here is that this kind of work is not institutionalized in the same way as in law, nor does it provide entrepreneurial opportunity in the same way.

4. Just like highly remunerated independent programming consultants, some temporary attorneys are highly specialized, in demand, and in control.

5. Henson and Rogers (1999) cover masculinity in temporary clerical work in greater detail.

6. This is not to be confused with "home work" in nonprofessional occupations. Typically in clerical and assembly jobs done at home, workers are paid on a piece-rate basis. In

contrast with professional home work, these jobs are low-paid and inflexible (Christensen 1989; Leidner 1988).

7. I am not able to indicate any relationship between race and temporary employment for lawyers simply because all the lawyers I interviewed were white. I had tremendous difficulty finding nonwhite temporary lawyers. Even when I asked the agency manager specifically to help me with finding a more racially diverse group of subjects, she could not come up with anyone. With low representation of people of color in law in general, my difficulty is not surprising. However, in a city with such a diverse population as Los Angeles, she should have been able to come up with a few people. Perhaps this is indicative of how the biases of agency representatives enter into the placement process in temporary law as in temporary clerical work.

8. I do not intend to characterize skill as an objective aspect of any job. By comparison, law is either materially higher-skilled or ideologically higher-skilled than most occupations. In other words, it may require more schooling and other training; however, it is also constructed as a highly skilled occupation because of male dominance. Lawyers have the power to define their jobs as skilled, while others (for instance, daycare workers) do not.

9. See Salzinger (1991) for an interesting analysis regarding the role of third-party organizations in shaping work experiences and opportunities.

10. Indeed, some labor organizations are going this route, but the practice is not yet widespread.

11. See DuRivage, Carré, and Tilly (1998) for more information on hiring halls and the role of labor law.

12. One agency that places truck drivers boasts that it "will do everything possible to assure you that these persons remain non-union."

Bibliography

Acker, J. 1990. "Hierarchies, Jobs, Bodies: A Theory of Gendered Organizations."
Gender and Society 4: 139–58.
———. 1992. "The Future of Women and Work: Ending the Twentieth Century."
Sociological Perspectives 35: 53–68.
Adler, Paul S. 1993. "The New 'Learning Bureaucracy': New United Motors
Manufacturing, Inc. In Barry Staw and Larry Cummings, eds., Research in
Organizational Behavior, 111–94. Greenwich, Conn.: JAI Press.
Albeda, W., et al. 1978. Temporary Work in Modern Society: A Comparative Study of
the International Institute for Temporary Work. Vols. 1–3. Zurich: Kluwer.
Ammot, T. A., and J. A. Matthaei. 1991. *Race, Gender, and Work: a Multicultural
Economic History of Women in the United States.* Boston: South End Press.
Andersen, M. L. 1993. *Thinking about Women: Sociological Perspectives on Sex and
Gender.* 3rd ed. New York: Macmillan.
Anleu, S. R. 1992. "The Legal Profession in the United States and Australia:
Deprofessionalization or Reorganization." *Work and Occupations* 19, no. 2 (May):
184–204.
"Bar Group's Ruling on Temporary Help Seen Aiding Agencies." 1988. *Wall Street
Journal,* 22 December, 5.
Beechy, V., and T. Perkins. 1987. *A Matter of Hours: Part-time Work and the Labor
Market.* Minneapolis: University of Minnesota Press.
Belous, R. 1989a. "How Human Resource Systems Adjust to the Shift toward
Contingent Workers." *Monthly Labor Review* (March): 7–12.
———. 1989b. *The Contingent Economy: The Growth of the Temporary, Part-time, and
Subcontracted Workforce.* Washington, D.C.: National Planning Association.
Blum, L. M. 1991. *Between Feminism and Labor.* Berkeley: University of California
Press.
Bookman, A., and S. Morgan. 1988. *Women and the Politics of Empowerment.*
Philadelphia: Temple University Press.
Braverman, H. 1974. *Labor and Monopoly Capital: The Degradation of Work in the
Twentieth Century.* New York: Monthly Review Press.
Burawoy, M. 1979. *Manufacturing Consent: Changes in the Labor Process under
Monopoly Capitalism.* Chicago: University of Chicago Press.

Callaghan, P., and H. Hartmann. 1991. *Contingent Work.* Washington, D.C.: Economic Policy Institute.

Cappelli, P., et al. 1997. *Change at Work.* New York: Oxford University Press.

Carey, M., and K. Hazelbaker. 1986. "Employment Growth in the Temporary Help Industry." *Monthly Labor Review* (April): 37–44.

Carnevale, A.; L. A. Jennings; and J. M. Eisenmann. 1998. "Contingent Workers and Employment Law." In *Contingent Work,* edited by Kathleen Barker and Kathleen Christensen. Ithaca, N.Y.: Cornell University Press.

Carré, F. 1998. Part-time and temporary work : Flexibility for whom? *Dollars & Sense,* 215 (January): 22–25.

Castro, J. 1993. "Disposable Workers." *Time,* 29 March, 43–47.

Christensen, K., and M. Murphree. 1988. *Flexible Workstyles: A Look at Contingent Labor.* Conference Summary for U.S. Department of Labor, Women's Bureau. Washington, D.C.: U.S. Department of Labor.

Clegg, S. 1994. " Power Relations and the Constitution of the Resistant Subject." In *Resistance and Power in Organizations,* edited by J. Jermier, D. Knights, and W. R. Nord, 274–325. London: Routledge.

Cockburn, C. 1983. *Brothers: Male Dominance and Technological Change.* London: Pluto Press.

———. 1985. *Machinery of Dominance: Women, Men, and Technical Know-how.* Boston: Northeastern University Press.

Cohany, S. R. 1996. "Workers in Alternative Employment Arrangements." *Monthly Labor Review* 119, no. 10: 31–45.

Colatosti, C. 1992. "A Job without a Future." *Dollars & Sense.* May, 9–11.

Collins, S. 1994. "The New Migrant Workers." *U.S. News & World Report,* 4 July, 53–55.

Collinson, D. 1994. "Strategies of Resistance: Power, Knowledge, and Subjectivity in the Workplace." In *Resistance and Power in Organizations,* edited by J. Jermier, D. Knights, and W. R. Nord, pp. 25–68. London: Routledge.

Committee on Government Operations. 1988. *Rising Use of Part-time and Temporary Workers: Who Benefits and Who Loses?* U.S. House of Representatives, 100th Congress. Washington, D.C.: U.S. Government Printing Office.

Committee on Labor and Human Resources. 1993. *Toward a Disposable Work Force: The Increasing Use of Contingent Labor.* U.S. Senate, 103rd Congress. Washington, D.C.: U.S. Government Printing Office.

Connell, R. W. 1987. *Gender and Power: Society, the Person, and Sexual Politics.* Stanford, Calif.: Stanford University Press.

Cook, C. 1994. "Temps: The Forgotten Workers." *The Nation,* 31 January, 125–28.

Cornfield, D. B. 1985. "Economic Segmentation and Expression of Labor Unrest: Striking versus Quitting in the Manufacturing Sector." *Social Science Quarterly* 66, no. 2: 247–65.

Crompton, R., and G. Jones. 1984. *White-collar Proletariat: Deskilling and Gender in Clerical Work.* Philadelphia: Temple University Press.

Daniels, A. K. 1987. "Invisible Work." *Social Problems* 34: 403–15.

Derber, C. 1982. *Professionals as Workers: Mental Labor in Advanced Capitalism.* Boston: G. K. Hall.

Diamond, T. 1992. *Making Gray Gold.* Chicago: University of Chicago Press.

Donaldson, L. E. 1992. *Decolonizing Feminisms: Race, Gender, and Empire Building.* Chapel Hill: University of North Carolina Press.

DuRivage, V. 1992. *New Policies for the Part-time and Contingent Workforce.* Armonk, N.Y.: M. E. Sharpe.

DuRivage, V.; F. Carré; and C. Tilly. 1998. "Making Labor Law Work for Part-time and Contingent Workers." In *Contingent Work,* edited by Kathleen Barker and Kathleen Christensen. Ithaca, N.Y.: Cornell University Press.

Edwards, P. K., and H. Scullion. 1982. *The Social Organization of Industrial Conflict.* London: Basil Blackwell.

Edwards, R. 1979. *Contested Terrain: The Transformation of the Workplace in the Twentieth Century.* New York: Basic Books.

Epstein, C. F. 1993. *Women in Law.* Garden City, N.Y.: Doubleday.

Epstein, C. F.; C. Seron; B. Oglensky; and R. Saute. 1999. *The Part-time Paradox: Time Norms, Professional Lives, Family, and Gender.* New York: Routledge.

Fanning, J., and R. Maniscalco. 1993. *Workstyles to Fit Your Lifestyle: Everyone's Guide to Temporary Employment.* Englewood Cliffs, N.J.: Prentice-Hall.

Feldberg, R. L., and E. N. Glenn. 1987. "Technology and the Transformation of Clerical Work." In *Technology and the Transformation of White-collar Work,* edited by R. E. Kraut. Hillsdale, N.J.: Lawrence Earlbaum Associates.

Ferguson, K. 1984. *The Feminist Case against Bureaucracy.* Philadelphia: Temple University Press.

Flexible Workstyles: A Look at Contingent Labor. 1988. Conference Summary for U.S. Department of Labor, Women's Bureau. Washington, D.C.: U.S. Department of Labor.

Flint, J. 1994. "A Different Kind of Temp." *Forbes,* 28 February, 54.

Freidson, E. 1973. *Profession of Medicine: A Study of the Sociology of Applied Knowledge.* New York: Dodd, Mead.

———. 1986. *Professional Powers: A Study of the Institutionalization of Formal Knowledge.* Chicago: University of Chicago Press.

Friedman, A. L. 1977. *Industry and Labour: Class Struggle at Work and Monopoly Capitalism.* London: Macmillan.

Game, A., and R. Pringle. 1983. *Gender at Work.* Sydney: Allen & Unwin.

Glenn, E. N. 1992. "From Servitude to Service Work: Historical Continuities in the Racial Division of Paid Reproductive Labor." *Signs* 18: 1–43.

Goffman, E. 1959. *The Presentation of Self in Everyday Life.* New York: Doubleday.

Golden, L., and E. Appelbaum. 1992. "What Was Driving the 1982–88 Boom in Temporary Employment: Preferences of Workers or Decisions and Power of Employers?" *Journal of Economics and Society* 51: 473–94.

Gonos, G. 1997. "The Contest over 'Employer' Status in the Postwar United States: The Case of Temporary Help Firms." *Law and Society Review* 31, no. 1: 81–110.

Gottfried, H. 1991. "Mechanisms of Control in the Temporary Help Service Industry." *Sociological Forum* 6: 699–713.

———. 1994. "Learning the Score: The Duality of Control and Everyday Resistance in the Temporary-Help Service Industry." In *Resistance and Power in Organizations,* edited by J. Jermier, D. Knights, and W. Nord, pp. 102–27. London: Routledge.

Gramsci, A. 1971. *Selections from the Prison Notebooks.* London: New Left Books.

Gutek, B. 1985. *Sex and the Workplace. The Impact of Sexual Behavior and Harassment on Women, Men, and Organizations.* San Francisco: Jossey-Bass.

Habermas, J. 1975. *Legitimation Crisis.* Translated by Thomas McCarthy. Boston: Beacon Press.

Hagan, J., and F. Kay. 1995. *Gender in Practice: a Study of Lawyers' Lives.* New York: Oxford University Press.

Hartmann, H.; R. E. Kraut; and L. A. Tilly, eds. 1986. *Computer Chips and Paper Clips: Technology and Women's Employment.* Washington, D.C.: National Academy Press.

Henson, K. D. 1996. *Just a Temp.* Philadelphia: Temple University Press.

Henson, K. D., and J. K. Rogers. 1999. "'Why, Marcia, You've Changed!' Male Clerical Temporary Workers and the Doing of Masculinity in a Feminized Occupation." Paper presented at the Annual Meeting of the American Sociological Association, Chicago, August 8.

Hipple, S., and J. Stewart. 1996. "Earnings and Benefits of Contingent and Noncontingent Workers." *Monthly Labor Review* 119, no. 10: 22–30.

Hochschild, A. R. 1983. *The Managed Heart: Commercialization of Human Feeling.* Berkeley: University of California Press.

———. 1989. *The Second Shift.* New York: Avon Books.

Hodson, R. 1994. "Loyalty to Whom? Workplace Participation and the Development of Consent." *Human Relations* 47, no. 8: 895–909.

———. 1995. "Worker Resistance: An Underdeveloped Concept in the Sociology of Work." *Economic and Industrial Democracy* 16: 79–110.

———. 1997. "Group Relations at Work: Solidarity, Conflict, and Relations with Management." *Work and Occupations* 24, no. 4: 426–52.

Howe, W. 1986 "Temporary Help Workers: Who They Are, What Jobs They Hold." *Monthly Labor Review* (November): 45–57.

Israel, J. 1971. *Alienation from Marx to Modern Sociology.* Boston: Allyn & Bacon.

Jermier, J. M. 1988. "Sabotage at Work." In *Research in the Sociology of Organizations,* vol. 6, edited by N. Ditomaso, pp. 101–35. Greenwich, Conn.: Jai Press.

Jermier, J.; D. Knights; and W. Nord, eds. 1994. *Resistance and Power in Organizations.* London: Routledge.

Kanter, R. M. 1977. *Men and Women of the Corporation.* New York: Basic Books.

Kaufman, B. E. 1993. *The Origins and Evolution of the Field of Industrial Relations.* Ithaca, N.Y.: ILR Press.

Kemp, A. A. 1994. *Women's Work: Degraded and Devalued.* Englewood Cliffs, N.J.: Prentice-Hall.

Knights, D., and H. Willmott. 1989. "Power and Subjectivity at Work: From Degradation to Subjugation in Social Relations." *Sociology* 23, no. 4: 535–58.

Kohn, M., and C. Schooler. 1983. *Work and Personality: An Inquiry into the Impact of Social Stratification.* Norwood, N.J.: Ablex.

Labaton, S. 1988 "Lawyers Debate Temporary Work." *New York Times,* 18 April, 2.

Layder, D. 1993. *New Strategies in Social Research.* Cambridge: Polity Press.

Lee, D. 1980. "Skill, Craft, and Class: A Theoretical Critique and a Critical Case." *Sociology* 15: 1.

Leidner, R. 1993. *Fast Food, Fast Talk.* Berkeley: University of California Press.

Leinberger, P., and B. Tucker. 1991. *The New Individualists: The Generation after the Organization Man.* New York: HarperCollins.

Lewis, W. M., and N. H. Malloy. 1991. *How to Choose and Use Temporary Services.* New York: AMACOM, American Management Association.

Lewis, W., and N. Schuman. 1988. *The Temp Worker's Handbook.* New York: AMACOM, American Management Association.

Machung, A. 1984. "Word Processing: Forward for Business, Backward for Women." In *My Troubles Are Going to Have Trouble with Me: Everyday Trials and Triumphs of Women Workers,* edited by K. B. Sacks and D. Remy. New Brunswick, N.J.: Rutgers University Press.

Mackensie, G. 1977. "The Political Economy of the American Working Class." *British Journal of Sociology* June: 244–52.

Mackinnon, C. 1979. *Sexual Harassment of Working Women.* New Haven, Conn.: Yale University Press.

McLellan, D. 1977. *Karl Marx: Selected Writings.* New York: Oxford.

Mansnerus, L. 1988. "Law Firms Too Hire Lawyers by the Hour." *New York Times,* 4 March, 10.

———. 1989. "Rule on Temporary Lawyers Changes Again." *New York Times,* 2 June, 6.

———. 1991. "Lawyer Layoffs: Boon to Temporary Job Agencies." *New York Times,* 3 May 11.

Martella, M. 1991. *'Just a Temp': Expectations and Experiences of Women Clerical Temporary Workers.* Washington, D.C.: U.S. Department of Labor, Women's Bureau.

Milkman, R. 1987. *Gender at Work: The Dynamics of Job Segregation by Sex during World War II.* Chicago: University of Illinois Press.

Mills, C. W. 1951. *White Collar.* London: Oxford University Press.

Morrow, L. 1993. "The Temping of America." *Time,* 29 March, 40–41.

National Association of Temporary Services. 1992. *Report on the Temporary Help Services Industry.* Alexandria, Va.: DRI/McGraw Hill.

Negrey, C. 1993. *Gender, Time, and Reduced Work.* Albany: State University of New York Press.

Oakley, A. 1981. "Interviewing Women: A Contradiction in Terms." In *Doing Feminist Research,* edited by H. Roberts. London: Routledge & Keegan Paul.

Ofstead, C. M. 1998. "Markets, Hierarchies, or Networks? Temporary Help Firms and Job Matching in Local Labor Markets." Paper Presented at the Annual Meeting of the American Sociological Association, San Francisco, August 21.

Ong, A. 1987. *Spirits of Resistance and Capitalist Discipline: Factory Women in Malaysia.* Albany: State University of New York Press.

Oppenheimer, M. 1973. "The Proletarianization of the Professional." *Sociological Review Monograph* 20: 213–27.

Parker, R. E. 1993. "The Labor Force in Transition: The Growth of the Contingent Workforce in the United States." In *The Labor Process and Control of Labor,* edited by B. Berberoglu. Westport, Conn.: Praeger.

———. 1994. *Flesh Peddlers and Warm Bodies: The Temporary Help Industry and Its Workers.* New Brunswick, N.J.: Rutgers University Press.

Pellicciotti, J. M. 1993. *Title VII Liability for Sexual Harassment in the Workplace.* Alexandria, Va.: International Personnel Management Association.

Phillips, A., and B. Taylor. 1980. "Sex and Skills." *Feminist Review* 6: 79–88.

Phipps, P. 1990. "Industrial and Occupational Change in Pharmacy: Prescription for Feminization." In *Job Queues, Gender Queues,* edited by B. Reskin and P. Roos. Philadelphia: Temple University Press.

Pierce, J. L. 1995. *Gender Trials: Emotional Lives in Contemporary Law Firms.* Berkeley: University of California Press.

Polivka, A. E. 1996. "A Profile of Contingent Workers." *Monthly Labor Review* 119, no. 10: 10–21.

Polivka, A., and T. Nardone. 1989. "On the Definition of Contingent Work." *Monthly Labor Review* (December 1989): 9–16.

Pringle, R. 1993. "Male Secretaries." In *Doing 'Women's Work': Men in Nontraditional Occupations,* edited by C. Williams. Newbury Park, Calif.: Sage Publications.

Pringle, Rosemary. 1988. Secretaries Talk: Sexuality, Power and Work. London: Verso.

Reich, R. 1992. *The Work of Nations.* New York: Vintage Books.

Reinharz, S. 1992. *Feminist Methods in Social Research.* New York: Oxford University Press.

Reskin, B. 1990. "Culture, Commerce, and Gender: The Feminization of Book Editing." In *Job Queues, Gender Queues,* edited by B. Reskin and P. Roos. Philadelphia: Temple University Press.

Reskin, B., and I. Padavic. 1994. *Women and Men at Work.* Thousand Oaks, Calif.: Pine Forge.

Reskin, B., and P. Roos, eds. 1990. *Job Queues, Gender Queues.* Philadelphia: Temple University Press.

Rizzo, J., et al. 1970. "Role Conflict and Ambiguity in Complex Organizations." *Administrative Science Quarterly* 15: 150–63.

Rogers, J. K. 1995. "Just a Temp: Experience and Structure of Alienation in Temporary Clerical Employment." *Work and Occupations* 22: 137–66.

———. 1999. "Deskilled and Devalued: Changes in the Labor Process in Temporary Clerical Work." In *Rethinking the Labor Process,* edited by M. Wardell, P. Meiksins, and T. Steiger. Albany: State University of New York Press.

Rogers, J. K., and K. D. Henson. 1997. "'Hey, Why Don't You Wear a Shorter Skirt?' Structural Vulnerability and the Experience of Sexual Harassment in Temporary Clerical Employment." *Gender and Society* (April): 215–37.

Rollins, J. 1985. *Between Women: Domestics and Their Employers.* Philadelphia: Temple University Press.

Romero, M. 1992. *Maid in the U.S.A.* New York: Routledge.

Rothschild, J., and J. A. Whitt. 1986. *The Cooperative Workplace.* Cambridge: Cambridge University Press.

Sacks, K. B., and D. Remy, eds. 1984. *My Troubles Are Going to Have Trouble with Me: Everyday Trials and Triumphs of Women Workers.* New Brunswick, N.J.: Rutgers University Press.

Salzinger, L. 1991. "A Maid by Any Other Name: The Transformation of 'Dirty Work' by Central American Immigrants." In *Ethnography Unbound,* edited by M. Burawoy et al., 139–60. Berkeley: University of California Press.

Sartre, J.-P. 1966. *Being and Nothingness.* New York: Washington Square Press.

Sassen-Koob, S. 1984. The New Labor Demand in Global Cities." In *Cities in Transformation,* edited by M. P. Smith. Beverly Hills, Calif.: Sage Publications.

Schmitt, R., and T. E. Moody. 1994. *Alienation and Social Criticism.* Atlantic Highlands, N.J.: Humanities Press.

Seeman, M. 1961. "On the Meaning of Alienation." *American Sociological Review* 26: 753–58.

Segal, L. 1990. *Slow Motion: Changing Men, Changing Masculinities.* New Brunswick, N.J.: Rutgers University Press.

Seron, Carroll. 1996. The Business of Practising Law: The Work Lives of Solo and Small-Firm Attorneys. Philadelphia: Temple University Press.

Smith, V. 1993. "Flexibility in Work and Employment: The Impact on Women." In *Research in the Sociology of Organizations.* Greenwich, Conn.: JAI Press.

——. 1994. "Braverman's Legacy: The Labor Process Tradition at 20." *Work and Occupations* 21: 403–21.

——. 1998. "Theorizing Power, Participation, and Fragmentation in the Contemporary Workplace: The Case of the Temporary Worker." *Social Problems* 45, no. 4: 411–30.

Sokoloff, N. J. 1992. *Black Women and White Women in the Professions: Occupational Segregation by Race and Gender, 1960–1980.* New York: Routledge.

Sosteric, M. 1996. "Subjectivity and the Labour Process: A Case Study in the Restaurant Industry." *Work, Employment, and Society* 10, no. 2: 297–318.

Spalter-Roth, R., et al. 1997. *Managing Work and Family: Nonstandard Work Arrangements among Managers and Professionals.* Washington, D.C.: Economic Policy Institute.

Spangler, E. 1986. *Lawyers for Hire.* New Haven, Conn.: Yale University Press.

Spragins, E. 1991. "The Art of Hiring Professional Temps." *Inc. Magazine,* June, 133–35.

Steinberg, R. J. 1992. "Cultural Lag and Gender Bias in the Hay System of Job Evaluation." *Work and Occupations* 19: 387–423.

Strauss, A. L. 1987. *Qualitative Analysis for Social Scientists.* Cambridge: Cambridge University Press.

Strober, M. H. 1984. "Toward a General Theory of Occupational Sex Segregation." In *Sex Segregation in the Workplace: Trends, Explanations, Remedies,* edited by B. Reskin, pp. 144–56. Washington, D.C.: National Academy Press.

Sturdy, A. 1992. "Clerical Consent: 'Shifting' Work in the Insurance Office." In *Skill and Consent,* edited by A. Sturdy, D. Knights, and H. Willmott. London: Routledge.

Sturdy, A., D. Knights, and H. Willmott. 1992. *Skill and Consent.* London: Routledge.

Sullivan, R. L. 1995. "Lawyers à La Carte." *Forbes,* 11 September, 44.

Taylor, L., and P. Walton. 1971. "Industrial Sabotage: Motives and Meanings." In *Images of Deviance,* edited by S. Cohen. London: Penguin.

Thomas, B. J. 1990. "Women's Gains in Insurance Sales: Increased Supply, Uncertain Demand." In *Job Queues, Gender Queues,* edited by B. Reskin and P. Roos. Philadelphia: Temple University Press.

Thomas, B. J., and B. Reskin. 1990. "A Woman's Place Is Selling Homes: Occupational Change and the Feminization of Real Estate Sales." In *Job Queues, Gender Queues,* edited by B. Reskin and P. Roos. Philadelphia: Temple University Press.

Thompson, P. 1983. *The Nature of Work.* New York: Humanities Press.

Thurow, L. R. 1975. *Generating Inequality.* New York: Basic Books.

Tiano, Susan. 1994. Patriarchy on the Line: Labor, Gender and Ideology in the Mexican Maquila Industry. Philadelphia: Temple University Press.

Tilly, C. 1990. *Short Hours, Short Shrift.* Washington, D.C.: Economic Policy Institute.

———. 1996. *Half a Job: Bad and Good Part-time Jobs in a Changing Labor Market.* Philadelphia: Temple University Press.

Tucker, W. 1994. "The Changing Face of America's Work Force." *Insight on the News*, 14 March, 10–13.

U.S. Bureau of the Census. 1994. *Statistical Abstract of the United States*. Washington, D.C.: U.S. Government Printing Office.

U.S. Department of Labor. 1988. *Flexible Workstyles: A Look at Contingent Labor*. Conference Summary for U.S. Department of Labor, Women's Bureau. Washington, D.C.: U.S. Department of Labor.

Vallas, S. P. 1991. "Workers, Firms, and the Dominant Ideology: Hegemony and Consciousness in the Monopoly Core." *Sociological Quarterly* 32, no. 1: 61–83.

Ward, K., ed. 1990. *Women Workers and Global Restructuring*. Ithaca, N.Y.: ILR Press.

Wardell, M. 1990. "Organizations: A Bottom-up Approach." In *Rethinking Organizations*, edited by M. L. Reed and M. Hughes. London: Sage.

West, C., and S. Fenstermaker. 1995. "Doing Difference." *Gender and Society* 9: 8–37.

West, J. 1990. "Gender and the Labor Process." In *Labor Process Theory*, edited by D. Knights and H. Willmott. London: Macmillan.

Westwood, S. 1985. *All Day, Every Day: Factory and Family in the Making of Women's Lives*. Urbana: University of Illinois Press.

Whyte, W. H. 1956. *The Organization Man*. New York: Simon & Schuster.

Wial, Howard. 1993. The Emerging Organizational-structure of Unionism in Low-wage Services. *Rutgers Law Review* 45, no. 3: 671–738.

Williams, C. 1992. "The Glass Escalator: Hidden Advantages for Men in the 'Female' Professions." *Social Problems* 39: 253–67.

———. 1993. "Temporary Workers: A Permanent Feature of Capitalism?" *Political Affairs* (September–October): 8–14.

———. 1995. *Still a Man's World: Men Who Do 'Women's Work.'* Berkeley: University of California Press.

Williams, H. 1989. "What Temporary Workers Earn: Findings from the New BLS Survey." *Monthly Labor Review* (March): 3–6.

Wood, S., ed. 1989. *The Transformation of Work?* London: Unwin & Hyman.

Index

Abuse, 52–53, 58, 81; resistance to, 97, 100
Age, 77, 152, 167
Agencies, temporary help service, 2, 4, 28, 30, 32, 34, 35–36, 43, 45–46, 50, 51, 52–54, 56–57, 58, 59, 60, 61, 62, 64, 66–67, 71, 72, 73, 75–76, 78–79, 87–89, 95, 99, 100, 101, 106–7; accountability of, 124; actions of, 120; as buffer, 156; and control, 157; identification with, 112; and law, 147; power of, 102; relationship between temporary workers and, 105, 158; role of, 164; as substitute for networks, 148; and temporary lawyers, 129–30; worker-owned, 169
Appearance, importance of, 71–72, 104
Appelbaum, Eileen, 30
Assignments, long-term, 50, 161
Attitude, negative, 75
Authenticity, 110

Babbage principle, 24–25, 32
"Bad client" stories, 47, 58–59. *See also* Control
"Bad temp" stories, 47, 57, 58, 87–88. *See also* Control
Benefits, employment, 55–56, 168, 172, 177 n. 10
"Boilerplate" tasks. *See* "Worker bee" assignments
Boredom, on the job, 81, 93–95, 97–98
Braverman, Harry, 7, 44
Burnout, 139, 153

Capital, professional, 128
Capitalism, 7–9, 44, 180 n. 1

Carré, Françoise, 126
Class, 70, 71–72, 76, 152, 166, 167; and good employees, 113–14; and resistance, 104, 126
Clerical work: degradation of, 153; versus industrial work, 5; versus legal work, 144, 149, 151–74, 176 n. 8; overrepresentation of women in, 156; and skills, 20
Client companies, 22, 28, 29, 31, 34, 43, 45–46, 47, 52, 56, 57, 58, 59, 65, 66, 67, 68, 72, 73, 78–79, 87–89, 106; identification with, 112; importance of, 124; as source of agency income, 102; and temporary lawyers, 129–30
Collinson, D., 96
Communication Workers of America, 169
Competition: between agencies, 52, 104, 109, 124; between temporary workers, 54–55, 87, 89–90, 103
Compliance. *See* Deference
Conception, separation from execution of, 44
Connell, R., 75
Consent, 44
Constraints, 51, 56, 84. *See also* Freedom: constraints on; Resistance: constraints on
Contingent workforce: definition of, 175 n. 2; growth of, 3
Control, 40, 43–80, 156–58; bureaucratic, 44, 45, 139–40; through collective action, 48–49; difference as, 47, 70–75, 79; direct, 157–58; discursive, 47, 62–70, 80, 120, 123; dual levels of, 84, 157; gendered, 45; over hours of work, 140–41; and ideology, 45; increased, 138–41, 165; indirect, 45;

nance of, 110–11, 112, 126, 163–64; mascu-
line, 115; reaffirming of, 125. *See also*
Stigma; Subjectivity
Incentive programs, 55
Individualization, 113–16, 125–26
Individuals, temporary workers as, 85, 96
Inequality, 8, 42, 163, 164, 167, 168–69, 170,
181 n. 8. *See also* Marginality; Minorities;
Naming practices
Insecurity, 49–52, 57, 90, 119, 164
Instability, 116, 163
Internal labor markets, access to, 38–39, 41,
177 n. 17
Irrationality, 90–91
Isolation, 180 n. 8; physical, 47–49, 85; so-
cial, 48, 85–88, 95–96

Job degradation, 9
Job matching, 63, 165
Jobs bridge. *See* Full-time job: bridge to
"Just a temp" strategy, 100–101

Kanter, Rosabeth Moss, 82
"Kelly Girl," 2, 78, 132
Knowledge, 123–26, 181 n. 18; of individualization, 125; of power imbalance, 126; of
structure of interests, 124–25; of temporary workers' position, 124

Labor power, 44
Labor process, 6–7, 44, 160–61; temporary,
7, 10
Labor process theory, 7, 8–9; feminist criti-
cism of, 9
Law, labor, 56, 66, 168, 170; improvements
of, 126
Law factories, 127, 139
Law profession: changes in, 127; versus cler-
ical work, 144, 149, 151–74, 176 n. 8; divi-
sion of, 128; feminization of, 131–32; and
men, 134, 141, 146, 147–48; and women,
127–29, 130–36, 141–44, 146, 147–48, 149,
150
Law professionals, status of, 127
Lawyers, assignments of, 130, 135–38, 140,
149. *See also* "Worker bee" assignments
Legitimation crisis, 153
Leidner, R., 110
Long-term assignments, 95
Loyalty, declining, 40

Management, 24
Managerialism, 145
Marginality, 88–89, 92, 105, 125, 133, 150, 153,
159, 162, 167, 168–69, 179 n. 24, 181 n. 4
Masculinity, 73–74, 114–15, 131, 141, 177 n. 16
Masculinization, 159, 161
Media, contemporary, 1–2, 12, 89
Minorities, 42, 71–73, 167
"Mommy jobs," 132–33, 161
Money-back guarantee, 51

Naming practices, 111–12, 181 n. 8
National Association of Temporary Ser-
vices, 64, 77
Networks, 146–49, 150
Nonpersonhood, 111–12

Ofstead, C. M., 177 n. 12
Outflanking, 111, 124, 126, 181 n. 14
Overflow work, 128–29, 147, 154, 157,
175 n. 8
Overqualification, 21, 27, 31, 104
Overrepresentation: of African Americans,
176 n. 10; of women, 129, 132–33, 149, 150,
158, 162

Parker, R. E., 4–5
Penalties, 53–54
Permanent job, 37–39, 68, 106, 153, 155; ben-
efits of, 119; compared to temporary job,
20, 117–18; pressures of, 118–19. *See also*
Full-time job
Permanent workers, 50
Placement, worker, 55
Policy, 34, 66
Popular culture, 2, 73, 89
Power, 84, 85; asymmetrical structure of,
103, 104–5, 107, 125–26, 158; discursive,
157; lack of, 103, 162, 166, 168; personal,
57; relations, 110, 111, 113, 117
Professionalism, 145, 157
Proletarianization, 19, 127
Quantification, 31–32
Queuing, 129

Race, 8, 19, 70, 71–72, 78, 96, 152, 159, 167, 176
n. 10, 179 n. 24; and good employees,
113–14; and resistance, 104, 126
Rationality, 47, 90–91; managerial, 63,
64–66

Rationalization, 45, 98, 153
Relationships, interpersonal, 57
Resistance, 81–108, 179 n. 2, 180 nn. 9–13;
  ad hoc, 90–92, 96, 108; change orientation, 96; collective, 89, 90, 108, 116, 125,
  126–27; constraints on, 92, 93, 102–8,
  124–25, 165; coping orientation, 96–101,
  108; definition of, 82; discursive, 125;
  and gender, 82, 93; individual, 85–89,
  108, 126; invisible, 107–8; nontraditional, 108; personal, 125; planned,
  90–91, 93–96, 108; prevention of, 63–64;
  research on, 83; and social change, 82;
  subjectivity of, 83; traditional, 81–82,
  108; of women, 83
Respect, 61
Revaluation, 103
Rollins, Judith, 59, 60
Romero, Mary, 59
Routinization, 110

Sabotage, 82, 91, 125
Science, 32, 33
Scientific management, 41, 44, 45, 178 n. 3
Scientism, 63–64
Screening process, 21–22, 28, 45, 63, 177 n.
  13. See also Skills: assessment of
Security, 153
Segregation, occupational, 24, 83–84, 129
Self-help books, 60, 75, 98
Semi-professionals, 127
Separation, 47
Sexual orientation, 159, 167. See also Gay
  men; Heterosexuals; Stereotypes: of gays
  and lesbians
Skills, 17–42; assessment of, 32; and degra-
  dation, 17; and disadvantaging women,
  9; "feminine," 19; ideologies of, 31, 34;
  matching, 31–34, 177 n. 12; polarization
  of, by gender, 9; social construction of, 9,
  19; uneven distribution of, 9. See also
  Deskilling; Screening process
Smith, V., 6
Socializing, 48–49
Solidarity, 90, 126; reduction of, 88. See also
  Resistance: collective
Solo practice, 130, 138, 145, 154, 157, 182 n. 12;
  hours of, 147; and men, 131; path to,
  146–47; similarities to temporary work,
  146; and women, 131, 142, 143

Stereotypes, 58, 84; co-opting of, 100; of
  gays and lesbians, 73–74, 115; of men, 93;
  rejection of, 98; of temporaries, 87, 89,
  92, 112, 125, 132; of women, 76, 82,
  92–93
Stigma, 58, 88, 114–16, 128, 132, 133, 134, 154,
  155–56, 161–62, 181 n. 10; gendered, 141,
  156; rejection of, 113, 125, 126, 139–40, 145,
  156, 163
Storytelling. See "Bad temp" stories; "Bad
  client" stories
Subjectivity, 111–12, 126, 158, 163–64, 180 n.
  7; perspectives of, 109–11
Submission. See Deference
"Supertemps," 58, 67, 88–89, 156
Supervision, 45

Taylor, Frederick, 41
Team-based system, 6
Teamsters, 172
Temporary help services (THS) industry,
  29, 30, 42, 75, 117, 126, 164; barriers
  constructed by, 120; growth of, 4, 7,
  25, 34, 54, 76; regulation of, 167–68,
  171–73
Temporary workers: benefits of, 34, 117; in-
  stability of, 3; involuntary, 3, 153, 171, 175
  n. 3, 177 n. 15, 179 n. 21; heterogeneity
  among, 6; problems of, 3–4, 5; and "side
  bet," 10; voluntary, 76, 171
Termination, 56, 78
Threats, latent, 57, 58, 89
Tilly, Chris, 126, 166
Training, 34–36, 177 n. 14
Trial period, 117

Underemployment, 128. See also Deskilling;
  Devaluing
Unemployment, 55, 67, 107, 124, 128, 167
Unionization, 108, 169–70; avoidance of,
  167; possibility of, 126; unlikelihood of,
  85, 101, 125, 154, 169–70; women and, 82,
  84, 179 n. 5
United Parcel Service, 172–73
Upbringing, emphasized, 113
Upgrading, 19, 20, 25, 28
Upward mobility, 34, 36–40, 41, 77, 157–58

Wages, 26, 27–28, 31, 32, 33, 39, 46, 57, 60, 62,
  63–64, 70, 79; increases in, 102, 106; as in-

dividualized phenomena, 86–87; low, 103, 145–46, 172; market determination of, 121; negotiations of, 102–5; reduction of, 107, 122–23; of temporary lawyers, 130, 137, 160; unfairness of, 123

"Worker bee" assignments, 135–38, 153, 155

Work ethic. *See* Work: desire to

Work process. *See* Labor process

Work: desire to, 47, 63, 66–67, 87; monotonous, 17, 19, 20–21, 23–24, 28, 29, 47, 99, 100, 153–54, 165; organization of, 83–84, 93, 120, 153–54; relationship, 95; skilled, 19, 25–27, 28, 138, 154–55, 162; unskilled, 17–18, 21, 31, 39

Jackie Krasas Rogers is Assistant Professor in Labor Studies Industrial Relations at the Pennsylvania State University. Her primary research interests are race, class, gender, and employment; contingent
employment; and work and family. Her other work on temporary
employment has appeared in *Work and Occupations* and *Gender and
Society*. Currently, she is looking at work and family in the lives of
substitute teachers.